Foreign Investment in Developing Countries

Also by H.S. Kehal

DIGITAL ECONOMY: Impacts, Influences and Challenges (*co-edited with Varinder Pal Singh*)

FOREIGN INVESTMENT IN THE PEOPLE'S REPUBLIC OF CHINA AND INDIA: Contrasts and Challenges

Foreign Investment in Developing Countries

Edited by

H.S. Kehal
University of Western Sydney, Australia

First published 2004 by
PALGRAVE MACMILLAN
Houndmills, Basingstoke, Hampshire RG21 6XS and
175 Fifth Avenue, New York, N.Y. 10010
Companies and representatives throughout the world

PALGRAVE MACMILLAN is the global academic imprint of the Palgrave
Macmillan division of St. Martin's Press, LLC and of Palgrave Macmillan Ltd.
Macmillan® is a registered trademark in the United States, United Kingdom
and other countries. Palgrave is a registered trademark in the European
Union and other countries.

ISBN 0–333–67080–9

This book is printed on paper suitable for recycling and made from fully
managed and sustained forest sources.

A catalogue record for this book is available from the British Library.

Library of Congress Cataloging-in-Publication Data
    Foreign investment in developing countries / edited by H.S. Kehal.
        p. cm.
    Includes bibliographical references.
    ISBN 0–333–67080–9
        1. Investments, Foreign – Developing countries. I. Kehal, Harbhajan, 1942–

HG5993.F597 2004
332.67'3'091724—dc22   2004042839

10   9   8   7   6   5   4   3   2   1
13   12   11   10   09   08   07   06   05   04

Printed and bound in Great Britain by
Antony Rowe Ltd, Chippenham and Eastbourne

*In memory of my parents Chaudhry Harkishan Singh Kehal
and Sardarni Harnam Kaur Kehal*

Contents

List of Tables

List of Figures

List of Boxes

Preface and Acknowledgements

It all started about eight years ago. The initial step to producing a book on foreign investment was when Mr T.M. Farmiloe offered me a contract on behalf of Macmillan to edit a book entitled *Foreign Investment in Developing Countries*. I am most grateful to him for his encouragement and sowing the seeds. The chapters in the volume were assembled from top professionals, academics and practitioners from all over the world in the field of foreign investment. Persistence pays, and has its own rewards. Despite various set backs I was given a fresh go ahead by Ms Amanda Watkins, Senior Commissioning Editor at Palgrave Macmillan in February 2003. She deserves and receives my highest appreciation, encouragement and goodwill. Ms Kerry Coutts, Editorial Assistant, Economics, Business and Management very ably supported my endeavours throughout 2003. A fresh call for chapters was issued, and the response from contributors was overwhelming. Contributors now come from the USA, Europe, Australia and Asia, from various backgrounds and with first-hand knowledge of the theory and practice of foreign investment.

I wish to thank all the contributors: Professor Dale Colyer was one of the original contributors who kept faith in the project, and I am most grateful to him for showing the virtue of persistence. A special vote of thanks is also due to Professor Richard Fletcher for making a valuable contribution within a very tight delivery schedule. The contributors also served as reviewers for other chapters in the book and assisted the Editor in producing a wonderful product. The chapters went through a double-blind review process and the reviewers did a exemplary job. Irrespective of their own congested schedules, they responded promptly and enthusiastically to all my requests. However, some of them need a special mention as their help set the benchmark. These include: Professor Alev M. Efendioglu and Professor Vincent F. Yip, University of San Francisco; Professor Yutaka Kurihara, Aichi University, Japan; Professor Earl Thompson, University of California, Los Angeles, USA; Dr Mark Wade, University of Tennessee, USA; Dr Andrew Sumner, University of East London, UK; Dr S.K. Singh, XLRI, Jamshedpur, India; Emeritus Professor Akira Ishikawa, Aoyama Gakuin University, Japan; Dr Naoko Shinkai, Economist, Development Studies, Japan Bank for International Cooperation Institute, Tokyo, Japan; and Dr Richard Dawson, University of Waikato, New Zealand among others.

A special vote of thanks is also due to those who provided us access to their networks, introducing us to potential authors and contributors and encouraging us to persist with the project to its successful completion. They are too numerous to mention by name.

In addition to the contributors and reviewers, the production of a book needs immense technical and organizational help. Here a special mention must be made of Harender Haresh Samtani for his technical help in the editing process and also for his very valuable computing and linguistic skills. His presence, perseverance and contribution to the development of this book raised its quality by many notches. His skill in organization of huge amounts of information was instrumental in keeping order among the deluge of materials. He was also of great help in the review process by ensuring that the schedule was adhered to and following up on various loose ends. His constant presence and persistence strengthened my resolve to see the project through.

I also wish to acknowledge the help and technical support provided by Varinder P. Singh and Dr Kiranjit Sohi during the final days of the project.

The journey on this path over the past eight years has been very arduous. Members of my family sustained my enthusiasm. My wife Harbans Kehal continued to encourage me to complete the work. My children Harjinder S. Kehal, Parminder Kaur, Harcharan Singh Kehal, my son-in-law Dr Kanwaljit Singh and my daughters-in-law Amanda and Paramdeep played a crucial role in maintaining a cheerful and happy family atmosphere. I am fortunate to be blessed with fine grandchildren Sahil, Simran, Sohan, Pia, Rohin, Cameron, Tej and Josh, all of them enjoy the fruits of more and more flow of investment funds from surplus to deficit countries and will also share in the future benefits of foreign investment with members of the world population living in the developing and developed countries. As a family, we are cosmopolitan and world travellers. My ancestral home is in a developing country. Over my lifetime, I have witnessed a profound change in the living standards of my native country. *Ceteris paribus*, this has happened because of the transfer of production technologies and know-how in agriculture and other sectors, strengthening of the industrial base and the host of other benefits that came with foreign investment. I take this opportunity to express my sincere thanks and gratitude to my family for their moral support, love, patience and kindness throughout the long gestation period of the project; without their forbearance, understanding and enthusiasm, it would never have reached fruition.

A collaborative project such as this does not exist in a vacuum and cannot be kept running without enormous support and help of many kinds. It is appropriate to acknowledge all of those people who have directly or indirectly shaped this work by contributing to its successful gestation. Many friends in Sydney, Australia and other countries have provided inspiration and support by reading and commenting on drafts. Mr J.S. Sawhney deserves special mention and also Professor Tejpal Singh and Dr G.S. Sidhu for providing valuable and constructive comments. Thanks are owed to many others too numerous to mention by name who spared their valuable time to contribute the project. This book is a culmination of fifty years of learning, teaching, researching, sharing and imparting knowledge of Economics and related subjects in developing countries and also in Australia, Japan and other developed countries. Particular mention must be made of the enrichment I have received from discussions with colleagues from Japan: Professor Minoru Harada, Kyushu University; Professor Saburo Saito, Fukuoka University; Professor Ken-Ichi Tanaka, President, Kitakyushu University; and many others who shared their ideas, insights and technical knowledge with me during my frequent sojourns in Japan. I also profited greatly from interactions with professionals, academics and researchers at professional meetings and gatherings, including the Western Economic Association International, Business and Economics Society International, International Food and Agribusiness Management Association, Indian Ocean Research Network, Economic Society of Australia, Australian Institute of International Affairs and many other professional organizations. My students, spread all over the world, always come in handy for sharpening my arguments. Discussions with Dr P. Dass, University of Manitoba, Canada, on various aspects of FDI strategy have clarified many issues.

A special environment at the University of Western Sydney, Australia, facilitated my work on this project. The cooperative attitude of all my colleagues there had a direct impact on the successful completion of this volume.

Special thanks finally go to the publishing team at Palgrave Macmillan, who through their timely emails prompted me to always meet the deadlines and keep the project on schedule. I acknowledge their unstinting support for the project.

H.S. KEHAL

Notes on the Contributors

Dale Colyer is Professor Emeritus of Agricultural and Resource Economics, Division of Resource Management, Davis College of Agriculture, Forestry and Consumer Sciences, West Virginia University, Morgantown, West Virginia, USA. He conducts research and consulting in the USA, Latin America and Africa on agricultural policy, economic development and international trade. Previous publications include books on agricultural policy in Ecuador and the international competitiveness of US agricultural commodities. He received his PhD from the University of Wisconsin in 1963.

Glauco De Vita is Principal Lecturer in International Business and Teaching Fellow at Oxford Brookes University (UK). His past experience includes working as senior analyst for an American MNC. A university lecturer since 1997, he has taught international economics, econometrics, industrial economics, international business, international management and strategy at undergraduate and postgraduate level. His research interests include international trade, FDI, capital mobility and models of exchange rate determination. He has published in *Economics Letters, Applied Economics*, The *Scottish Journal of Political Economy* and other peer-reviewed academic journals.

Richard Fletcher is principal author of a seminal text of international marketing, *International Marketing – An Asia-Pacific Perspective*, now in its second edition. He is currently completing a book on Global e-business marketing. His research interests focus on social sensitivity in international business and on doing business in emerging markets, including promotion in emerging markets, doing business with such markets via countertrade, the macro impacts of globalization, international ethical practices, environmental considerations, corporate citizenship in overseas locations, and sensitivity to national sovereignty. He has published in the *International Business Review*, the *Journal of Global Marketing, Industrial Marketing Management and* the *Australian Marketing Journal*. Prior to becoming an academic, he was a Senior Trade Commissioner for the Australian government and for over twenty-five years represented Australia's commercial interests in Bombay, Bangkok, Jakarta, Los Angeles, New Delhi and San Francisco.

Ashima Goyal is a Professor at the Indira Gandhi Institute of Development Research, Mumbai. She has taught courses in Development Theory and Policy, in Advanced Macroeconomics and Open Economy Macroeconomics, and visited the Economic Growth Center, Yale University, USA in 2000. Her research interests are in institutional macroeconomics, the open economy, international finance, development and gender. She is the author of a book on Developing Economy Macroeconomics, and has won international research awards. She is also active in the Indian policy debate, and writes a monthly column for the *Economic Times*.

Zubair Hasan has teaching and research experience spaning over forty-five years. Having worked in a number of educational institutions in India, mainly the University of Delhi, and abroad, he has been working as a Professor of Economics at the International Islamic University of Malaysia since 1990. His teaching and research areas include theoretical and applied economics, Islamic economics and finance and environmental economics. He has published extensively in these areas.

Simran Kahai is an Assistant Professor of Economics at John Carroll University in Cleveland OH (USA), and received her Bachelor of Arts in Economics (1987) from Punjab University, India and a Master of Science degree in Economics (1992) and a PhD degree in Economics (1995), both from Auburn University, Auburn, AL. She previously taught at Tuskegee University at Tuskegee (AL), University of Akron at Akron (OH) and at Kent State University (EMBA program) at Kent (OH). Her research has been published in the *Journal of Law and Economics, Transportation Research*, the *Review of Industrial Organization*, the *Antitrust Bulletin*, the *Business and Economic Review* and the *Journal of Applied Business Research* and she has also conducted numerous funded research projects.

Harbhajan S. Kehal is a Senior Lecturer in Economics at the University of Western Sydney, Blacktown Campus, New South Wales, Australia. He completed his PhD at the University of Western Australia, Perth. His research interests centre around the digital economy, foreign investment in developing countries and the economic relationships of Australia with Japan and other countries.

Kevin Lawler is Professor of Industrial Organization at the European School of Management (Rome, Italy), where he is Head of Research. He also teaches at Durham University (UK). Until 2002, he was Professor of Economics at Sunderland University (UK), and has worked as consultant with a number of large organizations. His current research interests include international trade and investment, the EU enlargement process and developments in e-commerce. He has written over a hundred articles, and published five books in the fields of international economics, industrial economics and applied econometrics.

Veena Keshav Pailwar received her PhD (University of Poona); MPhil (Cambridge University, UK) and MA (University of Poona), and is presently working in XLRI, Jamshedpur, as an Assistant Professor of Economics. She has previously worked in India with NIPFP, NCAER and NIFM in various capacities on various research and teaching projects. Her areas of interest are computable general equilibrium (CGE) modelling, financial sector modelling, the impact of financial, fiscal and external sector reforms, foreign capital and its export intensity and commercial banking.

Ramkishen S. Rajan is a Senior Lecturer at the School of Economics, University of Adelaide. He is concurrently a Visiting Fellow at the Institute of Policy Studies, Singapore. Dr Rajan has been in Adelaide Since 1999; since July 2003, he has been a Visiting Senior Lecturer and Freeman Asian Studies Scholar at the Department of Economics, Claremont McKenna College (CMC), California. He has published extensively on various aspects of international economics, especially with reference to Asia and received his BSocSci. (Hons) in Economics from the National University of Singapore, a MA in Economics from the University of Michigan, Ann Arbor and a MA and PhD from Claremont Mckenna College.

Bala Ramasamy is Associate Professor of International Business and Economics at the Nottingham University Business School, Malaysia Campus. He is also the Director of the Centre for Europe Asia Business Research (CEABuR). His research interests are in FDI, international trade, Asian economies, corporate social responsibility and tourism economics. He has published widely in the *Journal of Applied Economics,* the *Asia Pacific Journal of Economics and Business,* the *ASEAN Economics Bulletin* and the *Bulletin of Indonesian Economic Studies.*

Sadhana Srivastava is currently a Research Scholar pursuing her PhD in the South Asian Studies Programme at the National University of Singapore. She obtained her MPhil in Economics from Jawaharlal Nehru University (JNU) in 2000. Her current research interests include FDI and trade-related issues in the context of India and other Southeast Asian economies. Her recent publications include a chapter on the emerging economic opportunities between ASEAN and India (co-authored with Professor Mukul Asher and Rahul Sen) in Frederic Grare and Amitabh Mattoo (eds) *Beyond the Rhetoric: The Economics of India's Look-East Policy* (New Delhi, 2003).

Harender H. Samtani has masters' degrees in the fields of management, finance and accounting. His research interests lie in the fields of international finance and trade. His rich and varied professional experience has derived from various roles in a multinational bank before taking up a research position, and is currently focusing his research towards business developments in India. He has been actively involved in the editing of this book and played a key role in its development.

Jagjit S. Sawhney retired from the Indian Economic Service after a highly successful career. He was an Additional Economic Adviser to the Ministry of Commerce, Government of India and has held many other responsible positions in the Indian public service. He actively joined with the Editor of this book in reviewing the contributions.

Michael Thorpe has interests in international trade, investment and finance, especially in East Asian and Indian Ocean regions. His work has been published in *Economic Record, Applied Economics Letters,* the *Australian Quarterly,* the *Asia Pacific Journal of Economics and Business,* the *Global Business and Economics Review,* the *Asian Journal of Public Administration* and the *Australian Journal of Irish Studies.* He has undertaken research, teaching and consultancy in China (AusAid projects), Singapore, Vietnam, Hong Kong, the USA, the UK, South Africa (USAID economic development projects), Mongolia and Malaysia (as a United Nations consultant). He has been Visiting Fellow at the Institute of Southeast Asian Studies, Singapore (1991); Loughborough University of Technology UK (1993); the University of Natal, South Africa (1995); University College Dublin, Ireland (1997) and the University of International Business and Economics in Beijing (2001). He assumed the position of President of the Economic Society of Australia (WA) in mid-2002. He was formerly a Senior Research Fellow with the Institute for Research into International Competitiveness (IRIC) at Curtin in 1994 and 1995; and is at present the Director of the Curtin Business School's International Business Unit. He is also chair of the University's China Reference Group. He currently sits on several editorial boards and is the book review editor for the *Australia Pacific Journal of Economics and Business.*

P.K. Vasudeva is a retired colonel of the Indian Army and is presently Director Principal, College of Communication and Management, Bharatiya Vidya Bhavan, Chandigarh. He is also Visiting Professor on International Trade, Panjab University, Chandigarh, Immediate Past President of the Chandigarh Management Association and Senior Research Fellow of the Strategic Research Centre, Chandigarh. He has authored four books on the WTO and international marketing, 123 research papers and more than 500 articles in national and international journals and Newspapers.

Matthew Yeung received his PhD in Marketing from the University of Nottingham, UK. He is currently Lecturer at the School of Business and Administration, Open University of Hong Kong. He is also a Research Fellow at the Centre for Europe Asia Business Research, University of Nottingham, Malaysia Campus. His research interests are in FDI, tourism economics and international marketing. He has published in journals such as the *Asia Pacific Journal of Economics and Business* and the *Asia Pacific Management Review.*

Kevin Honglin Zhang received his PhD in Economics from the University of Colorado, and was a post-doctoral fellow at Harvard University and a consultant of Harvard Institute of International Development for a year, before joining Illinois State University. His research field is international economics, focusing on FDI, trade and development. He has co-edited four books and published over thirty articles in leading journals such as *the Journal of Development Economics, Economic Development and Cultural Change, the Journal of Development Studies, Economia Internazionale/International Economics*, and *Urban Studies*. In 2000–1 and 2002–3, he was vice president of the Chinese Economists Society (CES), a US-based worldwide academic organization of economists for the Chinese economy.

List of Acronyms and Abbreviations

ACFTA	ASEAN–China Free Trade Area
ADB	Asian Development Bank
ADR	American Depository Receipt
AFTA	Asian Free Trade Area
AIA	ASEAN Investment Agreement
ASEAN	Association of South East Asian Nations
B2B	Business-to-business
BKPM	Investment Coordinating Board (Indonesia)
BOP	Balance of payments
BPO	Business process outsourcing
CEC	Comprehensive Economic Cooperation (ASEAN–India)
CECA	Comprehensive Economic Cooperation Agreement (India–Singapore)
CEE	Central and Eastern European
CII	Confederation of Indian Industry
CPE	Centrally planned economy
EAI	Enterprise for ASEAN Initiative
EC	European Community
ETDZ	Economic and/or technology development zone
EU	European Union
FDI	Foreign direct investment
FDICI	Foreign direct Investment Confidence Index
FED	Foreign exchange expenditure
FEE	Foreign exchange earnings
FEMA	Foreign Exchange Management Act
FI	Foreign investment
FIB	Foreign Investment Board
FIE	Foreign invested enterprise
FII	Foreign institutional investor
FIIA	Foreign Investment Implementation Authority (India)
FIPB	Foreign Investment Promotion Board (India)
FPI	Foreign portfolio investment
FSU	Former Soviet Union
FTA	Free trade area
FTZ	Free trade zone
GATS	General Agreement on Trade in Services
GATT	General Agreement on Tariffs and Trade

GDP	Gross domestic product
GDR	Global Depository Receipt
GFCF	Gross fixed capital formation
GNP	Gross national product
HRD	Human resource development
HS	Harmonized system (tariff classification)
ICOR	Incremental capital–output ratio
ICT	Information and communications technology
ICTs	Information and communication technologies
IFI	International financial institution
IMF	International Monetary Fund
IP	Intellectual property
IPR	Intellectual property right
ITC	Information and communications technology
ITES	Information technology enabled services
JACIK	Japan, ASEAN, China, India, Korea (regional integration)
JSQ	Joint Study Group (India–Singapore)
JV	Joint venture
LDC	Least developed country
M&A	Merger and acquisition
MERCOSEN	Mexico–Central America FTA
MFA	Multifibre Arrangement
MFN	Most favoured nation
MNC	Multinational corporation
MNE	Multinational enterprise
MTI	Ministry of Trade and Industry
NAFTA	North American Free Trade Area
NFEE	Net foreign exchange earnings
NIC	Newly industrialized country
NRI	Non-resident Indian
NRNR	Non-resident (non-repatriable) (rupee)
NTB	Non-tariff barrier
NTZ	New and high-technology development zone
ODI	Overseas direct investment
OECD	Organisation for Economic Co-operation and Development
OFED	FED other than imports
OFEE	FEE other than exports
OLI	Ownership, location and internalization
PAC	Pre-Accession Countries
PCA	Principal Component Analysis
PPP	Purchasing power parity
PRC	People's Republic of China
PROCAMPO	Mexican agricultural programme
QR	Quantitative restriction

R&D	Research and development
RBI	Reserve Bank of India
RCA	Revealed comparative advantage
RTA	Regional trade agreement
SCP	Structure–Conduct–Performance (paradigm)
SDO	Standards development organization
SECOFI	Secretaria de Comercio y Fomento Industrial (Mexico)
SETC	State Economic and Trade Commission
SEZ	Special economic zone
SIA	Secretariat for Industrial Assistance
SME	Small and medium-sized enterprise
SOE	State-owned enterprise
TRIMs	Trade-Related Investment Measures Agreement
TRIPs	Trade-Related Intellectual Property Rights Agreement
UNCTAD	United Nations Conference on Trade and Development
UNCTC	United Nations Centre on Transnational Corporations
WDI	*World Development Indicators*
WTO	World Trade Organization
Y2K	Year 2000

Introduction

Harbhajan S. Kehal, Harender H. Samtani and Jagjit S. Sawhney

1 The digital era

Foreign investment can play a crucial role in the development of the economies of the developing countries. It can supplement the host country's resources and provide a valuable injection in the capital formation process. In addition, it can lead to the introduction of new technologies and widening of markets for the products of the host countries. Foreign investment can take the form of official or non-official flows. The non-official flows include foreign direct investment (FD1) and portfolio investment. Foreign investment brings with it a host of benefits such as the transfer of production technologies and know-how, employment, strengthening of the industrial base and competitiveness and acceleration of development in various sectors and regions. Among other benefits, foreign investment helps to bridge the savings–investment gap in the economy and brings additional resources, technology, management know-how and access to export markets.

There is a tide of rising expectations all over the world, especially in the developing countries as they have come to be closely linked with the developed world through the digital revolution. While paying attention to the current status of the interlocking issues of technology, product standards, policy and legal matters related to foreign investment, the focus in this book will be on the economic aspects of foreign investment. Thus this book covers local and global production, trade and investment in the digital era. The effects of the Internet on the flow of information, computing and communication has greatly influenced the local as well as the world economy, accelerating the flow of FD1 and portfolio investment to developing countries.

In the emerging 'digital economy' the players as well as the rules of the game are changing quickly and a lot of confusion and uncertainty has been generated in the developing countries about foreign investment. Most of the literature on these changes has been concerned with the experiences of advanced economies; however, the economies of Asia and the emerging economies of Eastern Europe and the formes USSR are also producers and users of information technologies. The digital revolution has influenced the government as well as the private sector, creating a borderless environment which changes the responsibilities of both private sector and the governments and may bring unknown problems in relation to foreign investment. This book aims to provide relevant theoretical frameworks and latest empirical research findings, catering to the needs of professionals and many others who wish to improve their understanding of foreign investment in the developing countries in the digital era.

In addition to academics, students and other practitioners, this book is intended for the business people who are involved in the development process in various ways, as suppliers of development goods and services and as partners in development activities in the developing countries around the world. If the reader is already directly involved in international trade in development goods and services and business to business (B2B) transactions, as manufacturer, distributor, exporter, importer, customs broker and freight forwarder, financier or diplomat, then this book is for them. If the reader is involved in the international field – perhaps as an employee of an international institution directly or indirectly involved in foreign investment, a consultant, lawyer, trade and investment show organizer, developer, business school professor, executive educator or advise to international companies directly or indirectly involved in foreign investment in developing countries, the book will be equally valuable.

2   Structure of the book

Chapters 1 and 2 present a comprehensive investigation of the determinants of the flow of FDI across the globe. The general nature of the analysis means that its application is relevant to all situations.

Many theoretical and applied studies have been conducted since the 1970s on the determinants of FDI. However, despite the abundance of research, no unanimity reigns and unresolved issues remain as to the importance of particular FDI determinants for both developed and developing countries. In Chapter 1, the authors survey this vast literature in an attempt to identify the major contributions to the debate on the forces attracting FDI, and examine whether any general direction for consensus may be found. Their review confirms the existence of a rather fragmented theoretical landscape. The available evidence suggests that although the main hypotheses are not mutually exclusive and that many rather than a single or even a few factors are likely to affect investment decisions, the determinants identified in the literature cannot all be simultaneously relevant. The 1990s debate on the potential changes in the relative significance of traditional and non-traditional determinants as a result of globalization, though very promising, is still in its infancy, and needs to mature before conclusive inferences can be drawn. What is clear, however, is that the relative importance of factors determining a country's propensity to attract foreign investment will continue to be highly contextual, and dependent upon the specific type of FDI involved.

FDI was a key factor in shaping the world economy during the 1980s and '90s, and has now come to be widely recognized as major contributor to growth and development. In the year 2000, FDI grew by 18 per cent but due to the world's recession declined in 2001 for the first time in a decade. Developing countries still attract less than a third of world FDI flows, and these flows are concentrated in only a small number of developing countries. In 2000, the forty-eight least developed countries (LDCs) received just 1.5 per cent of FDI. For these countries whose future growth depends upon successful participation in the world economy, it is important that they understand the criteria that multinational corporations (MNCs) apply when investing abroad.

The purpose of Chapter 2 is to examine the role of foreign capital in the form of FDI in enabling developing countries to obtain access to the resources and markets needed for restructuring their economies, thereby creating new opportunities for growth and development. The chapter includes a comprehensive review of theoretical and empirical studies that have made important contribution to understanding the role of FDI and its determinants in the developing countries. It also points out the importance of FDI in today's global economy.

Chapters 3 and 4 concentrate on the impact of FDI on the Chinese economy, bringing out the role of the Chinese Diaspora in contributing to FDI in China. Besides Hong Kong and Taiwan, significantly large Chinese business communities have settled in South Asian countries, flourishing through the interaction with western economies and benefiting from their close ties with the western banking system. Since they were keen to invest in areas where labour costs were at a minimum and foreign trade was liberal, it suited them when the Chinese mainland opened up its economy for foreign investment with special incentives for export manufacturing. With few language or cultural barriers these communities could take advantage of China's 'open door' policy and geographical proximity to their countries of adoption and settlement made it advantageous for them to set up manufacturing units on the mainland. The western banking system with which they had been dealing for decades made it possible to raise funds in US dollars which were most welcome in China. Thus, under these particular circumstances, the opening of the Chinese economy by Deng Xiaping in 1979 had a catalytic impact on the flow of foreign investment into China.

China instituted its 'open door' policy in 1979 and opened its economy to the outside world in a carefully managed and phased approach. While foreign portfolio investment is restricted, FDI inflows grew steadily over the 1980s and accelerated through the 1990s, to the extent that China now ranks behind only the USA as the most favoured host nation for FDI. The forces driving FDI into China are myriad and include the perceived opportunities for foreign firms from domestic market access and the availability of cheap labour as well as being a response to distortions in the domestic economy.

In line with China's gradualist policy, FDI has been concentrated in the eastern and southern coastal regions. While the inflows of capital have been closely linked with China's expanding trade performance and general economic development, regional disparities are significant and policies are being instituted to widen the geographic spread of investment. By 2001 FDI accounted for 25 per cent of China's domestic investment, with foreign companies responsible for around 48 per cent of exports and 27 per cent of industrial production. Overseas Chinese, particularly in the east Asian region were initially very important in providing FDI and this was primarily focused in labour-intensive manufacturing industries. Since the mid-1990s foreign MNCs from the USA, Japan and the European Union (EU) have increased their presence, leading to a significant rise in large-scale capital and technology-intensive investment projects. With China's entry into the World Trade Organisation (WTO), the sources of FDI inflows and the industries into which the funds are flowing have become increasingly diversified, and future growth sectors will include services and automobiles. Although impediments still exist, China continues to be a growing destination for investment by foreign firms, despite a sharp downturn in investment flows globally since 2000.

FDI may be a catalyst to economic growth in developing countries. Yet its benefits do not automatically accrue and flow evenly across countries. Chapter 4 attempts to shed light on the question of how a developing country can maximize the benefits from FDI and minimize its cost, based on China's experience. As one of the largest recipients of FDI in the world, China seemed to stumble onto a FDI strategy that has proved remarkably successful, enhancing economic growth and helping the country move quickly to a market-based system. Two groups of questions are addressed in Chapter 4. First, what benefits and opportunities can FDI bring to China's development process, and what risks and dangers accompany it? Second, what policies and strategies did China design to attract FDI and to use it effectively? In particular, how did China at the same time capture the benefits of FDI and avoid its dangers?

Chapters 5 and 6 deal with foreign investment in India. The importance of FDI in India was realized only after its spectacular success in China and India has thus lagged behind in its efforts to attract FDI. Nor has been India as lucky as China in attracting its Diaspora in making big contributions. Indeed, non-resident Indians are predominantly professionals and hence have migrated in the recent past. Many are still struggling to get established in business or professions abroad. Their potential to invest in their home country is not yet as large as that of the Chinese Diaspora. As a democracy, India has not been able to quickly shift its policies from the restrictive regime of the 1960s and 1970s to meet the liberalization and globalization of the 1980s and 1990s. The policy shifts have met with wide spread dissent and opposition particularly in the area of labour reforms and incentives to foreign investors. Political instability and the law and order situation have not been congenial for attracting FDI, whereas China, with one-party rule, could introduce reforms with a stroke of pen, particularly in the special economic zones (SEZs) and other designated areas. India is still struggling to achieve a political consensus on a reform programme: even policies already put in place suffer from a threat of reversal with a change in the political set up and thus discourage potential investors.

India has a strong tradition of private enterprise in both the large and small sectors of production. Any foreign investor has to take into account a stiff competitor in many manufacturing activities whereas in China the field was fairly 'green' as private enterprises were suppressed under the Communist regime. Small investors from Hong Kong, Taiwan and Macao found it very tempting to enter an open market with little competition in the small manufacturing area for exports for which they already had the market. However, India offers attractive opportunities in terms of acquisitions of established businesses and portfolio investment was the first and immediate attraction for the foreign investor in India, who might in due course also get interested in FDI. India's superiority in the field of information and communications technology (ITC) and the outsourcing of information technology enabled services (ITEs) from India is widely recognized, and these areas have enormous potential for attracting FDI. Not that the potential in other areas has been exhausted: in fact, with growing interaction with western enterprises the scope for further FDI inflow is expanding, and will take off as soon as the necessary infrastructure and a congenial legal framework is put in place. As and when holistic improvement in the manufacturing and investment paradigm in India proceeds, the profit differential in India compared to competing countries will make FDI more rewarding in India as compared to the competing Asian countries.

In India, the 'pull' factor attracting FDI has been intensifying, although a weakening of the worldwide 'push' factor led to a slackening of inflows towards the end of 1990s. There is a consensus about FDI's desirability and the need for changes in regulation, at both central and state level, to smooth the entry process. The share going to services and electronics has risen, reflecting the fast growth and huge potential of Indian software and ITEs. FDI has contributed to improvements in industrial processes, qualities and standards. A revision in line with international accounting concepts shows that FDI has been underestimated. Other inflows have shown more volatility, and their contribution has been less than their potential, because macroeconomic policies maintained a large and volatile interest rate differential. As a result, investment fluctuated, and inflows fed a large forex reserves accumulation. A softening of interest rates and strong infrastructure spending stimulated an industrial revival, so that in 2003 India seemed to have succeeded in triggering the 'virtuous cycle'.

Using data for the post-reform period, Chapter 6 examines the impact of FDI inflows on saving and investment behaviour in India. The study indicates that the correlation between domestic saving and FDI and domestic investment and FDI is still weak. Though the fear that FDI may be replacing domestic saving is not supported by the data, the apprehension that FDI may crowd out investment by domestic agents was not refuted by the study. FDI flows in the post-liberalized era seem to be replacing investment by domestic participants at the margin. The policies pursued in the 1990s were able to boost the level of investors' confidence and create an investment friendly environment.

Chapters 5 and 6 further examine the performance of FDI companies *vis-à-vis* non-FDI companies operating in India in terms of such things as export intensity, import intensity, net foreign exchange earning intensity, profitability, and efficiency in the post-liberalized era. Though on number of parameters – such as profitability, overall efficiency, skill intensity, R&D intensity, net foreign currency earnings – FDI companies fared better than the non-FDI companies, the percentage difference in the performance level caused by most of these parameters is only marginal. Capital cost efficiency and import intensity of exports are the two important parameters where FDI companies fared significantly better than the non-FDI companies operating in India. However non-FDI companies in India have been found to be more labour cost-efficient and they closely compete with the FDI companies in skill intensity and export intensity of sales. The profitability and efficiency levels in India seems to be more affected by cyclical fluctuations within the country as well as the ups and down in the global economy and not much can be attributed to the FDI inflows. The marginal improvement in the export and import intensity of sales and import intensity of exports by the companies operating in India in the second half of the 1990s can also be largely attributed to the various tax and non-tax incentives granted by the government to the companies engaged in export activities and are not the result of FDI flows *per se*. The study also indicated that the strategic focus of the FDI and non-FDI companies operating in India is on the short run rather than the long run, as reflected in the higher and higher advertisement intensity and more or less stagnant R&D intensity. Thus, though a marginal improvement in the profitability and efficiency of the Indian companies can be expected from the higher inflow of foreign capital, India cannot depend entirely on these flows on improving its efficiency and productivity levels and plugging the country's foreign exchange gap.

Chapters 7 and 8 deal with the two important ASEAN countries, Indonesia and Malaysia. These countries have long-standing links with investing countries. Indonesia since its colonial days has benefited from FDI and Malaysia started early to attract FDI. However, the benefits to the two countries from FDI have been uneven. Malaysia through a conscious policy effort succeeded in attracting FDI in improved technology areas and emerged from the 1997–8 financial crisis rather quickly. Indonesia, on the other hand, attracted FDI in resource-seeking activities with the increase in mobility of resources caused by a phenomenal advancement in global transport, and the importance of resources as an attraction for FDI declined with the financial crisis. Indonesia is therefore still struggling to overcome its adverse impact.

Malaysia made bold efforts in providing incentives for FDI, putting in place congenial rules and regulations and above all an infrastructure that creates a significant first impression on potential investors. It emulated Singapore in many ways in creating attractions for FDI and had great success in its efforts. The competition among developing countries for attracting FDI is hotting up, and each country will have to redouble its efforts to increase the FDI inflow. Indonesia and Malaysia, being close geographic neighbours, are natural competitors and will have to watch each other's moves very carefully.

The 1997 financial crisis and its aftermath made FDI more important to the Indonesian economy than ever before. Chapter 7 deals with Indonesia's largest investor, the EU. The EU accounted for more than a third of FDI to Indonesia between 1996 and 2000, the UK, Germany, the Netherlands and France accounting for 95 per cent of this FDI. The purpose of Chapter 7 is to identify the determinants of EU FDI in Indonesia as well as the countries that pose a threat to the FDI inflow. The regression analysis found that EU FDI was both market- and resource-seeking and that infrastructure development played a significant role in attracting EU FDI. Based on a Principal Component Analysis (PCA), the geographical analysis indicated that Vietnam and the Philippines were Indonesia's major threat in the ASEAN region, while Brazil and Chile were its South American threat. The direct threat to Indonesia's FDI from the EU stemmed from the transition countries of Central and Eastern Europe (CEE). As the FDI tournament intensifies, it is imperative that Indonesia stabilizes its political environment and gives more attention to the development of physical and human resources if it is to remain as a major recipient of EU FDI in the region.

Chapter 8 reviews the literature identifying the determinants of the FDI flows to these countries, and attempts to lay bare the theories that underlie them. A simple regression model is set up to assess the efficacy of the determinants selected for Malaysia. The literature review finds the classical theory of factor endowment differences relevant but deficient in explaining FDI flows across national borders, for the latter are more volatile than the former. Other factors have also tended to assume greater importance with the passage of time. These include changes in foreign exchange rates, exports, external trade, infrastructure development expenditure, incentive schemes, removal of unnecessary restrictions, market size, rate of GDP growth, political and economic stability, labour cost, extent of openness, current account balance and capital flight. The relevant factors from this list for Malaysia are foreign exchange rate, exports, infrastructure development expenditure, rate of GDP growth, current account balance and capital flight. The Data used are expressed in terms of local currency. It was found that a relatively weak foreign exchange rate, export expansion and infrastructure development played a major role in attracting FDI flows to Malaysia, while rate of GDP growth, capital flight and current account balance, although significant, were of smaller consequence. The model explains 90 per cent of variation in FDI for Malaysia. Causality tests indicate that over the range of regression, rates of exchange, exports, infrastructure expenditure and rate of growth have been important in that order, and all have led the FDI flow; the reverse is not true.

Malaysia had location advantage, and rapidly created a social and physical infrastructure anticipating the foreign investors' expectations. The uniqueness of the response has been the readiness to design and adjust the modern sectors of the economy in accordance with the foreign investors' changing requirements. Malaysia readily switched its priorities from manufacturing to the expansion of the services sector foreign capital flowed in abundance to take advantage of the profit-earning opportunities the country offered. Among developing economies, Malaysia was one of the top five recipients of FDI during 1970–96. The tide turned after the 1997–8 financial crisis. The argument that the cause of the reversal was the wasteful use of resources or the imposition of capital controls is untenable. Malaysia still remains an attractive place for FDI flows from an economic viewpoint, but tends to lose due to increased competition for the funds, and new world order compulsions. A search for more diversified avenues for trade and investment may help; the country certainly has domestic saving rates high enough to carry her through a sticky patch.

Chapters 9 and 10 make a very interesting study of the Chinese success in a massive absorption of FDI and consistent high annual rate of growth since the 1970s, and the effects on Association of South East Asian Nations (ASEAN) countries and particularly on India. Such a simultaneously development going on in many neighbouring countries obviously raises doubts about their mutual competition. No doubt a degree of competition does exist, and each country is out to make best of the emerging opportunities for attracting FDI, but at the same time opportunities for mutual cooperation and creation of complementarities are emerging and efforts are being made to take advantage of them. India, which has remained more or less isolated from this area, has entered into Free Trade Agreements (FTAs) with the ASEAN countries and made a declaration of comprehensive cooperation with China.

Some of the ASEAN countries, such as Malaysia and Singapore, were early entrants in the field of development and may in due course move over to more technology-intensive areas. India, with its edge in communications and IT, may be seen as a help by others in this areas. China, with its near-inexhaustible supply of cheap labour, may benefit from continuing to concentrate on labour-intensive light manufacturing industries for which it has created markets not only in developed countries like the USA, the EU and Australia, but also in ASEAN countries. India has also been importing increasingly large amounts of these products from China. With a conscious effort, these countries can together develop into higher-income countries just as the western countries all developed almost simultaneously despite stiff competition from one another.

With the phenomenal growth of the People's Republic of China (PRC) since the 1980s, the country has emerged as a major economic power in Asia. An important and vigorous ongoing policy debate concerns the impact of the economic rise of China on the rest of developing Asia. The general perception is that there is a likelihood of substantial diversion of FDI from other developing countries in Asia towards the PRC in order to service its large domestic market and in a search for more cost-efficient production locations. Members of ASEAN are expected to face particularly intense competitive pressures from China in view of the overlap in relative factor endowments, export markets (the USA) and heavy reliance on FDI inflows from similar sources. The economic emergence of the PRC may also significantly impact on another large emerging economy in Asia, India. India has been positioning itself relatively favourably to attract and benefit from FDI since 1991, the year when wide-ranging measures were introduced to liberalize the economy.

Chapter 9 examines the relative performances of the PRC, selected ASEAN countries (Indonesia, Malaysia, the Philippines, Singapore and Thailand) and India since the 1980s, as well as the intensity and changing dynamics of their intra-regional economic interactions. The focus is on trends and patterns in merchandise trade, trade in commercial services and FDI flows, and the potential impact of the PRC's continued economic emergence on ASEAN and India. The chapter also charts the comparative advantage positions of these countries in the manufacturing and services sectors. The chapter concludes that the PRC's economic emergence is likely to provide as many opportunities as threats for both the ASEAN countries and India in not only attracting FDI inflows but also in the area of trade, particularly services trade, which is emerging as a major component of international trade involving these economies. However, in order to reap benefits from the PRC's economic emergence, ASEAN needs to strengthen itself as a regional grouping, and would significantly benefit by engaging in an Asia-wide economic cooperation effort involving both the PRC and India. The chapter clearly indicates that, unlike in the past, direct bi-lateral ties are now being forged between India and the PRC, and the need for third countries to act as middlemen appears to be fast diminishing.

Chapter 10 deals with World Trade Organisation (WTO) issues in addition to various aspects of FDI in India and China. There has been an unprecedented build-up of foreign exchange reserves in India (to the tune of US$ 85 billion, October 2003) after the repayment of more than US$ 2 billion debt by the Reserve Bank of India (RBI), but a healthy increase in FDI inflows in India during a global slowdown cannot hide the fact that India accounts for an extremely small share of FDI inflows. China attracts 80 per cent of the FDI inflows in Asia, against India's 5.5 per cent. Although FDI inflows have risen, they continue to be way behind those of China. India's share of FDI, among the developing countries, is only 1.7 per cent, compared to China's 17 per cent. India also attracts significantly lower FDI than many other South-East Asian countries such as South Korea, Thailand and Malaysia. According to the Foreign Direct Investment Confidence Index (FDICI) report (2002), India now has to face a nearly 20 per cent decline in the likelihood of receiving the FDI. India's attractiveness has, however, improved significantly in non-financial services, where investment likelihood increased by 28 per cent during 2001. Telecoms and utilities investors, for example, consider India as their twenty-fifth most attractive investment destination.

The reasons for low FDI inflows are first that India excludes reinvested earnings (which are part of foreign investor profits that are not distributed to shareholders as dividends and are reinvested in the affiliates in the host country) when estimating actual FDI inflows. Second, India excludes overseas commercial borrowings, whereas according to International Monetary Fund (IMF) guidelines financial leasing, trade credits, grants, bonds, etc. should be included in FDI estimates. India's failure to adopt such international guidelines on measuring FDI statistics means that aggregate FDI data are not directly comparable to those of other countries. The IMF report found that between 1980 and 2000 India's trade openness had increased by about 50 per cent compared to about 150 per cent for China over the same time period. Total FDI inflows to India during 2002 were US$ 4.4 billion (Rs 21,286 crore) including ADRs (American Depository Receipts)/GDRs (Global Depository Receipts) and advance pending issue of shares. Progressively liberal policies have led to increasing inflows of foreign investment, in terms of both FDI and portfolio investment. The IMF report noted that, China's exports reached US$ 320 billion in 2001, compared to India's US$ 35 billion. China also boasted more social investments than India.

UNCTAD reported that ranking of countries in terms of foreign investment (relative to the size of the economy) for the period 1998–2000 was 119 for India and 47 for China. The study also found that the quantum of FDI inflow in China and India, as a proportion of their respective FDI, was roughly comparable.

The other main reasons for decline of FDI inflows in India highlighted by various agencies are: (1) terrorism in Jammu and Kashmir and communal riots; (2) fiscal deficit; (3) poor infrastructure; (4) severe drought in several parts of the country due to shortfall of rains; (5) high trade barriers, which the IMF feels need to be slashed by 12 per cent; and (6) inadequate labour reforms hiring and tiring. Among these, the lack of infrastructure, inadequate openness of economy, aggressive marketing in exports and FIIS', permission to invest seem most important.

Chapter 11 on Mexico makes a very interesting study of a poor economy sitting next to a very prosperous and highly developed one, but failing to take advantage of its proximity to so much surplus investible wealth. For decades, Mexico feared exploitation of its natural resources by its powerful neighbour but when opened its economy the reality turned out to be not that bleak. After initial pitfalls, FDI proved to be a powerful engine of growth in all sectors, including that of natural resources. Rapid improvements in technology and management brought in by FDI are making production in all sectors more competitive internationally, helping Mexico to make full use of opportunities opened to it by its membership of the North American Free Trade Area (NAFTA). Historically, FDI in Mexico's primary sector was constrained and discouraged as the country followed import substitution-oriented economic policies. However, after the debt crisis in 1982, the government of Mexico began to shed autarkic policies, turn away from state control and open its economy to international economic forces. The reforms included reinterpretations of legal requirements on investment, passage of new laws, negotiation of treaties such as NAFTA and a constitutional amendment. These reforms made FDI easier and more attractive, although controls remain for petroleum and forestry. Foreign investments in the economy and the primary sector grew rapidly. Until 1993, foreign investments, while permitted, were severely restricted under a 1973 law, but after 1982 most of the anti-investment regulations were revised and FDI was encouraged. To consolidate and codify the revisions, a new law regulating foreign investment was enacted in 1994. FDI in the primary sector of Mexico grew rapidly after liberalization. FDI in agriculture, forestry and fisheries, while small in terms of the totals, rose from about US$ 800,000 in 1984 to over US$ 80 million in 1999 and 2000. FDI in the extractive sector increased from about US$ 5.7 million in 1984 to US$ 181 million in 2000. With NAFTA and other trade agreements, FDI can be expected to continue to play an important role in the nature and extent of the restructuring of the agricultural and mining sectors.

Chapter 12 deals with the cultural gap between countries and societies that can have a great impact on their economic interaction. People with 'cultural closeness' find it easy to invest in each other's economies – people in English-speaking countries like the UK, the USA, Canada, Australia, New Zealand. for example, experience little inhibition in moving from one country to another and investing there. With the advent of globalization, this 'cultural gap' is generally diminishing and people are coming culturally closer to each other. The MNCs have developed a 'culture' of their own which enables them to function freely in an environment of varying national cultures. Consumption patterns are also acquiring increasing uniformity and as a consequence of the cross-border mobility of investable funds, the world is fast becoming a 'global village'. Chapter 12 highlights the cultural differences between emerging and developed markets overseas and the extent to which cultural differences impact on market selection for siting an investment and negotiating it, locating investment partners, managing an investment and withdrawal from an investment activity. Aspects of culture in terms of its impact on investment in emerging markets are fully explored and illustrated by an analysis of communication in such markets: securing investment approvals and efficient investment operations overseas mandate effective communication. The chapter concludes by reviewing the impact of culture on investment in emerging markets in relation to each phase of the investment process.

The book provides a compilation of some of the latest literature on the subject of FDI, especially related to the important developing countries such as China, India and the ASEAN group. The policy measures adopted by these countries for attracting FDI has been excellently documented and a picture of things to come has been well drawn. The book serves the invaluable purpose of pointing to the developmental waves generated by FDI in these countries, along with the problems being encountered by them and the potential future opportunities. The changes in this region are being seen as so phenomenal that just in a few decades the whole area, accommodating the bulk of the world's poor population, may come to stand among the family of well-off nations. The impact on global poverty is expected to be equally dramatic and in the process may give rise to a further developmental push to the rest of the world, particularly the remaining lagging areas of the globe. Viewed from this perspective, the area will continue to be the focus of growth and developmental activities for many decades to come and will attract FDI on an increasingly larger scale. The relevance of the book to such a topical area of economic development subject should be self-evident.

1
Foreign Direct Investment and its Determinants: A Look to the Past, A View to the Future

Glauco De Vita and Kevin Lawler

1 Introduction

Foreign Direct Investment (FDI) has long been a subject of interest. This interest has been renewed in recent years due to the strong expansion of world FDI flows recorded since the 1980s, an expansion that has made FDI even more important than trade as a vehicle for international economic integration. Given this fact, it should come as no surprise that a large number of theoretical explanations as to the very existence of FDI have been advanced over the years, with many studies focusing on the investigation of the determinants of such investment. However, despite the abundance of research, there is at present no universally accepted model of FDI, there is still some confusion over what are the key factors capable of explaining a country's propensity to attract investment by multinational enterprises (MNEs) and it is not yet clear how globalization is likely to influence the determinants of, and motivations for, FDI. These unresolved issues are of special importance to developing countries that now more than ever seek to attract FDI to fuel economic growth.[1]

This chapter surveys the vast literature in this area in an attempt to identify the major contributions to the development of the debate on the forces attracting FDI, and examine whether any general direction for consensus may be found. We begin in Section 2 by clarifying the precise contours of the concept of FDI by discussing how its definition and measurement have changed over time. Section 3 provides a comprehensive and up-to-date critical review of both theoretical and empirical studies on the factors expected to have an influence on a country's propensity to attract foreign investment. It first examines the determinants of FDI identified in traditional hypotheses that assume perfect markets. It then considers hypotheses in which the assumption of full or nearly full competition in factor and product markets is dropped, and hypotheses that view FDI as a function of the exchange rate. Finally, it discusses other specific determinants not explicitly included in the theories reviewed earlier. In Section 4, we turn our attention to the relevance of the various determinants of FDI in the context of developing countries, and assess emerging trends and future prospects in light of globalization. The final Section 5 concludes with a brief summary of the overall discussion, and suggestions on profitable avenues for future research.

2   The definition and measurement of FDI

Generally speaking, the concept of FDI refers to the setting up of an overseas operation (greenfield investment) or the acquisition of an existing enterprise located within another economy. FDI implies that the investor exerts a significant degree of influence on the management of the enterprise resident in the host country. The *management dimension* is what distinguishes FDI from other forms of investment such as foreign portfolio investment (FPI), which includes equity and debt securities, and financial derivatives.

A closer look at the concept of FDI, however, reveals that, partly due to the complex nature of this phenomenon, its definition has changed considerably over time. One of the earliest definitions can be found in the 1937 inward investment survey conducted by the US Department of Commerce, which aimed to measure 'all foreign equity interests in those American corporations or enterprises which are controlled by a person or group of persons … domiciled in a foreign country' (US Department of Commerce, 1937, p. 10). No specific definition of 'control' was provided in this report, although control was the main criterion for the foreign inward investment classification. In the subsequent survey of outward investment, 'the United States equity in controlled foreign business enterprises' (US Department of Commerce, 1953, p. 4), control was explicitly defined on the basis of four investment categories, only some of which would still constitute measures of FDI.

As noted by Lipsey (1999), the current definition of FDI, as endorsed by the IMF (1993) and the OECD (1996), seems to have shifted its emphasis away from the idea of 'control', toward a 'much vaguer concept' (Lipsey, 1999, p. 310) of 'lasting interest'. According to this new benchmark definition, FDI 'reflects the objective of obtaining a lasting interest by a resident entity in one country ("direct investor") in an entity resident in an economy other than that of the investor ("direct investment enterprise"). The lasting interest implies the existence of a long-term relationship between the direct investor and the enterprise and a significant degree of influence on the management of the enterprise' (OECD, 1996, pp. 7–8).

In spite of the efforts of international agencies to push for uniformity, it is important to acknowledge that definitions and measurements of FDI still differ among countries. Indeed, different countries often have diverse conventions as to what constitutes ownership of a company from the point of view of the management of its assets. For example, while in the USA an equity capital stake of 10 per cent of shares would suffice to indicate foreign ownership, in the UK a stake of 20 per cent or more would be regarded as a more appropriate indicative threshold. Most importantly, there are serious practical difficulties in the compilation of FDI data, particularly in the case of developing countries which often lack the necessary technology and systems to collect such data on a systematic basis. For this reason, even UNCTAD's *World Investment Reports* often contain statistics derived through the use of proxies. It is due to this kind of problem that published FDI statistics of most countries, but particularly the developing ones, are subject to considerable errors and omissions. This also explains why reported data on FDI inflows and outflows, that should theoretically be equal to each other, always tend to show discrepancies.

3   FDI determinants: theory and evidence

Theories assuming perfect markets

Differential rates of return

Until the 1960s, FDI was largely assumed to exist as a result of international differences in rates of return on capital investment, with capital moving across countries in search of higher rates of return. Although the hypothesis appeared to be consistent with the pattern of FDI flows recorded in the 1950s (when many US MNEs obtained higher returns from their European investments), its explanatory power declined a decade later when US investment in Europe continued to rise in spite of higher rates of return registered for US domestic investment (Hufbauer, 1975). The implicit assumption of a single rate of return across industries, and the implication that bilateral FDI flows between two countries could not occur, also made the hypothesis theoretically unconvincing.

Portfolio diversification

The search for an alternative explanation of FDI soon revolved around the application of Markowitz and Tobin's portfolio diversification theory. This approach contends that in making investment decisions MNEs consider not only the rate of return but also the *risk* involved. Since the returns to be earned in different foreign markets are unlikely to be correlated, the international diversification of an MNE's investment portfolio would reduce the overall risk of the investor. Empirical studies have offered only weak support for this hypothesis. This is not surprising when one considers the failure of the model to explain the observed differences between industries' propensities to invest overseas, and to account for the fact that many MNEs' investment portfolios tend to be clustered in markets with highly correlated expected returns.

Market size

The market size hypothesis, which has its roots in neoclassical investment theory, focuses on the role of both the absolute size of the host country's market and its growth rate. The hypothesis states that the larger the market, the more efficient the investors' utilization of resources will be and, consequently, the greater their potential to lower production costs through the exploitation of scale economies. In his survey of earlier work on the determinants of FDI, Agarwal (1980) found the size of the host country's market to be one of the most popular factors influencing a country's propensity to attract inward investment, and most of the subsequent empirical literature has provided further support to the market size hypothesis (see, among others, Tsai, 1994; Billington, 1999; Chakrabarti, 2001).

Theories assuming imperfect markets

Industrial organization and oligopolistic reaction

The industrial organization approach (Hymer, 1960) is based on the idea that due to structural market imperfections, some firms enjoy advantages *vis-à-vis* competitors. These advantages (including brand name, patents, superior technology, organizational know-how and managerial skills) allow such firms to obtain rents in foreign markets that more than compensate for the inevitable initial disadvantages (for example, inferior market knowledge) to be experienced when competing with local firms within the alien environment. Firms, therefore, invest abroad to capitalize on such advantages. Hymer (1970) also argued that this conduct by firms, which often results in 'swallowing up' competition, affects market structure and allows MNEs to exploit monopoly and oligopoly powers.

The industrial organization hypothesis has received some support in subsequent literature. Graham and Krugman (1989), for example, used it to explain the growing inflow of FDI in the US post-1975, given the concomitant decline of US technological and managerial superiority over that period. The hypothesis, however, is not altogether cogent. More specifically, it fails to explain why firms need to engage in FDI to capitalize on their advantages when cheaper forms of expansion (for example, exporting) would allow them to compete equally successfully in international markets.

The offensive and defensive strategies of firms operating within imperfect markets have also been examined by Knickerbocker (1973). He concluded that it is the interdependence, rivalry and uncertainty inherent in the nature of oligopolies that explains the observed clustering of FDI in such industries. Higher industrial concentration causes increased oligopolistic reaction in the form of FDI except at very high levels, where an equilibrium is reached to avoid the overcrowding of a host country market.

Internalization

The market imperfection approach was further extended by Buckley and Casson (1976), who focused on the gains from internalization available in the presence of market failures. Internalization entails the acquisition of control, through vertical integration, over activities that would otherwise be carried out inefficiently through market transactions. Buckley and Casson (1976) identified several types of market imperfections, such as time lags and trans-action costs, that call for internalization, and listed a number of markets where such imperfections were more likely to be present. According to Buckley and Casson (1976), it is the internalization of markets across national boundaries that explains the very existence of international production.

Since the inception of the internalization hypothesis, much debate has taken place over the question of whether we are, in fact, in the presence of a 'general theory'. By focusing primarily, if not exclusively, upon the firm's motivation for producing abroad (hence partly neglecting the host country's macroeconomic factors that may affect a country's propensity to attract inward investment) the internalization approach should at best be referred to as a 'general theory' of the MNE rather than of FDI.

While, at the theoretical level, the comprehensive treatment of the rela-tionship between knowledge, market imperfections and the internalization of markets for intermediate products offered by the hypothesis has received much support, due to its high degree of generality, no direct empirical tests have been conducted.

The product cycle

The product cycle hypothesis (Kuznetz, 1953; Posner, 1961; Vernon, 1966) postulates that an innovation may emerge as a developed country export, extend its life cycle by being produced in more favourable foreign locations during its maturing phase and ultimately, once standardized, become a developing country export (developed country import). FDI, therefore, occurs when, as the product matures and competition becomes fierce, the innovator decides to shift production in developing countries because lower factor costs make this advantageous. Vernon's (1966) model of the product cycle was primarily intended to explain the expansion of US MNEs in Europe after the Second World War and, at the time of its inception, could account for the high concentration of innovations in, and technological superiority of, the USA.

Although during the late 1960s and early 1970s a number of empirical studies provided results consistent with the hypothesis' insightful description of the dynamic process of product development, the model is now regarded by many as largely anachronistic. First, as acknowledged by Vernon (1979) himself, the technological gap between the USA and other regions of the world (most notably Europe and Japan) has been eroded. Second, the product life extension which characterizes the maturity phase is difficult to reconcile with MNEs' tendency to produce the new product where factor costs are at their lowest from the start, and opt for a simultaneous introduction phase of the product worldwide. Most importantly, the hypothesis appears to be at odds with the fact that most FDI flows have been, and continue to be, between developed countries. Indeed, rather than moving toward truly global production relations, available evidence suggests a tendency toward a regionalization of international production primarily concentrated within the three major regional blocks of the 'Triad' (the USA, the EU and Japan). If these trends of intra-regional growth in FDI persist, we are likely to witness a further consolidation of the Triad members. The extent to which similar regional dynamics will emerge in the developing world largely depends upon the ability of developing countries to both close the gap on more advanced industrial economies (Kozul-Wright and Rowthorn, 1998), and cement regional cooperation with neighbouring countries.

The Uppsala internationalization model and psychic distance

The product cycle theory identified income and cost levels of would-be-host countries as the key factors affecting firms' ability to expand internationally. Work conducted by a group of Scandinavian researchers at Uppsala University, however, questioned the explanatory power of the product cycle theory by emphasising the limited knowledge of the individual investing firm as the most significant determinant.

In examining the increasing outward involvement of four Swedish organizations, Johanson and Wiedersheim-Paul (1975) identified a four-stage sequence leading to international production. Firms begin by serving the domestic market, then foreign markets are penetrated through exports. After some time, sales outlets are established abroad until, finally, foreign production facilities are set up. Johanson and Vahlne (1977) qualified the underlying logic of this sequential internationalization process, arguing that this stepwise, evolutionary development is based on the gradual acquisition of knowledge of the foreign market, and use of foreign-based sources of intelligence. It is this process of incremental, experiential learning that justifies and determines successively greater levels of commitment to foreign markets.

Research at Uppsala also observed that the typical FDI pattern of Swedish firms was that they first set up foreign production facilities in one of the closest Nordic countries, such as Norway. Later on, they established subsidiaries in countries such as Germany, Holland and the UK. And only then, if still successful, they would venture into 'psychically distant' markets. Although the concept of 'psychic distance' can be traced back to the mid-1950s (see Beckermann, 1956), its use in this context was operationalized in terms of uncertainty about would-be-host markets due to differences in culture, language and levels of education and economic development. Some studies have confirmed the existence of a gradual process characterising firms' international expansion (see, for example, Yoshihara, 1978), while others have provided support to the idea that psychic distance makes firms shy away from full-ownership foreign involvement (Gatignon and Anderson, 1988). Kogut and Singh (1988) also showed that firms are more likely to choose a joint venture (Jv) entry mode over wholly owned subsidiaries as means of reducing their uncertainty in relation to investments in psychically distant markets.

The Uppsala model, however, has not escaped criticism. Millington and Bayliss (1990), for example, found that the postulated stepwise development did not reflect the actual internationalization process of UK companies expanding in the European Community (EC). This was because knowledge based on experiential learning could be leveraged and translated across countries and product markets, and these economies of scope allowed firms to bypass some or all of the intermediate stages of the postulated sequential process. Like the product cycle theory, the Uppsala model is also incapable of explaining the emerging phenomenon of firms that are 'born global'. These are small to medium-sized companies which rather than slowly building their way into foreign markets, almost from inception expand by investing overseas. This is often evident in operations whose market entry strategy is driven by franchising, and the investment element is exemplified in their having to establish wholly owned subsidiaries in the overseas markets as a prelude to franchising in other markets. According to an Australian report by McKinsey & Co. (1993) 80 per cent of the firms studied 'view the world as their marketplace from the outset' (p. 9). McDougall, Shane and Oviatt (1994) also found that none of the 241 firms in their sample pursued a gradual incremental process when going international. It is important to note that, much, if not all, of the literature treating the 'born global' phenomenon has thus far focused on the activities undertaken by such firms in developed markets, particularly within new industries and high-technology-based sectors.

The eclectic approach

Dissatisfied with the fragmentation of previous explanations of FDI, Dunning's search (1977, 1979, 1981, 1988a, 1988b, 1998) for a generalized framework capable of integrating the existing hypotheses resulted in the eclectic theory, later renamed 'paradigm', of international production. Dunning's framework states that firms will engage in FDI if conditions of ownership, location and internalization (OLI) advantages are satisfied. Like those described by Hymer (1970), ownership advantages can give a firm competitive advantage *vis-à-vis* rivals. This approach, however, distinguishes between asset-based advantages, which arise from proprietary ownership of specific assets, and transaction-based advantages, that can be gained only if internalized. If the possession of ownership advantages offers internalization incentives across countries, and if there are additional location-specific factors which favour overseas production over production at home (access to natural endowments, lower factor costs and so on), then the three conditions for FDI are satisfied.

By virtue of its eclectic nature, which combines elements of various theories, Dunning's approach to explaining the 'why', 'how' and 'where' of international production can still be regarded as the most comprehensive FDI framework that has emerged to date. The strength of its explanatory power, however, also constitutes the main weakness of the approach in that, by including so many factors that are expected to influence both a firm's motivation to engage in foreign production and a country's propensity to attract inward investment, it loses any operationality. Indeed, no testable predictions can be deduced from the 'paradigm', and while location variables can easily be included in FDI regressions, it is much more difficult to estimate the relevance of motives linked to the ownership and internalization advantages underlying the OLI triad. Its application in the UNCTAD's (1998) *World Investment Report* as the framework used to analyse FDI determinants is a case in point, where only location advantages were considered. Interestingly, the reported econometric estimates of the role of location factors in attracting FDI led to the conclusion that market variables, such as physical infrastructure and political stability, are more relevant for explaining inward investment in developed than developing countries.

The level and variability of the exchange rate

Interest on the impact of the exchange rate on investment decisions can be traced back to the work of Aliber (1970). He suggested that weak-currency countries are likely to attract FDI due to the higher purchasing power and more efficient hedging capacity of investors operating from strong-currency countries. Despite Aliber's (1970) early work, it was not until the late 1980s and early 1990s that serious consideration started to be given to the exchange rate as a potential FDI determinant. This new research impetus was prompted by Caves (1989). He examined inward investment flows into the USA from over a dozen different countries, and found that the strength of a country's currency relative to the US dollar was an important explanatory variable for that country's direct investment in the USA. Since then, several hypotheses have emerged in the search for an explanation of the relationship between FDI and both the level and variability of the exchange rate.

With respect to the level of the exchange rate, two main models have stood out. The first one is that by Froot and Stein (1991). They present an unambiguous connection between exchange rates and FDI, when globally integrated capital markets are subject to informational imperfections. Their model considers US target firms sold at auction to the highest bidder. Informational asymmetries about an asset's payoffs cause external financing to be more expensive than internal financing and, because of this, the more net wealth the bidder can bring to such an 'information-intensive' investment, the lower will be his total cost of capital. As explained by Froot and Stein (1991, p. 1194) 'to the extent that foreigners hold more of their wealth in non-dollar denominated form, a depreciation of the dollar increases the relative wealth position of foreigners, and hence lowers their relative cost of capital', so that, *ceteris paribus*, more foreign investors win auctions.

Empirically, Froot and Stein (1991) found that when regressing inflows of FDI and other forms of capital inflows into the USA against the real value of the US dollar, FDI was 'the only type of capital inflow that is statistically negatively correlated to the value of the dollar' (Froot and Stein, 1991, p. 1209).

While a number of studies have provided evidence confirming the significance of the exchange rate as a key determinant of FDI (Klein and Rosengren, 1994; Gopinath, Pick and Vasavada, 1998), Froot and Stein's (1991) results have not received unanimous support. Stevens (1998) challenged the implied negative relationship between the flow of FDI and the exchange rate by specifically questioning the structural stability of the estimates obtained by Froot and Stein. He showed that their results were not robust for sub-samples within their chosen sample, and that when the original sample was extended to 1991, the exchange rate coefficient became insignificantly related to the direct investment ratio. Dewenter (1995) used transaction-specific data on foreign acquisitions of US target firms to examine the relationship between the value of the dollar and both the flow and prices of cross-border acquisitions. While confirming that a depreciating US dollar is associated with higher levels of foreign acquisitions and higher foreign takeover premia for US targets, Dewenter's (1995) results also showed that, after controlling for overall investment levels and relative corporate wealth, 'the measure of foreign investment relative to domestic investment shows no significant exchange rate sensitivity' (p. 415), a finding which casts further doubt on Froot and Stein's (1991) hypothesis that the exchange rate link is based on asymmetries between domestic and foreign investors.

The second model aimed at establishing why the level of the exchange rate matters has been advanced by Blonigen (1997). He argued that acquisitions involve firm-specific assets (such as product and process innovation, technology and so on) that can generate returns in currencies other than that used for purchase, yet do not involve a currency transaction as does the initial purchase of the asset. For instance, suppose that a firm intends to purchase knowledge-rich foreign assets in one currency (say, dollars), and by leveraging this knowledge in its home market expects to generate returns in its own currency (say, yen) as a result of this acquisition. Evidently, under this scenario, given that the foreign firm's costs and returns are in different currencies, a depreciation of the dollar would increase the foreign firm's dollar-denominated reservation bid for the knowledge-rich US asset (relative to US firms' reservation bid), thus increasing its likelihood to win the auction. Blonigen (1997) empirically tested his model's predictions and found that real depreciations of the dollar lead to substantial increases in acquisition FDI in industries that more likely have firm-specific assets, namely, manufacturing industries with high R&D.

Conflicting evidence, however, comes from Seo, Tarumun and Suh (2002) who investigated the impact of exchange rate levels on inward FDI to Korea. While all their estimated regressions show that the real exchange rate exerts a positive influence on FDI inflows, they interpret this evidence as consistent with Froot and Stein's (1991) wealth-effects hypothesis. They argue that, given the 'status quo of Korea's technology capacity' (p. 15), foreign acquisitions of Korean real assets are not for the purpose of acquiring firm-specific assets that may increase the foreign investor's global productivity.

As noted earlier, the theoretical underpinning for the impact of exchange rate variability on FDI has also been recently developed. Cushman (1985) considered a model where the firm maximizes the 'certainty equivalent' of its future real profits expressed in domestic currency terms. He analysed the effects of real exchange rate risk and expectations on direct investment for four different cases, depending on where inputs were purchased, where output was produced, where financial capital was raised and where output was sold. Using data on bilateral direct investment flows from the USA to the UK, France, Germany, Canada and Japan, Cushman found that increases in real exchange rate variability raise direct investment, partly because in the presence of exchange rate risk FDI is preferred to exports as a means to serving the foreign market. Cushman (1988) finds an analogous relationship between exchange rate variability and inward US FDI.

Goldberg and Kolstad (1995) developed a two-period model in which firms produce under constant marginal costs but make production decisions before uncertainty in exchange rates and in demand are resolved. The model showed how, if investors are risk averse, the share of investment resources located abroad increases as short-term volatility rises. Goldberg and Kolstad tested their theoretical proposition using US bilateral FDI data (with Canada, Japan and the UK) and obtained empirical results consistent with their model's prediction.

Using Dixit's (1989) option pricing framework – according to which as the exchange rate becomes more volatile, the greater the incentive to postpone entry – Campa (1993) estimated the effects that exchange rate variability and industry-specific sunk costs have on entry by foreign firms into the USA. He found exchange rate variability to be negatively correlated with the number of events of entry by foreign firms, and that this effect becomes even more pronounced in industries where sunk costs are relatively high. Campa (1993) also examined the impact of the level of the exchange rate on entry into the USA and, contrary to Froot and Stein (1991), found a positive relationship which he justified by arguing that the higher the level of the dollar, the higher would be inward investment as the expectation of future profits is higher.

Other specific determinants

Socio-political instability

Although the intuition behind the argument that an unstable social and political environment may deter inward investment is self-explanatory, the empirical significance of socio-political instability, and its relative importance among FDI determinants, is somewhat unclear. Indeed, while survey studies have consistently shown socio-political instability to be one of the major concerns of company executives, the evidence from econometric studies is much more ambiguous. Schneider and Frey (1985) found a statistically significant negative relationship between the number of strikes and riots in host countries and inward FDI. Conversely, Bennet and Green (1972), Chase, Kuhle and Walther (1988) and Wheeler and Mody (1992) found that direct investments did not appear to be a function of socio-political instability in host countries.

The conflicting evidence may be partly explained by the operational difficulties inherent in measuring social unrest and political risk. As originally pointed out by Kobrin (1981), socio-political instability is a complex qualitative phenomenon for which it is difficult to obtain reliable estimates, especially given that most of the available proxies can only indicate the presence or absence of certain political or social events rather than their potential manifestation as constraints upon foreign investors' operations. Equally, only some confidence can be placed upon commercially available indices. Another difficulty originates from the fact that the perceived degree of risk stemming from socio-political events in host countries may vary depending on the country of origin of the investment, the time at which the investment was made and the composition of the MNE's investment portfolio since a portfolio balancing effect aimed at diluting risk may well motivate MNEs to also invest in countries characterized by a high degree of socio-political instability.

Export orientation, openness to trade and tariff-jumping

Export orientation and openness to trade are other factors that typically enter the determination of the FDI function. The widespread perception is that MNEs are attracted to export-oriented countries, first, for their intrinsic export potential, and second, because 'open' economies tend to instil greater confidence in foreign investors by virtue of their better performance record and generally more stable economic climate.

Export orientation and openness to trade have received considerable support in the empirical literature (see, for example, Culem, 1988; Chakrabarti, 2001). It is interesting to point out that the relevance of these variables constitutes evidence inconsistent with the tariff-jumping hypothesis, which views FDI as the result of MNEs' attempt to circumvent trade barriers. It should be recognized, however, that as more and more countries liberalize their import regimes, the tariff-jumping motive for FDI is bound to become less relevant. This argument is supported by the relatively recent evidence provided by Blonigen and Feenstra (1996), who found trade barriers to have no significant impact on FDI.

Wage costs and labour skills

Theoretical backing for the role of labour costs in the determination of FDI comes from the product cycle hypothesis and the eclectic paradigm. The standard hypothesis holds that lower relative wage costs will encourage investment by MNEs who seek efficiency gains. Most of the empirical literature, however, suggests that, for industrial countries, labour costs are not a significant determinant of FDI. This may be due to the fact that wage rate differentials are not particularly strong across developed countries.

When the cost of labour is relatively insignificant, labour skills are expected to influence a country's propensity to attract FDI. Due to measurement difficulties, however, the existing evidence, much of which is of an indirect nature, is inconclusive.

Government incentives

Governments have rarely held a neutral position towards FDI. Some governments, perceiving the net benefits to be negative, have sought to restrict inward investment through the establishment of various protectionist barriers, which have ranged from the slow processing of authorizations for FDI to its outright prohibition. Other governments, on the other hand, have offered incentives in order to attract investment by MNEs. Since the mid-1980s, there has been a drastic shift in policy towards the latter approach, with many countries that had traditionally opted for widespread controls on FDI engaging in radical reforms of their investment regimes aimed at facilitating and promoting inward investment through incentives (De Vita, 2001). These incentives include, in addition to more liberal operating conditions, fiscal benefits, such as tax concessions, and financial benefits, such as grants and subsidized loans. Some governments also provide less transparent benefits, such as public sector investment on specific infrastructure likely to raise the expected returns from a given investment project. But do these incentives play a significant role in the determination of FDI? Overall, the evidence would seem to indicate that incentives have no major impact (see Porcano and Price, 1996), especially when they are established, or perceived to be established, to compensate for continuing comparative disadvantages of the host country. As suggested by UNCTAD (1998), although government incentives may influence the choice of location within a country once the investment decision has been made, they are not to be regarded as an actual determinant of FDI.

4   FDI determinants in developing countries and future prospects

Although, in relative terms, FDI remains heavily concentrated in developed countries, the 1990s witnessed a substantial growth in investment flows to developing countries, with FDI increasing from $ 24 billion in 1990 to $ 178 billion in 2000 (World Bank, 2001). This boom would seem to indicate that MNEs are increasingly considering developing countries to be profitable investment locations. But are the key factors that influence direct investment flows to developing countries the same as those pertaining to developed countries? Unfortunately, the empirical evidence does not provide an altogether conclusive answer to this question.

Variables that appear to be particularly significant in explaining developing countries' propensity to attract FDI include: market size (Torrisi, 1985; Shamsuddin, 1994; Pistoresi, 2000); export orientation, particularly in the manufacturing sector (Singh and Jun, 1995; Gastanaga, Nugent and Pashamova, 1998; Taylor, 2000) and relative wage costs (Flamm, 1984; Lucas, 1993; Sader, 1993).

Unfortunately, research on the potential impact of exchange rate movements on FDI in the context of developing countries is almost inexistent. Bénassy-Quéré, Fontagné and Lahrèche-Révil (2001) attempted to begin to fill this gap by estimating a panel of forty-two developing countries receiving FDI from seventeen OECD countries over the 1984–96 period. Their model considers the case of a risk averse MNE which contemplates producing in two alternative foreign locations in order to re-export, the location choice being dependent upon the host country price competitiveness (proxied by the relative real exchange rate of the potential host country against the investing country), the effect of nominal exchange rate variability and whether the correlation of the exchange rates of the alternative locations against the investing country's currency is positive or negative. Their empirical results indicate that: (1) a depreciation (rise in the real exchange rate) of the host country against the investing country increases FDI inflows; (2) an increase in nominal exchange rate variability reduces inward FDI; and (3) when the exchange rate of a host country is positively correlated to that of alternative locations, an improved competitiveness in those locations reduces FDI inflows to that country (the substitution effect). While bearing in mind that these findings have yet to prove robust to the test of future replication studies, they point to fairly significant policy implications for developing countries. Since exchange rate volatility induced by a free-floating regime is detrimental to FDI inflows, the first policy implication is that developing countries should consider the adoption of a currency board which, by holding the nominal exchange rate stable, would be the best way of attracting FDI. Bénassy-Quéré, Fontagné and Lahrèche-Révil (2001) also suggest that such a stabilization should be done against the currency of the country or area expected to be the major FDI supplier. As they themselves conclude 'this would mean a polarization of exchange-rate regimes consistent with economic geography (given that the impact of exchange rate variables increases with proximity), hence a step toward monetary regionalism' (p. 192).

With respect to incentive programmes and promotional activities, the effect on the level of FDI also appears to be rather weak in relation to developing countries. In the early 1990s, Bangladesh and Pakistan implemented policy reforms aimed at facilitating inward investment but still failed to attract significant flows. Most econometric studies have corroborated the view that the impact of government incentives and promotional activities is rather limited. The most recent evidence comes from Wint and Williams (2002) who, using a stratified random sample of thirty-six developing countries, found that their proxy for 'effectiveness of investment promotion activity' did not have a statistically significant effect on FDI flows. Interestingly, they attribute the relative insignificance of promotion to the changes in governmental attitudes toward FDI and, more specifically, to the convergence among the promotional efforts of developing countries. As they put it: 'As countries converge toward best practice in promotion, it becomes more difficult for any particular country to gain a differential advantage in relation to attracting FDI' (2002, p. 370).

As to the remaining variables, the evidence remains fairly ambiguous. For instance, mixed results seem to characterize the role of socio-political instability in influencing FDI in developing countries. In their analysis of fifty-eight developing countries, Root and Ahmed (1979) found that, aside from constitutional changes in government leadership, other measures of socio-political instability (e.g. internal armed attacks) did not have a significant effect on FDI. Nigh (1985) examined the impact of political risk on FDI undertaken by US MNEs in both developed and developing countries using panel data on inter-country and intra-country conflict and cooperation. He found that while for developed countries only inter-country events were significant determinants of FDI, for investments in developing countries US MNEs responded to both intra-country and inter-country events. Lucas (1993) adopted an altogether different approach. He made use of episodic dummies associated with 'good' socio-political events, such as the Olympic games in Korea, and 'bad' events, such as Marcos' martial law in the Philippines. He found that while good socio-political events were positively associated with FDI, episodes of the latter kind had a negative impact on inward investment. More recently, however, Jaspersen, Aylward and Knox (2000) and Asiedu (2002) found no significant relationship between measures of political instability and FDI flows. This may be partly due to the fact that many nations now offer government-backed insurance policies to cover various types of FDI risk in politically unstable countries of the developing world. Risks insurable through these policies include the risk of expropriation of assets, war losses and losses stemming from the inability of repatriation of profits.

Overall, this lack of a clear and conclusive pattern of results as to the relative importance of the determinants of FDI may be explained by a number of factors ranging from the challenges associated with the collection of reliable FDI data discussed at the beginning of this chapter, to differences in estimation techniques and model specifications. Indeed, as shown by Chakrabarti's (2001) extreme-bound-analysis robustness tests, estimates of the many controversial determinants of FDI 'are highly sensitive to small alterations in the conditioning information set' (p. 108) of FDI equations.

Against this backdrop, it is not easy to formulate expectations of future trends on both the geography of FDI and possible shifts in the relative significance of variables determining the location of multinational activities. Some experts have argued that the process of globalization has already started to change the relative importance of traditional and non-traditional determinants. As reported by UNCTAD (1996, p. 97) 'one of the most important traditional FDI determinants, the size of national markets, has decreased in importance. At the same time, cost differences between locations, the quality of infrastructure, the ease of doing business and the availability of skills have become more important.'

The study by Noorbakhsh, Paloni and Youssef (2001) partially corroborates the view that non-traditional determinants, particularly labour skills and knowledge, are becoming increasingly more important as a result of globalization. Specifically, their results show that in the context of developing countries 'the estimated coefficients of the variables used as proxies for human capital as well as their t ratios increase in magnitude across the consecutive sample periods' (p. 1602). On the other hand, in his analysis of the impact of globalization-induced changes on the determinants of FDI in developing countries, Nunnenkamp (2002) argues that traditional market-related determinants are still dominant factors in shaping the geography of FDI, and that with the exception of the availability of local skills, non-traditional determinants such as labour costs and openness to trade have not become more important. Finally, Dunning (2002) points out that while in large developing countries traditional economic determinants such as cheap labour, natural resources and market size, remain important, in the more advanced industrialized countries 'MNEs are increasingly seeking complementary knowledge intensive resources and capabilities, a supportive and transparent commercial, legal communications infrastructure, and government policies favourable to globalization, innovation and entrepreneurship' (pp. 12–13). Dunning (2002) also suggests that the new globally integrated economic environment is likely to affect the geography of FDI in two main ways. First, by placing a higher premium on uncertainty and environmental risk, it may steer MNEs' investments towards locations politically friendly towards their home country regimes. This, in turn, is likely to make socio-political instability more relevant as a determinant of FDI. Second, the increasing global integration of markets and competition is likely to force MNEs to improve their cost efficiency by relocating some of their plants in low (real)-cost locations. Under this scenario, the nature of investment flows from developed to developing countries may well shift from market-seeking and resource-seeking FDI to more (vertical) efficiency-seeking FDI.

5 Conclusions

Our review of the various hypotheses of FDI has revealed a rather fragmented theoretical landscape. While the main hypotheses are not mutually exclusive, and many rather than a single or even a few factors are bound to affect

FDI, it is also obvious that the determinants identified in the literature cannot all be simultaneously relevant. Lack of a consensus on a unique all-encompassing model capable of guiding empirical work has produced a very heterogeneous plethora of empirical studies. Partly due to differences in the underlying frameworks and methodologies employed, most findings stemming from these studies are not directly comparable and often present conflicting evidence from which it is not possible to discern a conventional wisdom.

The recent debate on the potential shifts in the relative significance of traditional and non-traditional determinants of FDI in the context of globalization, though very promising, is still in its infancy and has yet to mature before reliable conclusions can be drawn. What is clear, however, is that the relative importance of factors determining a country's propensity to attract FDI will continue to be highly contextual. For example, the main forces believed to drive inward investment in the transition economies of the CEE area (see Resmini, 2000) will inevitably continue to differ from those attracting FDI in sub-Saharan Africa (see Asiedu, 2002).

The significance of specific determinants also appears to be dependent upon the type of FDI. While some determinants such as socio-political stability could well be relevant for every kind of investment, other determinants may not be capable of explaining all types of FDI. For example, the size of domestic demand and income growth cannot explain investment in small, low-income developing countries. Such investment, therefore, is unlikely to be of the market-seeking type. Similarly, labour costs are unlikely to be very relevant in the case of (natural) resource-seeking FDI.

In light of the above considerations, in order to gain a better insight into the contextual significance of FDI determinants, future research should make use of data disaggregated by market of destination and sectors of economic activity while controlling for the type of investment being examined. Time series econometric studies that test for structural breaks and the significance of the estimated coefficients across consecutive sample periods would also be valuable in enhancing our knowledge of possible shifts in the relative importance of traditional and non-traditional FDI determinants.

As to the role of governments as they seek to attract inward investment, although the evidence reviewed suggests that the effectiveness of incentives and promotional campaigns cannot be taken for granted, and may not lead to a country-specific differential advantage, it is equally evident that especially developing countries should continue their special attraction efforts if they want to avoid experiencing differential disadvantages. As a guideline to policymakers, it seems reasonable to suggest that the encouragement of inward investment should take forms that also add value to domestic investors, and bring long-term benefits to the host country's economy. These may include the upgrading and extension of infrastructure and public expenditure on education and training.

Note

1. An important lesson of the recent financial crises in the Asian emerging economies has been increased awareness of the destabilising effect of short-term capital flows. By contrast, FDI is widely perceived as a stable source of financing for developing countries.

References

J.P. Agarwal, 'Determinants of Foreign Direct Investment: A Survey', *Weltwirtschaftliches Archiv*, 116 (1980): 739–73.

R.Z. Aliber, 'A Theory of Direct Foreign Investment', in C.P. Kindleberger (ed.), *The International Corporation: A Symposium* (Cambridge, MA: MIT Press, 1970): 17–34.

E. Asiedu, 'On the Determinants of Foreign Direct Investment to Developing Countries: Is Africa Different?', *World Development*, 30 (2002): 107–19.

W. Beckermann, 'Distance and the Pattern of Intra-European Trade', *Review of Economics and Statistics*, 28 (1956): 31–40.

A. Bénassy-Quéré, L. Fontagné and A. Lahrèche-Révil, 'Exchange-Rate Strategies in the Competition for Attracting Foreign Direct Investment', *Journal of the Japanese and International Economies*, 2 (2001): 178–198.

P.D. Bennet and R.T. Green, 'Political Instability as a Determinant of Direct Foreign Investment in Marketing', *Journal of Marketing Research*, 9 (1972): 162–186.

N. Billington, 'The Location of Foreign Direct Investment: An Empirical Analysis', *Applied Economics*, 31 (1999): 65–76.

B.A. Blonigen, 'Firm-Specific Assets and the Link between Exchange Rates and Foreign Direct Investment', *American Economic Review*, 87 (1997): 447–65.

B.A. Blonigen and R.C. Feenstra, 'Effects of US Trade Protection and Promotion Policies', Working Paper, 5285 (Cambridge, MA: National Bureau of Economic Research, 1996).

P.J. Buckley and M.C. Casson, *The Future of the Multinational Enterprise* (London: Macmillan, 1976).

J.M. Campa, 'Entry by Foreign Firms in the United States under Exchange Rate Uncertainty', *Review of Economics and Statistics*, 75 (1993): 614–22.

R.E. Caves, 'Exchange-Rate Movements and Foreign Direct Investment in the United States', in D.B. Andretsch and M.P. Claudon (eds), *The Internationalization of US Markets* (New York: New York University Press, 1989): 199–228.

R.E. Caves, *Multinational Enterprises and Economic Analysis*, 2nd edn (Cambridge: Cambridge University Press, 1996).

A. Chakrabarti, 'The Determinants of Foreign Direct Investment: Sensitivity Analyses of Cross-Country Regressions', *Kyklos*, 54 (2001): 89–114.

C.D. Chase, J.L. Kuhle and C.H. Walther, 'The Relevance of Political Risk in Direct Foreign Investment', *Management International Review*, 28 (1988): 31–8.

C.G. Culem, 'The Locational Determinants of Direct Investment among Industrialized Countries', *European Economic Review*, 32 (1988): 885–904.

D.O. Cushman, 'Real Exchange Rate Risk, Expectations, and the Level of Foreign Direct Investment', *Review of Economics and Statistics*, 67 (1985): 297–308.

D.O. Cushman, 'Exchange-Rate Uncertainty and Foreign Investment in the United States', *Weltwirtschaftliches Archiv*, 124 (1988): 322–35.

G. De Vita, 'Foreign Direct Investment and Multinational Enterprise', in K. Lawler and H. Seddighi (eds), *International Economics: Theories, Themes, and Debates* (London: Prentice-Hall, 2001): 353–65.

K.L. Dewenter, 'Do Exchange Rates Drive Foreign Direct Investment?', *Journal of Business*, 68 (1995): 405–33.

A. Dixit, 'Entry and Exit Decisions under Uncertainty', *Journal of Political Economy*, 97 (1989): 620–38.

J.H. Dunning, 'Trade, Location of Economic Activity and the MNE: A Search for an Eclectic Approach', in B. Ohlin, P.O. Hesselborn and P.M. Wijkman (eds), *The International Allocation of Economic Activity* (London: Macmillan, 1977): 395–418.

J.H. Dunning, 'Explaining Patterns of International Production: In Defence of the Eclectic Theory', *Oxford Bulletin of Economics and Statistics*, 41 (1979): 269–95.

J.H. Dunning, *International Production and the Multinational Enterprise* (London: Allen & Unwin, 1981).

J.H. Dunning, 'The Eclectic Paradigm of International Production: A Restatement of Some Possible Extensions', *Journal of International Business Studies*, 19 (1988a): 1–29.

J.H. Dunning, 'Location and the Multinational Enterprise: A Neglected Factor?', *Journal of International Business Studies*, 29 (1998b): 45–66.

J.H. Dunning, 'Determinants of Foreign Direct Investment: Globalization Induced Changes and the Role of FDI Policies', Paper presented at the Annual Bank Conference on Development Economics in Europe, Oslo (2002): 1–17.

K. Flamm, 'The Volatility of Offshore Investment', *Journal of Development Economics*, 16 (1984): 231–48.

K. Froot and J. Stein, 'Exchange Rates and Foreign Direct Investment: An Imperfect Capital Markets Approach', *Quarterly Journal of Economics*, 106 (1991): 1191–1217.

V.M. Gastanaga, J.B. Nugent and B. Pashamova, 'Host Country Reforms and FDI Inflows: How Much Difference Do They Make?', *World Development*, 26 (1998): 1299–1314.

H. Gatignon and E. Anderson, 'The Multinational Corporation's Degree of Control over Foreign Subsidiaries: An Empirical Test of a Transaction Cost Explanation', *Journal of Law, Economics and Organization*, 2 (1988): 305–36.

L. Goldberg and C. Kolstad, 'Foreign Direct Investment, Exchange Rate Variability and Demand Uncertainty', *International Economic Review*, 36 (1995): 855–73.

M. Gopinath, D. Pick and U. Vasavada, 'Exchange Rate Effects on the Relationship Between FDI and Trade in the US Food Processing Industry', *American Journal of Agricultural Economics*, 80 (1998): 1073–9.

E.M. Graham and P.R. Krugman, *Foreign Direct Investment in the United States* (Washington, DC: Institute for International Economics, 1989).

S. Hirsch, 'The United States Electronic Industry in International Trade', *National Institute Economic Review*, 24 (1965): 92–7.

G.C. Hufbauer (1975) 'The Multinational Corporation and Direct Investment', in P.B. Kenen (ed.), *International Trade and Finance: Frontiers for Research* (Cambridge: Cambridge University Press, 1975): 253–319.

S. Hymer, *The International Operations of National Firms: A Study of Direct Foreign Investment*. PhD thesis, MIT, 1960.

S. Hymer, 'The Efficiency (Contradictions) of Multinational Corporations', *American Economic Review*, 60 (1970): 441–8.

IMF, *Balance of Payments Manual*, 5th edn (Washington, DC: International Monetary Fund, 1993).

F.Z. Jaspersen, A.H. Aylward and A.D. Knox, 'The Effects of Risk on Private Investment: Africa Compared with Other Developing Areas', in P. Collier and C. Pattillo (eds), *Investment and Risk in Africa* (New York: St Martin's Press, 2000): 71–95.

J. Johanson and J.E. Vahlne, 'The Internationalization Process of the Firm: A Model of Knowledge Development and Increasing Foreign Market Commitments', *Journal of International Business Studies*, 8 (1977): 22–32.

J. Johanson and F. Wiedersheim-Paul, 'The Internationalization of the Firm: Four Swedish Cases', *Journal of Management Studies*, 12 (1975): 305–22.

M. Klein and F. Rosengren, 'The Real Exchange Rate and Foreign Direct Investment in the United States: Relative Wealth vs. Relative Wage Effects', *Journal of International Economics*, 36 (1994): 373–89.

F.T. Knickerbocker, *Oligopolistic Reaction and Multinational Enterprise* (Cambridge, MA: Harvard University, 1973).

S. Kobrin, 'Political Risk: A Review and Reconsideration', *Journal of International Business*, Spring (1981): 67–80.

B. Kogut and H. Singh, 'The Effect of National Culture on the Choice of Entry Mode', *Journal of International Business Studies*, 3 (1988): 411–32.

R. Kozul-Wright and R. Rowthorn, 'Spoilt for Choice: Multinational Corporations and the Geography of International Production', *Oxford Review of Economic Policy*, 2 (1988): 74–93.

S. Kuznetz, *Economic Change* (New York: Norton, 1953).

R.E. Lipsey, 'The Role of Foreign Direct Investment in International Capital Flows', in M. Feedstein (ed.), *International Capital Flows* (Chicago: University of Chicago Press, 1999): 307–31.

R.E.B. Lucas, 'On the Determinants of Direct Foreign Investment: Evidence from East and SouthEast Asia', *World Development*, 21 (1993): 391–406.

P.P. McDougall, S. Shane and B.M. Oviatt, 'Explaining the Formation of International New Ventures', *Journal of Business Venturing*, 9 (1994): 469–87.

McKinsey and Co., *Emerging Exporters* (Melbourne: Australian Manufacturing Council, 1993).

A.I. Millington and B.T. Bayliss, 'The Process of Internationalization: UK Companies in the EC', *Management International Review*, 2 (1990): 151–61.

D. Nigh, 'The Effect of Political Events on US Direct Foreign Investment: A Pooled Time Series Cross-Sectional Analysis', *Journal of International Business Studies*, 16 (1985): 1–18.

F. Noorbakhsh, A. Paloni and A. Youssef, 'Human Capital and FDI Inflows to Developing Countries: New Empirical Evidence', *World Development*, 29 (2001): 1593–1610.

P. Nunnenkamp, 'Determinants of FDI in Developing Countries: Has Globalization Changed the Rules of the Game?', Kiel Institute for World Economics, Kiel Working Papers, 1122 (2002).

OECD, *Benchmark Definition of Foreign Direct Investment*, 3rd edn (Paris: Organisation for Economic Co-operation and Development, 1996).

B. Pistoresi, 'Investimenti diretti esteri e fattori di localizzazione: L'America Latina e il Sud Est Asiatico', *Rivista di Politica Economica*, 90 (2000): 27–44.

T.M. Porcano and C.E. Price, 'The Effects of Government Tax and non-Tax Incentives on Foreign Direct Investment', *Multinational Business Review*, 4 (1996): 9–20.

M. Posner, 'International Trade and Technical Change', *Oxford Economic Papers*, 13 (1961): 323–41.

L. Resmini, 'The Determinants of Foreign Direct Investment in the CEEs: New Evidence from Sectoral Patterns', *Economics of Transition*, 8 (2000): 665–89.

F. Root and A. Ahmed, 'Empirical Determinants of Manufacturing Direct Foreign Investment in Developing Countries', *Economic Development and Cultural Change*, 27 (1979): 751–67.

F. Sader, 'Privatisation and Foreign Investment in the Developing World', World Bank, Policy Research Working Papers, 1202 (1993).

F. Schneider and B.S. Frey, 'Economic and Political Determinants of Foreign Direct Investment', *World Development*, 13 (1985): 161–75.

J.S. Seo, S. Tarumun and C.S. Suh, 'Do Exchange Rates Have any Impact on Foreign Direct Investment Flows in Asia: Experiences of Korea', Paper presented at the first annual conference, Korea and the World Economy (Seoul, Korea Yonsei University, 21–22 July 2002): 1–18.

A.F.M. Shamsuddin, 'Economic Determinants of Foreign Direct Investment in Less Developed Countries', *The Pakistan Development Review*, 33 (1994): 41–51.

H. Singh and K.W. Jun, 'Some New Evidence on Determinants of Foreign Direct Investment in Developing Countries', World Bank, Policy Research Working Papers, 1531 (1995).

G.V.G. Stevens, 'Exchange Rates and Foreign Direct Investments: A Note, *Journal of Policy Modeling*, 20 (1998): 393–401.

C.T. Taylor, 'The Impact of Host Country Government Policy on US Multilateral Investment Decisions', *World Economy*, 23 (2000): 635–47.

C.R. Torrisi, 'The Determinants of Direct Foreign Investment in a Small LDC', *Journal of Economic Development*, 10 (1985): 29–45.

P.L. Tsai, 'Determinants of Foreign Direct Investment and Its Impact on Economic Growth', *Journal of Economic Development*, 19 (1994): 137–63.

United Nations Conference on Trade and Development (UNCTAD), *World Investment Report 1996* (New York: United Nations, 1996).

United Nations Conference on Trade and Development (UNCTAD), *World Investment Report 1998: Trends and Determinants* (New York: United Nations, 1998).

US Department of Commerce, *Foreign Investments in the United States* (Washington, DC: Bureau of Foreign and Domestic Commerce, 1937).

US Department of Commerce, *Direct Private Foreign Investments of the United States, Census of 1950* (Washington, DC: Office of Business Economics, 1953).

R. Vernon, 'International Investment and International Trade in the Product Cycle', *Quarterly Journal of Economics*, 80 (1966): 190–207.

R. Vernon, 'The Product Cycle Hypothesis in a New International Environment', *Oxford Bulletin of Economics and Statistics*, 41 (1979): 255–67.

D. Wheeler and A. Mody, 'International Investment Location Decisions, the Case of US Firms', *Journal of International Economics*, 33 (1992): 57–76.

A.G. Wint and D.A. Williams, 'Attracting FDI to Developing Countries. A Changing Role for Government?', *The International Journal of Public Sector Management*, 15 (2002): 361–74.

World Bank, *Global Development Finance* (New York: World Bank, 2001).

K. Yoshihara, 'Determinants of Japanese Investment in South-East Asia', *International Social Science Journal*, 2 (1978): 1–20.

2
The Role of Foreign Direct Investment and its Determinants

Simran Kahai[1]

1 Introduction

Foreign direct investment (FDI) was a .key factor in shaping the world economy during the 1980s and 1990s. During this period, it grew faster than trade and domestic production, with the world stock of FDI having reached nearly $ 6 trillion in 2000, ten times the level of 1980 (*The Economist*, 24 February 2001). FDI has now come to be widely recognized as major contributor to growth and development. Global FDI inflows measured $ 865 billion in 1999, compared with $ 209 billion in 1990 (World Bank, 2000). FDI grew by 18 per cent in 2000, faster than other economic aggregates such as world production, capital formation and trade.

Since the mid-1990s, FDI has become the largest component of external financing for developing countries. It is estimated that FDI to developing countries increased to about $ 200 billion in 2000 from $ 183 in 1999 (World Bank, 2000). During this period, FDI flows on a net basis (inflows less out-flows), were the only positive component of private flows going to developing countries. FDI declined in 2001, this was the first decline since 1991 and was the result of recession affecting the world's major economies. Most of this decline was on FDI going to the developed countries. FDI declined by 59 per cent in the developed economies, compared to 14 per cent in the developing countries (UNCTAD, 2002). This disparity in decline can be attributed to the fact that since the mid-1990s cross-border mergers and acquisitions (M&As) have been the main vehicle of FDI in developed countries. The slower economic growth in the developed countries discouraged firms from making cross-border investment in developed countries and made them look for low-cost locations in developing countries to meet competitive pressure.

Foreign private capital inflow into developing countries can take three principal forms: commercial borrowing from overseas markets, portfolio investment and FDI. Over the years the composition of capital flows has shifted away from bank loans and toward FDI and portfolio investment.

During the 1978–81 period loans accounted for 80 per cent of total private capital flows, with FDI and portfolio investment accounting for the remaining 20 per cent. By 1990–5, the share of loans had decreased to 36 per cent, with FDI and portfolio investment accounting for the remaining 64 per cent (Loungani and Razin, 2001). There is now general consensus that FDI is a better form of private form of capital inflow to developing countries compared to portfolio equity investments. This is because portfolio investment has been found to be sensitive to financial market conditions around the globe, in contrast, FDI flows driven by structural factors in the host country are relatively more stable. For instance, FDI was remarkably stable in East Asian countries during the global financial crises of 1997–8. On the other hand, other forms of private capital flows – portfolio equity and debt flows – were subject to large reversals during the same period (Dadush, Dasgupta and Ratha, 2000; Lipsey, 2001). Also, while any of the three forms of capital inflows can help to bridge the savings–investment gap in the economy, it is FDI that almost always brings additional resources – technology, management know-how and access to export markets (Romer, 1993). Capital associated with FDI can enhance the performance of a country because it not only provides assets directly used in production of goods and services, but can also act as a catalyst for domestic investment, either by contributing to the mobilization of financial and other resources of indigenous firms or as a signal of confidence for future investment opportunities (Bloom, 1992).

The current pattern of capital flows from developed to developing countries is similar to the pattern observed in the late nineteenth century. During that period, investment from Europe exploded into new world countries such as the USA, Argentina and Australia. For example, Britain was running a current account surplus of around 8 per cent of GDP that it invested in bonds to finance the construction of foreign railways and other projects in the new world. During each year of the last quarter of the nineteenth century, British capital accounted for more than 5 per cent of GDP in Argentina, Australia, Canada and the USA (*The Economist*, 3 May 2003). This capital flow was a major contributor to the development of the new world.

The development of the newly industrialized countries (NICs) also depended heavily on foreign financing in the form of commercial and official loans. However, today's fast-growing countries, such as China, Malaysia, Singapore, Taiwan and Thailand rely more on FDI and portfolio investment. Between 1990 and 1994, the value of total private capital flows to developing countries more than tripled, with FDI constituting the largest single component (UNCTAD, 1995).

The trend of FDI in the developing countries can be seen in Figure 2.1. During the decade covered in Figure 2.1, only two years saw a decline in FDI going to the developing countries. The smaller decline in 1998 was the result of the global financial crises of 1997–8. The larger decline was in the year 2001, and this was the result of recession in the major economies of the

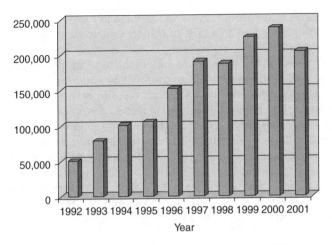

Figure 2.1 FDI inflows in developing countries, 1992–2001 ($ million)

world. Uncertainties resulting from the recession made the firms in these countries hesitant in making investment in domestic and overseas markets. In spite of the substantial liberalizing measures of the 1990s, developing countries still attract less than a third of world FDI flows, and these flows are concentrated only in a small number of developing countries. The forty-eight LDCs receive just 1.5 per cent of FDI (Micklethwait and Wooldridge, 2000). In 2001, the five largest host countries in the developing world received 62 per cent of total inflows and the ten largest received three-quarters. For developing countries whose future growth depends upon successful participation in world economy, it is important that they understand the criteria that MNCs apply when investing abroad. The increase in investment flows is to a large extent the result of expansion in international production. International production by MNCs continues to grow in importance for both developed and developing countries. Over the years researchers have used the concept of value-chain to describe how a firm organizes and performs discrete activities that add value to its production of goods and services (Dunning, 1993; Hamel and Prahlad, 1994; Porter,1990). According to this analysis, with reductions in transportation costs and the spread of new technologies in today's world, MNCs evaluate all activities in the value-chain as potential candidates for being performed by one or more affiliates outside the country. At the centre of the emerging integrated international production system are MNCs which have established worldwide affiliates. In 2001,more than 65,000 MNCs with over 850,000 affiliates were engaged in cross-border production of goods and services and accounted for 54 million employees, compared to 24 million in 1990 (UNCTAD 2002). Indeed international production today is more important than exports when it comes to delivering goods and services to foreign markets. In 2001 foreign affiliates sales of almost $ 19 trillion were more than twice as high as world exports.

The purpose of this chapter is to examine the role of foreign capital in the form of FDI in enabling developing countries to obtain access to resources and markets needed for restructuring their economies, thereby creating new opportunities for growth and development. Specifically, the chapter includes a comprehensive review of theoretical and empirical studies that have made important contribution to the understanding of the role of FDI and the determinants of FDI in the developing countries. The chapter is organized the following manner. Section 2 focuses on the importance of FDI in today's global economy and Section 3 discusses the current literature on the benefits of FDI to developing countries. Section 4 reviews the determinants of FDI. Section 5 concludes the chapter.

2   Benefits of FDI to developing countries

The role of FDI

In the 1980s and 1990s a number of developing countries took advantage of the MNCs' desire to engage in international production. These countries had had a high growth rate up to the time of the Asian financial crisis in the second half of the 1990s. Studies have shown that economic growth in these countries was associated with industrialization and export promotion (Chow and Kellman, 1993). Many of these fast-growing countries restructured themselves by forming important linkages with foreign firms that undertake international production. This resulted in an increased flow of trade, capital and technology. However, many of these developing countries did not finance their investment through domestic savings; in fact, they relied upon foreign sources of capital to bridge the gap between investment and domestic savings.

Over the years a number of studies have presented evidence that FDI has a beneficial impact on developing host countries (Bosworth and Collins, 1999; Feldstein, 2000; Loungani and Razin, 2001). These studies have shown that, as opposed to other sources of foreign capital, FDI in a developing country has been most important in providing access to foreign markets and tangible and intangible resources to the recipient country. These resources include capital, R&D, technology, human capital development through employee training, increased export earnings and organizational and managerial practices.

The role of FDI as a source of capital needed in the growth of developing countries can be seen from the experience of the five fastest-growing countries during the 1990s. Table 2.1 provides figures on FDI stock as a percentage of gross domestic product (GDP) capital in these five countries in 1990–2000. Since a developing country is likely to have accumulated less

Table 2.1 Inward FDI stock as a percentage of GDP in a select group of fast-growing countries, 1990–2000

Year	Singapore	Malaysia	China	Hong Kong	Taiwan
1990	77.9	23.4	7.0	198.1	6.1
1995	71.5	32.3	19.6	125.0	5.9
2000	103.8	58.8	32.3	263.8	9.0

Source: Based on data from various surveys by UNCTAD in *World Investment Reports*.

capital per worker than a developed country, returns to capital should be high in a developing country and it would thus make sense for a developing country to import capital for its development. From Table 2.1, we can see examples of countries that followed this strategy for development in the 1990s. For each of these countries FDI had an increasingly important role throughout the period covered in the table.

For the growth of the developing countries, it is important to understand that capital inflows are more likely to prove sustainable if they are channelled into investment rather than consumption. This is evidenced by the fact that, since 1985, the ratio of investment to GDP has risen faster than the ratio of consumption to GDP in the successful economies of East Asia and South East Asia. It should also be noted that many of the East Asian countries had rapid economic growth before they began saving more; these countries had to rely on foreign capital sources for initial development. For example, in 1960, the savings rate in Singapore was only 6 per cent of GDP compared to 50 per cent in 1995 (*The Economist*, 9 December 1995). Between 1965 and 1985, South Korea ran a large current account deficit to meet the shortfall of savings to investment and its net capital inflows averaged 9 per cent of GDP each year from 1953 to 1980.

Global links and FDI

The current globalization of the world economy has expanded opportunities for developing countries to access physical and financial capital accumulated in other countries. In a global economy, the economic development of a country depends to a large extent on the links its economic units establish with the rest of the world. If one uses shares of foreign affiliates in the exports of a country as a measure of its linkages with the global economy, one will observe that the rapidly growing countries of recent years restructured themselves by forming important linkages with foreign firms that undertake international production (UNCTAD, 1998). These linkages resulted in an increased flow of trade, capital, and technology to the countries.

Linkages with foreign firms through FDI also bring market access through intra-firm transactions and a greater reach into international markets for manufactured goods. For example, in 1960, non-value added goods such as

Table 2.2   Share of foreign affiliates in dollar value of manufacturing of fast-growing economies, 1990–5

Year	Singapore	Malaysia	Hong Kong	Taiwan	China
1990	76.9	44.1	22.6	17.8	2.3
1991	75.4	45.4	26.0	19.2	5.3
1992	74.7	47.6	27.0	20.9	7.1
1993	74.8	48.6	30.8	18.7	9.1
1994	75.1	52.6	35.7	21.5	11.3
1995	76.6	50.1	43.5		14.4

Sources: World Investment Report (2000); UNCTAD (2000).

rubber, palm oil, timber and tin constituted over 90 per cent of Malaysia's $ 1.2 billion total exports. By 1994, however, exports of *manufactured* goods had captured almost 80 per cent of the $ 58.8 billion of export volume. Even in China, a large fast-growing economy, FDI has been a major contributor toward increasing exports. In 1994, foreign affiliates and other related affiliates of transnational corporations accounted for $ 34.8 billion in exports from China (International Trade Centre, 1995). Table 2.2 gives shares of foreign affiliates in manufacturing for rapidly growing countries in the early 1990s. As can be seen from Table 2.2, foreign affiliates had a large share in manufacturing of the fast-growing countries before the financial crisis of the middle and late 1990s. This share started increasing again after 2000. For example, in China, sales of foreign affiliates in manufacturing were 31.3 per cent in 2000.

During the 1950s and 1960s, a large number of development economists believed that protectionism and import substitution were key to economic growth. But in the late 1970s and 1980s, economists began to recommend development strategies based on market-oriented reforms that emphasized exports. Using data from the individual country studies, Krueger (1978) tested two hypotheses: (1) more liberal (open) regimes result in higher rates of growth of exports, and (2) a more liberalized trade sector has a positive effect on aggregate growth. With respect to GNP growth, Krueger (1978) argued that her estimates provided strong evidence in favour of an indirect effect of liberalization on growth – i.e. higher exports positively influenced GNP growth.

In a highly influential paper, Michaely (1977) used simple rank correlations on a forty-one-country sample from 1950–73 to analyse the effect of growth of exports on GDP growth. He found that the correlation coefficient was significantly positive (0.308) for the sample as a whole. It was larger (0.523) for a sub-sample of middle-income countries.

Two other studies also examined the relationship between high growth and exports. Chow and Kellman (1993) examined the reasons behind the success of newly industrialized countries (NICs). They came to the conclusion that increased exports has been the vehicle of growth in these countries. A study by Sara, Newhouse and Cheng (1995) essentially came to a similar conclusion concerning the success of four other Asian countries – Indonesia, Malaysia, the Philippines and Thailand – that grew growing rapidly during the two 1980s and 1990s. FDI has played an important role in the export expansion of these countries.

Another factor that can influence the economic growth of the developing countries is the intensity of FDI in gross fixed capital formation (GFCF). Among the developing countries, the fast-growing East Asian economies grabbed 60 per cent of FDI in 1995 compared to 41 per cent in 1993 (*The Economist*, 16 March 1996). Even since 2000, a disproportionate share of FDI is going to fast-developing countries. The share of FDI in the GFCF of all developing countries more than doubled between 1986 and 1992. Table 2.3 provides the share of inward FDI flow as a percentage of GFCF for some of the fast-growing developing countries during the 1990s. It also shows FDI flows as a percentage of GFCF for all developing countries.

The above discussion implies that foreign capital inflows, especially in the form of FDI, can enhance the productivity and growth of developing countries by providing much-needed capital, technology, access to markets, organizational and managerial practices and induced investment.

Among the factors most consistently mentioned for the success of the developing economies is investment performance. For example, Leipziger and Thomas (1994) have pointed out that the increase in GFCF as a share of GDP in the East Asian countries since the 1970s has been one of the main reasons for rapid growth of these countries. Several other researchers have also argued that the East Asian experience to some extent can be explained on the basis of rapid increases in investment (Young, 1993; Krugman, 1994). Table 2.3 shows that over the years FDI has played a very important role in meeting the investment needs of these countries.

Table 2.3 Share of inward FDI flows in GFCF, 1990–9 (per cent)

Year	Singapore	China	Hong Kong	Malaysia	Taiwan	All developing countries
Annual av. 1990–5	30.5	9.8	15.3	19.8	2.5	5.7
1996	24.6	14.3	21.7	17.0	3.0	9.1
1997	29.4	14.6	19.8	14.7	3.4	11.1
1998	20.8	12.9	30.0	14.0	0.4	11.4
1999	42.4	11.3	60.2	22.0	4.4	13.4

Source: UNCTAD (2000).

3   Negative impact of FDI

Many of the developing countries have been caught in a love–hate relationship with FDI. On the one hand, they recognize the benefits that accrue to their economies from FDI, on the other hand, they fear the negative impacts that FDI brings in political, cultural and economic arenas. Some of the major areas of concern are as follows:

(1) Interference in domestic affairs
(2) Cultural change
(3) Technological dependence
(4) Crowding out of local capital
(5) Industrial dominance and crowding out of local products
(6) Tax concessions to MNCs
(7) Transfer pricing and tax avoidance
(8) Pollution of the environment
(9) Balance of payments effects.

Even though some of the concerns listed above have been diminishing, the literature indicates that some researchers feel that developing countries need to control FDI to minimize potential negative effects. MNCs bring about change not only by introducing new business practices in host countries (*Business Week*, 1986), but also through the new and different products and services they offer. This causes cultural change that may lead to conflict among members of a society. Concerns have also been expressed about interference by MNCs in the political and economic affairs of the host countries (Nye, 1974). The concern here is that the host country's national interests will suffer if an MNC makes decisions on the basis of its own global objectives.

The issue of technology transfer by MNCs has been a sensitive issue in many developing countries (Asheghian and Ebrahimi, 1990). There are two concerns in this area. The first is that the technology transferred by MNCs is 'inappropriate' for the conditions existing in the developing countries. That is, it does not take into account the host country's factors of production. For example, it is argued that technology transferred to the developing countries does not take into account that these countries have high unemployment. As a result, labour-saving technology might not be appropriate in these countries. The second concern is related to the monopolistic position of the MNCs doing business in the developing countries (Vernon, 1971). The reasoning here is that MNCs' monopolistic power over the technology they transfer to a developing country makes that country dependent on future flows of technology. As a result, the MNCs can dictate terms that are favourable to them.

The 'crowding out' argument against FDI has been made in regards to domestic investment and domestic products. In the first case the argument is made that FDI, rather than augmenting investment in a developing country, may actually replace investment by local firms (UNCTAD, 1999). This can occur if FDI reduces the availability of capital or raises the cost of capital in the domestic market. In addition, by hindering local entrepreneurial development, FDI may discourage investment by domestic firms. The second case of 'crowding out' is said to occur if FDI adversely affects the growth and learning processes of local firms. As a result, the capabilities of the local firms are not fully developed. In the long run, this can have a negative effect on the growth of the economy of the host country.

Governments of countries often compete to attract FDI. This is true of both developed and developing countries. One common method used in this competition is to offer special tax incentives to MNCs. The effect of this can be inequitable and distorting since eventually the cost will be borne by the local economy (UNCTAD, 1998). This in essence means that there is a transfer of income from the local community to MNCs.

Another major problem with FDI centres on the use of transfer pricing to evade taxes paid in the host country. 'Transfer pricing' refers to the prices charged for the movement of goods and services between the parent company and its affiliates or between the affiliates themselves. Since transfer prices are set by the parent company or its affiliates, they may not reflect the market prices. This means that an MNC may use transfer pricing to minimize taxes or even to bypass foreign exchange controls that restrict or prohibit the repatriation of funds. Abuse of transfer pricing has declined as tax rates have fallen around the globe and countries are increasingly permitting full repatriation of profits.

Many developing countries have limited regulation on the environment and little capacity for effective enforcement. Some have accused MNCs of exploiting these to avoid stringent environmental standards in the developed countries. The large volume of publicity regarding this issue is prompting many MNCs to conform to higher environmental standards, so this may not be a major concern in the future.

The balance of payments effects of FDI have been discussed quite extensively in literature (Gray, 1993; Lall and Streeten, 1997). The thinking here has been that even though FDI will initially result in foreign exchange inflow, in later years outflows will exceed inflows as MNCs repatriate profits, repay loans to the parent company and import goods and services. This issue was more pressing in the 1970s and 1980s when many developing countries faced severe foreign exchange problems. Today there is much more capital mobility around the globe and export growth in many developing countries has made this a less pressing problem. But it does remain a concern for some of the developing countries that have not expanded their exports.

4   Determinants of FDI

Since FDI is largely driven by the constant quest by firms to increase their competitiveness, an increased awareness by the developing countries about the nature of locational determinants is of critical importance if they wish to attract investment. While the main traditional factors driving FDI location – large markets, the possession of natural resources and access to low-cost labour – remain relevant, they are diminishing in importance, particularly for the most dynamic industries and functions. Location decisions by MNCs are increasingly based on the ability of the host countries to complement traditional factors with institutions that create a friendly business climate.

Determinants of inward FDI are complicated, and not always susceptible to accurate measurement. There are essentially three categories. The first includes traditional economic variables, such as market size of the host country, growth potential, purchasing power, cost of production, geographic location and natural resources. The second includes factors that are related to the political, social and cultural environment of the host countries. The third measures the factors that are related to the transaction costs from assumptions of 'bounded rationality' and 'opportunism' in FDI decisions. In his study of organization design, Simon (1957) used the term 'bounded rationality' to indicate that economic actors have limited knowledge. Under such circumstances, a person will be willing to enter into a contract only after spending a great deal of time on researching, negotiating and carefully writing a contract. All this increases the transaction cost of the firm. In the case of MNCs, the assumption of bounded rationality means that they will be willing to invest in a country that has a climate of certainty. The assumption of 'opportunism' holds that there will always be some economic agents who are dishonest and untrustworthy. As a result, the MNCs will seek a country in which national laws and regulations provide standards for conduct of business and thus protection against dishonest local agents.

Based on the above discussion, we can classify the factors that can affect FDI in a three-part breakdown.

Traditional economic variables

(1) Market size
(2) Market growth
(3) *Per capita* income
(4) Market structure
(5) Consumer preferences
(6) Availability of raw material
(7) Cost and availability of labour (skilled and unskilled)
(8) Quality, availability and cost of infrastructure inputs.

Market size, market growth and *per capita* income are important determinants of FDI. Everything else equal, MNCs are more likely to go to countries with larger market size, higher growth potential and higher purchasing power than to countries with smaller market size, slow economic growth and low purchasing power. The FDI literature suggests that a host country's economic health – namely, its economic size and growth rate – is important in determining a country's FDI inflows (Tsai, 1994).

Market structure is also an important factor in determining the FDI inflow in developing countries. MNCs are likely to enter markets where entry is relatively easy and where host countries encourage foreign capital with favourable investment and banking policies. Relaxed regulation in many of the industries in India and China has led to increase in the inflow of FDI in these countries, for example.

Consumer preference is an important determinant of FDI, especially in service and manufacturing industries. If the MNCs are looking to supply the local markets in the host countries, then the preferences of the local consumers become very important. Many MNCs are successfully able to modify their product or service to suit local consumers' preferences. In India, for example, McDonald's offers chicken burgers instead of hamburgers and use vegetable oil in the preparation of French fries to accommodate vegetarians.

Availability of raw material, availability of labour (skilled and unskilled) and cost and quality of labour are important in determining the inflow of FDI in host countries. Empirical research has found relative labour costs to be a statistically significant determinant of FDI, particularly for foreign investment in labour-intensive industries and for export-oriented subsidiaries (Wheeler and Mody, 1992). Much of the investment in the labour-intensive industries comes from a response to integration strategies driven by cost/price competition. Such FDI may be used to produce and sell in the local host country market or to export to the home country and elsewhere.

Availability, quality and cost of infrastructure inputs are also very important determinants of FDI. Infrastructure covers many dimensions, ranging from physical assets such as roads, sea ports, railways and telecommunications, to institutional development, such as accounting and legal services. In order to present an attractive setting for MNC operations, it is important that the country's infrastructure be sufficiently developed to support various activities to be carried out by the company. An indispensable condition for global competition among MNCs is the ability to link affiliates through adequate infrastructure facilities. A country may have low-cost labour, but if it does not have the necessary supporting services or infrastructure MNCs will not locate in that country.

Political, social, cultural environment variables

(1) Political, economic and social stability
(2) Tax policy

(3) Privatization policy
(4) Trade policy.

In evaluating host developing countries, MNCs also look for the political, economic and social stability. The range in the level of political risk that exists in these countries is significantly large. In evaluating political risk in a country, MNCs should consider many dimensions of risk that may exist. The PRS Group, Inc. publishes an overall political risk rating in many of the countries, calculated by summing up the points awarded to twelve components: government stability, socioeconomic conditions, investment profile, internal conflict, external conflict, corruption, military in politics, religious tensions, law and order, ethnic tensions, democratic accountability and bureaucracy quality. For example, this latter variable ranges from 44 (Russia) to 93 (Netherlands). The countries with higher political risk receive a higher ranking (smaller values) and countries with lower political risk receive a lower ranking (bigger values) on this variable.

Tax, privatization and trade policies are also considered to be important determinants of FDI in developing countries. The extent to which the government of a host country interferes with international commerce can negatively impact on the gains from specialization and trade. MNCs should take into account non-tariff barriers (NTBs) and the level of corruption in the customs services in addition to average tariff rate in the host countries. Other things being constant, higher the level of government control on trade the lower the level of FDI by the foreign MNCs.

The extent of the fiscal burden of the host government on its citizens can also have an impact on the attractiveness of FDI. The rate of income tax, corporate tax and the share of government expenditure are some indicators of these factors. The share of private resources that a government consumes does have a negative impact on the available resources for the private sectors; MNCs are more likely to take their investment to countries where tax rates are lower and private sector plays a greater role in the production of goods and services. The extent of government-owned enterprises in developing countries can play a crucial role in attracting FDI. Government-owned enterprises generally crowd out private initiatives and investment, and MNCs are more likely to avoid countries where the government controls the production of major goods and services.

The level of FDI can also depend on the government's control of monetary policy. If a tight monetary policy is maintained by a government – i.e. the money supply is kept in line with money demand – then the rate of inflation is kept under control and individuals and businesses in the countries are free from the problems associated with high inflation and thus free to engage in productive economic activities.

Transaction cost variables

(1) Fair and equitable legal structure, including equity in the application of law
(2) International dispute settlement, including arbitration
(3) Consistent and stable laws for the repatriation of earnings and capital
(4) Laws on compensation if a firm is nationalized
(5) Easy access to government agencies
(6) Post-approval services
(7) Simple requirements for visas, work permits and import licenses
(8) A stable and unambiguous commercial code to protect against dishonest local agents
(9) Intellectual property rights that are strictly enforced
(10) Level of corruption.

In many developing countries and LDCs, government regulations are one of the major hindrances to profitable business. In some countries, obtaining a business licence requires businesses to bribe government officials and follow time-consuming procedures. A country with stable business environment will probably also have a steady inflow of FDI.

Determinants of FDI also include the level of restrictions on banks. In most developing countries banks are the major financial sources for economic expansion. Banks also provide various services, such as real estate, insurance and securities investments. One would expect that a host country with fewer restrictions on the banking systems would have higher level of FDI.

There is a potential effect of the degree of legal protection of property rights on the attractiveness of FDI. MNCs will evaluate the extent to which the government protects and enforces laws to protect private property in host countries.

A number of studies have argued that the level of corruption in a country has an effect on the level of FDI. Corruption makes dealing with government officials to obtain local licences and permits, for example, less transparent and more costly, particularly for foreign investors. A high level of corruption in a country increases transaction costs, and thereby discourages FDI. Due to the illegal and 'shadow' nature of corruption, it is difficult to get a precise measure of this variable. Transparency International (TI), an international non-governmental organization (NGO) dedicated to fighting corruption, compiles one of the most widely known indexes of corruption, which pools information from ten different surveys of business executives, risk analysts and the general public. Kahai (2004) uses a corruption perception variable to measure a country's level of perceived corruption as computed by TI. For example, in 2000 Nigeria received 1.6 and Denmark received 10. A country with a high perceived corruption level among business executives receives a high-ranking score (smaller value on this variable).

Evidence from Kahai's study suggests that corruption can lead to lower level of FDI going into these developing countries.

Most of the research on FDI in developing countries has concentrated on the first category of factors (Kahai, 2004). These factors are quantitative in nature and are easy to measure. But, increasingly, researchers are coming to the conclusion that FDI is strongly influenced by determinants that are *qualitative* in nature and not always susceptible to easy measurement. These factors contribute to what might be called a country's 'business environment' and they can often be gauged only through surveys of investors. Some of the factors in the second category, and factors related to transaction costs, can be classified as qualitative factors.

The author has attempted to include both traditional and non-traditional determinants of FDI in estimating an empirical model of FDI *per capita* inflow for fifty-five developing countries. Inward FDI *per capita* in US dollars in each country was used as the dependent variable. The traditional variables included in the model were the number of telephone lines per 1,000 people (a proxy for the quality of infrastructure in the country), GDP *per capita*, the annual real GDP growth rate, exports and annual labour cost per worker in manufacturing in US dollars. To capture the variations in developing countries' economic climate, the rate of inflation and the exchange rate were included. Independent non-traditional variables used in this study were not easily quantified. Cross-country comparisons of these variables are made on the basis of surveys of business firms or experts in fields related to each variable. Economic freedom (the absence of government constraints), trade (a measure of trade restrictions) and the corruption perception index were included in the study. This research finds that non-traditional variables, which affect the transaction costs of conducting business in a developing country, are important determinants of observed FDI flows. Traditional variables typically used to explain FDI also play a key role. An important lesson to be learned from the experiences of countries that have attracted FDI is that a country desiring to attract greater levels of foreign capital benefits from undertaking structural adjustments and policy reforms designed to reduce transaction costs for MNCs.

5   Conclusion

FDI decisions by MNCs involve a process with several distinct stages that can be broadly classified into two phases. In the first phase the firm undertakes a *strategic planning decision* to expand internationally and select priority regions for this expansion. Decisions in the second phase involve the *site selection* in the priority region identified in the first phase. The criteria used for the two phases will not be the same. In the first phase the firm chooses a region based upon factors that may not be entirely economic in nature. For example, regional trade agreements (RTAs) or market proximity may be most important during the first phase. A 1998 survey of Japanese MNCs showed that their top priority region for overseas investment was Asia/Pacific. In the same survey, the region of top priority for western European companies was locations in western Europe (Hatem, 1998). In the second phase the final selection between countries in the chosen region is based on detailed business plans. At this stage, the firm usually has an idea of the region it wants to target. The next step is to draw up an initial list of potential sites. Some of these sites are quickly eliminated because of their failure to meet critical requirements such as access to a particular raw material, host country policies on which sectors of the economy are off-limits to foreign firms, etc. The choice between the remaining sites is then based on analysis that takes into account the political, social, cultural and transaction cost variables listed above.

Since attracting FDI is now an accepted policy for countries at all levels of development, governments are increasingly seeking to create an environment that is friendly to foreign firms. In today's global economy, successful MNCs gain competitive advantage by dispersing economic activities around the globe to optimize their positions and to take advantage of the opportunities offered by developing economies (Sara and Newhouse, 1995). This gives opportunities to developing countries with foresight to improve their productivity by attracting global firms that can make use of resources in those countries. A country desiring foreign capital must undertake structural adjustments and policy reforms in which firms – both foreign and domestic – can prosper. This means that a developing country must streamline its bureaucracy, simplify licensing, remove restrictions on foreign ownership, improve access to imported inputs and upgrade the infrastructure and relevant skills of the workforce. Only those developing countries which move from inward-looking to outward-looking policies that create a climate of certainty and friendly policies towards FDI will be able to emulate the success of the rapidly growing economies of the early twenty-first century.

Note

1. Some of the discussion of the role of FDI is taken from and based on the author's previous work (Kahai and Sara, 2001). The discussions on the determinants of FDI are taken from and based on the author's forthcoming paper (Kahai, 2004).

References

Ashegian, P. and B. Ebrahimi, *International Business* (New York: HarperCollins, 1990).
Bloom, M., *Technological Change in the Korean Electronics Industry* (Paris: OECD, 1992).
Bosworth, Barry, P. and Susan M. Collins, 'Capital Flows to Developing Economies: Implications for Saving and Investment', *Brookings Papers on Economic Activity*, 1 (1999): 143–69.
Business Week, 14 July (1986): 51–2.
Chow, Peter, C.Y. and Mitchell H. Kellman, *Trade: The Engine of Growth in East Asia* (Oxford: Oxford University Press, 1993).

Dadush, U., D. Dasgupta and D. Ratha, 'The Role of Short-Term Debt in Recent Crises', *Finance and Development*, 37 (2000): 54–7.

Economist, The, 9 December (1995): 15.

Economist, The, 16 March (1996): 72.

Economist, The, 24 February (2001): 14.

Economist, The, 3 May (2003): 10.

Feldstein, Martin, 'Aspects of Global Integration: Outlook for the Future', NBER Working Paper N. 7899 (Cambridge, MA: National Bureau of Economic Research, 2000).

Gray H. Peter (ed.), *Transnational Corporations and International Trade and Payments*, United Nations Library on Transnational Corporations, 8 (London and New York: Routledge, 1993).

Hamel, Gary and C.K. Prahlad, *Competing for the Future* (Cambridge, MA: Harvard Business School Press, 1994).

Hatem, F., *International Investment: Towards the Year 2002* (New York: United Nations, 1998).

International Trade Center, UNCTAD/GATT, *TNCs Market Access and Competitiveness: The Experience of China* (New York: United Nations, 1995).

Kahai, S., 'Traditional and Non-Traditional Determinants of Foreign Direct Investment in Developing Countries', *Journal of Applied Business Research* (Winter 2004).

Kahai, S. and T. Sara, 'The Impact of Foreign Capital Inflows on Economic Growth of Developing Countries: Empirical Evidence from 1984–1992', *Business and Economic Review*, 15 (1) (2001): 35–53.

Krueger, A. O., *Foreign Trade Regimes and Economic Development: Liberalization Attempts and Consequences* (Cambridge MA: Ballinger for NBER, 1978).

Krugman, P., 'The Myth of Asia's Miracle', *Foreign Affairs*, November/December 1994.

Lall, S. and P. Streeten, *Foreign Investment, Transnationals and Developing Countries* (London: Macmillan, 1977).

Leipziger, D. and V. Thomas, 'Roots of East Asia's Success', *Finance and Development* (March 1994).

Lipsey, Robert E. 'Foreign Direct Investors in Three Financial Crises', NBER Working Paper No. 7400 (Cambridge, MA: National Bureau of Economic Research, 2001).

Loungani, P. and A. Razin, 'How Beneficial is Foreign Direct Investment for Developing Countries', *Finance and Development* (June 2001).

Michaely, M., 'Exports and Growth: An Empirical Investigation', *Journal of Development Economics*, 4 (1) (1977): 49–53.

Micklethwait, John and Adrian Wooldridge, *A Future Perfect* (New York: Crown Business Publishers, 2000).

Nye, Joseph S., 'Multinational Corporations in World Politics', *Foreign Affairs*, 53 (1974).

Romer, P.M., 'Two Strategies for Development: Using Ideas and Producing Ideas', *Proceedings of World Bank Annual Conference on Development Economics* (Washington, DC: World Bank, 1993).

Sara, T., B. Newhouse and W. Cheng, 'Global Strategy in Changing Cost of Production', *Journal of Business and Economic Studies* (Winter 1995).

Simon, H.A., *Models of Man: Social and Rational Mathematical Essays on Rational Human Behavior in Social Setting* (New York: John Wiley, 1957).

Tsai, P. 'Foreign Direct Investment and Income Inequality: Future Evidence', *World Development*, 23(33) (1995): 469–830.

United Nations Conference on Trade and Development (UNCTAD), *World Investment Report: Transnational Corporations and Competitiveness* (New York: United Nations, 1995–2000).

United Nations Conference on Trade and Development (UNCTAD), *World Investment Report: Trends and Determinants* (New York: United Nations, 1998).

United Nations Conference on Trade and Development (UNCTAD), *World Investment Report: Foreign Direct Investment and the Challenge for Development* (New York: United Nations, 1999–2000).

United Nations Conference on Trade and Development (UNCTAD), *International Investment Towards the Year 2002* (New York: United Nations, 2002).

Vernon, Raymond, *The Multinational Spread of the US Enterprise* (New York: Basic Books, 1971).

Wheeles, D. and A. Mody, 'International Investment Location Decisions. The Case of US Firms', *Journal of International Economics*, 33 (1992): 57–76.

World Bank, *Global Development Finance: Analysis and Summary Tables* (Washington, DC: World Bank, 2000).

Young, A., 'Lessons from the East Asian NICs: A Contrarian View', NBER Working Paper 4482 (Cambridge, MA: National Bureau of Economic Research, 1993).

3
Inward Foreign Investment and the Chinese Economy

Michael Thorpe

1 Introduction

In 1979 China instituted its 'open door' policy and has gradually opened its economy to the outside world in a carefully managed and phased approach. Since that time the economy has increased in size fivefold and *per capita* income has risen fourfold (*The Economist,* 2001).[1]

China's impressive economic growth performance has been accompanied by a rapidly expanding export sector (Figure 3.1). While foreign direct investment (FDI) inflows to China increased steadily over the 1980s as restrictions on the entry of foreign companies were eased, since the 1990s inflows of foreign capital have accelerated in line with more general global trends (Table 3.1). While the rate of growth of world FDI flows averaged just over 20 per cent per year over 1991–5, over the remainder of the decade growth averaged an annual 40 per cent (UNCTAD, 2002a).[2] China has increased its inflow of foreign capital to the extent that it now ranks number two behind the USA as the most favoured destination country for FDI.[3] The stock of investment in China now exceeds that in Mexico and Brazil, which opened up to investment decades before China.

In 2001 China accounted for 23 per cent of all FDI inflows to developing countries. China's share of global flows reached a peak of 11.3 per cent in 1995 and in 2001 was 6.4 per cent. This compares with the EU and the USA which had shares of 43.9 and 16.9 per cent, respectively, in 2001.

In 1982 the value of FDI inflows globally was USD 59 billion and by 2000 it had reached USD 1,491 billion. There was a precipitous fall of 51 per cent in 2001, the largest fall since the 1970s and the first decline in inflows since the world economic downturn in 1991. The flow to developed economies halved, while that to developing economies fell by 14 per cent. Preliminary figures have indicated that FDI inflows globally will show a decline of a further 27 per cent in 2002 (UNCTAD, 2002a,b). The falls reflect a general global economic slowdown as well as a series of major corporate financial scandals. However, China was one of only a few countries which increased

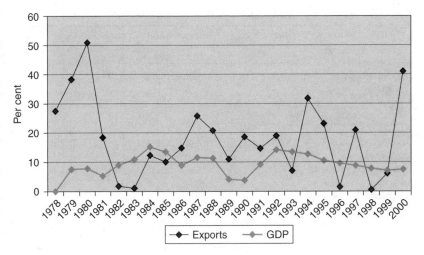

Figure 3.1 China's trade and output growth, 1978–2000 (per cent p.a.)
Source: Asian Development Bank, *Asian Development Outlook* (various years).

Table 3.1 Global FDI, annual growth rate 1986–2001 (per cent)

	1986–90*	1991–5*	1996–2000	1998	1999	2000	2001
FDI inflows	23.0	20.8	40.1	44.9	55.2	18.2	−50.7
FDI outflows	26.2	16.3	36.7	52.8	41.3	14.3	−55.0

Note: * Annual average.
Source: UNCTAD (2002a).

its inflow of FDI in 2001 (Table 3.2).[4] This was a turnaround in the trend of relative decline during the previous few years which reflected developments in China's East Asian neighbours following the regional financial crisis of 1997e/8. At that time, these countries accounted for around 40 per cent of FDI inflows into China.

A further pickup in investment also looks likely to continue over the immediate future, driven by China's accession to the World Trade Organization (WTO) which will provide improved access for foreign investors in new and existing areas as well as eliminating some of the legal and regulatory barriers that have created difficulties in the past (Li, 2002). While a 12 per cent reduction in inflows of FDI to developing Asia is expected for 2002 due to a slowing in flows from Europe and the USA, China is expected

Table 3.2   Regional distribution of FDI inflows, 1989–2001 (USD billions)

	1989–94*	1995	1996	1997	1998	1999	2000	2001
Developed countries	137.1	203.5	219.7	271.4	483.2	829.8	1227.5	503.1
EU	76.6	113.5	109.6	127.6	261.1	487.2	808.5	323.0
Japan	1.0		0.2	3.2	3.3	12.7	8.3	6.2
USA	42.5	58.8	84.5	103.4	174.4	283.4	300.9	124.4
Developing countries	59.6	113.3	152.5	187.4	188.4	225.1	237.9	204.8
East Asia	34.3	71.7	85.7	93.6	82.5	93.1	134.3	90.1
Latin America	17.5	32.3	51.3	71.2	83.2	110.3	86.2	85.0
Africa	4.0	4.7	5.8	10.7	9.0	12.8	8.7	17.2
China**	13.9	37.5	40.2	44.2	43.8	40.3	40.8	46.8
World	200.1	331.1	386.1	478.1	694.5	1088.3	1491.9	735.1

Notes: * Annual average.
** Included in East Asia.

Source: UNCTAD (2001, 2002a).

to experience an increase, with USD 50 billion estimated for 2002 and average annual inflows forecast at around USD 65 billion over 2003–7(*The Economist*, 2003).[5]

This chapter commences with an overview of the historical development and relative economic importance of FDI inflows into China (Section 2). The sources of FDI are also examined along, with the regional sectoral distribution of FDI. A comment on the mode of operation of foreign firms in China is provided and the role that they play in China's external trade and economic development generally (Sections 3–7). Factors driving FDI inflows are assessed in the context of the literature dealing with factors driving the FDI decision of firms (Section 8–9). The potential effect of China's entry to the WTO is briefly reviewed (Section 10) along with the presentation of a short case study of the automobile industry in China (Section 11). Section 12 briefly concludes.

2   FDI inflows to China: historical development

In 1979, as part of the 'open door' policy initiated by Deng Xiaping aimed at transforming China from an essentially controlled and closed economy into a nation actively engaged with the international economy, the first steps were taken to attract FDI in order to promote exports, introduce new technology and transfer management skills and capital (Story, 2003). The approach has been a cautious and gradual process of opening up, in terms of the geographical and sectoral restrictions on FDI inflows within China as well as with respect to the mode of entry and the operating environment generally.

China's FDI policy can be considered as comprising four phases. The first covers the period from the initial moves to liberalize, up to 1985. This is followed by the period to 1992 with the third phase leading up to the changes heralded by China's entry to the WTO in December 2001. In the wake of the accession agreements made by China, a new wave of investment is expected to follow in areas previously out of bounds to foreign companies.

The introduction of a law on joint ventures (Jvs) in 1979, stipulating that foreign capital must account for at least 25 per cent of the total capital of any operation (with no restriction on the maximum), was followed in 1980 by the creation of special economic zones (SEZs) in the southern coastal provinces. These areas provided for a range of inducements for foreign companies and operated outside of most government planning controls.[6]

Initially four SEZs were established in the provinces of Guangdong (in Shenzhen, Zhuhai and Shantou) and Fujian (in Xiamen). It was expected that proximity and cultural ties would initially encourage capital inflows from neighbouring Hong Kong and Taiwan (Wang, 2001). In 1984 another fourteen coastal cities were set up as 'open cities' that offered investment incentives similar to those in the SEZs. These included Dalian, Shanghai and Guangzhou (Zhou, Delias and Yang, 2002). In 1985 the Yangtze River delta, the Pearl River delta and the Minnan region were opened up as development zones, while in 1988 Hainan was added as a fifth SEZ. These moves broadened the reach of FDI considerably. Another type of zone, the economic and/or technology development zone (ETDZ), was also created after the establishment if the coastal cities, but concessions applied only to small areas within cities. However these were established widely across China.[7] The tight focus allowed the government to regulate and control the opening up of the economy, while learning how best to accommodate and use the investment inflows. This approach also provided an opportunity for those in government sceptical of the reform process to observe what was happening and assisted in policy development. As Chow (2002, p. 59) observes, the Chinese leader Deng Xiaoping had advised: 'Seek truth from facts.'[8]

Initially investment came mainly from Hong Kong and Macau, in areas of labour intensive manufacturing and in the hotel and restaurant sector. Outdated communication and transport and delivery systems, restrictive labour practices, the lack of a market for land, foreign exchange and foreign personnel restrictions and the finite life of Jv arrangements all meant that FDI grew very slowly in the early reform period. FDI inflow was USD 1 billion in 1978 and 2 billion in 1985, but had reached 41 billion by 2000 (Figure 3.2).

In 1986 laws were introduced under which wholly owned foreign enterprises and cooperative ventures were permitted. The easing of exchange

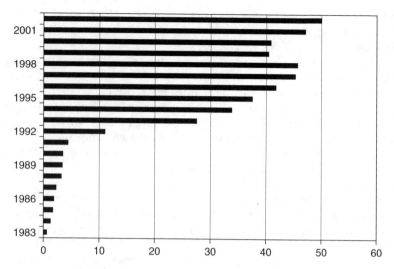

Figure 3.2 China's FDI inflows 1993–2001 (USD billion)
Source: UNCTAD, *World Investment Report* (various years).

restrictions and a clarification of the legal position for foreign companies stimulated further investment. New incentives in respect of reduced duties on imported materials, equipment and vehicles, together with additional tax breaks for technology-oriented Jvs were also introduced (Zhang, 2002; Zhou, Delios and Yang, 2002). The allowing of wholly owned companies proved particularly attractive to western companies.

In 1988 a law protecting against expropriations and allowing wider access to local markets and more equitable profit distribution arrangements was introduced. Developments since then have progressively clarified arrangements and eased restrictions on foreign companies (Story, 2003). In 1996, for example, China introduced full currency convertibility on current account. Foreign firms were able to convert domestic currency profits into foreign exchange and remit them abroad.

Gradually, following the successful economic expansion and modernization in the coastal regions, moves were made in the early 1990s to further extend the reach of FDI into the hinterland and the western provinces of China (Zhou, Delios and Yang, 2002). A wider regional spread of FDI resulted as restrictions on the location of foreign companies were eased with the advent of new and high-technology development zones (NTZs).[9] Unlike in SEZs, the focus in these areas has been less on exports and more on technology development and transfer. Provinces were also given greater control over FDI approvals during this time.

Since 1992, foreign multinationals have begun to have a greater presence in China with a significant rise in large-scale capital and technology-intensive projects.[10] By the mid-1990s FDI in China accounted for around 25 per cent of domestic investment, 13 per cent of industrial output, 31 per cent of exports, 11 per cent of tax revenues and 16 million jobs.

3   The relative importance of FDI in China

The ratio of FDI stock to GDP for most countries is relatively modest. In 1995 the figure for the EU was 13.4 per cent and for the USA 7.7 per cent. Japan's figure was very low relative to most countries at 3.3 per cent, reflecting the limited role allowed for FDI in that country (UNCTAD, 2001).[11] China tends to be at the high end of the range, with a ratio of 32.3 per cent (2000). The figure for the UK, generally regarded as an industrialized economy with a high dependence on FDI, was 28 per cent in 1995. FDI as a share of gross fixed capital formation (GFCF) in China averaged around 15 per cent each year over the mid-1990s and was 10.5 per cent in 2000. This compares with a world average of 16.3 per cent in 1999, 5.9 per cent for the USA, 6.8 per cent for the EU, 12.4 per cent for the UK, 2.8 per cent for Taiwan and 0.1 per cent for Japan. The relative importance of FDI in China, despite its high rate of domestic savings (by world standards) and current account strength over the 1990s might initially be at odds with expectations. FDI, however, reflects both *push* and *pull* factors, as discussed below.[12]

FDI has been a major source of external funding for China. From 1992 to 1998, FDI provided 70 per cent of total external resources supplied to the economy (Story, 2003). However, large inflows of FDI over the 1990s did not raise China's overall rate of investment, rather, they supported the build-up of substantial foreign exchange reserves (and increasing capital outflows) allowing China to comfortably manage its external debt position (Lardy, 2003).[13] Domestic savings were sufficient to finance domestic investment.[14] Despite the fact that the rate of capital formation did not increase due to FDI, in the future, as increased investment flows to service areas such as telecoms, distribution and the financial sector, it is expected that reduced costs and productivity gains in these areas will spread more widely across the economy, benefiting local firms as well as consumers. Increased foreign competition will also create ongoing pressures for improved efficiencies by local firms.

4   FDI by source

The cumulative stock of FDI in China at the end of 2001 was around USD 390 billion, almost exclusively in Greenfield projects (Chen, 2002).

A large number of China's so-called foreign invested enterprises (FIEs) are owned by investors from Hong Kong, Taiwan Province of China (Taiwan) and Singapore (Table 3.3). These are mainly small and medium-sized businesses that are export-oriented and involved in assembly and processing

Table 3.3 FDI inflows by source,
1983–2000 (per cent of total)

Source	(%)
Hong Kong and Macao	49.6
Taiwan	7.5
Singapore	4.8
South Korea	2.9
USA	8.6
Japan	8.1
EU	7.7

Source: SSB, *China Statistical Yearbook*
(Beijing, 2001).

operations. The import content of these exports is high (around 50 per cent).[15] Overseas Chinese investors currently hold about 80 per cent of the stock of FDI in China (Story, 2003).

In 1999 the leading investors were Hong Kong (and Macao), the USA, Japan, the Virgin Islands, Singapore, Taiwan, Germany, the Republic of Korea, the UK and France (Chow, 2002). As a group the EU is second, ahead of the USA.

Hong Kong is the largest source of investment funds in China, having provided a stock of USD 311 billion up to the end of 1999, The USA, the EU, Japan, Taiwan and Singapore are next in terms of importance. Altogether, these economies have accounted for almost 90 per cent of FDI inflows to China (UNCTAD, 2001). FDI from the USA, the EU and Japan has been focused in large import substituting areas such as automobiles and off-shore petroleum and other natural resource sectors.

While the importance of Hong Kong, Singapore and Taiwan as sources of FDI diminished over the 1990s as investment from the industrialized economies increased, they together continue to account for around half of all FDI inflows (Table 3.4). This is likely to change following the liberalization moves in service areas and automobiles by China following its accession to the WTO.

At the start of the reform period in 1979, China pursued an outward orientation with emphasis on exports. Initially use was made of trading skills from Hong Kong, shipping manufactured goods through the city. However, through the 1980s Hong Kong and Taiwan became crucial as sources of capital, trade links and commercial know-how, fostering the restructuring of the Chinese economy for export (Nolan, 2001).

Huang (2002) identifies the role that government support has played in directing funds to the (inefficient) state-owned enterprises (SOEs), together with the preferential treatment afforded foreign firms, in driving the reliance of Chinese economy on foreign capital. Despite China having one

Table 3.4 Top ten foreign investors in China, 1999 (USD billion)

Country/region	Contracted	Utilized
Hong Kong	13.3	16.4
USA	6.0	4.2
Japan	2.6	3.0
Virgin Is.	3.5	2.7
Singapore	2.3	2.6
Taiwan	3.4	2.6
Germany	0.9	1.4
S. Korea	1.5	1.3
UK	1.1	1.0
France	0.5	0.9

Source: www.chinabusinessreview.com/0011/gelb.html.

of the highest savings rates in the world, intra-regional flows of capital have been restricted, along with the ability for local firms to invest outside their regional jurisdiction. With no such restrictions on foreign firms, a foreign partner became an attractive proposition for local firms in order to obtain finance and convert to foreign firm status for the benefits that provided.[16]

5   Regional distribution of FDI

The geographical spread of FDI flows across China reflects the history of liberalization, deregulation and government policy, as noted above.[17] An important part of managing the reform process in China has been to restrict foreign investment to specific areas.[18] As a result, the coastal (or eastern) region which accounts for around 65 per cent of China's GDP accounted for around 88 per cent of FDI inflows in 1999, with the central region taking around 9 per cent and the western region only 2 per cent (Table 3.5). The government introduced The West Development Strategy in 1998, aimed at directing more public and private investment to the hinterland where income levels and general physical and social infrastructure levels are significantly lower than elsewhere (Chen, 2002). The region does have a comparative advantage in natural resources and cheap labour, while spending power is rising among consumers. Environmental problems do remain an issue, however. Some central provinces (e.g. Jilin, Hubei and Hunan) and Shaanxi and Sichuan in the west have had significant increases in FDI since the mid-1990s.

Zhou, Delios and Yang (2002) argue that restrictions on the location of foreign firms' policy differences across provinces and regions are becoming increasingly less important in influencing the pattern of FDI across China as firms seek greater penetration of the local market and the development

Table 3.5   Regional distribution of FDI in China, 1983–99 (per cent)

Region	1983–5	1989–91	1992–4	1999
Coastal	92.6	92.05	88.2	87.8
Guangdong	61.1	42.9	28.9	29.2
Fujian	6.7	10.1	11.2	10.1
Jiangsu	2.2	4.2	11.3	15.2
Shanghai	5.8	6.6	8.6	7.1

Source: SSB, *China Statistical Yearbook* (Beijing, 2000).

of regional production networks. With FDI inflows following the WTO accession agreements likely to favour the eastern region, it is important that efforts to foster a wider geographic spread of capital across the country are actively pursued.

6   FDI distribution by sector

In the early 1980s the bulk of FDI went to geological exploration (such as oil and gas) and into real estate (including hotels and industrial sites) and tourism-related activities. Following the regulatory change in 1986, more investment was directed to export-oriented industries, primarily processing and assembly operations. Following the reforms in 1992, the growing levels of FDI extended more widely to retail, wholesale and other service areas. There was also a shift to electronics, precision machinery and transportation equipment (Story, 2003).

China's commitments under WTO entry will encourage a new wave of investments in service sector areas previously prohibited, with foreign entry increasing in financial areas, insurance, transport, legal and accounting fields, education, advertising and health.

About 56 per cent of FDI goes to manufacturing (Table 3.6). Around half of this is directed to labour-intensive manufacturing which includes textiles and clothing, food processing, furniture, travel goods, toys and handicrafts. Another half has gone to technology- and capital-intensive areas such as pharmaceuticals, petroleum refining and chemicals. The significant foreign involvement in what can be considered areas of comparative advantage for China such as simple handicrafts may appear somewhat surprising, particularly given the relatively high domestic savings rate in China and the history of local enterprise in these activities. This reflects in large degree the distortions in local capital markets, including the direction of funds towards the (SOEs) and the impediments to intra-regional capital flows within China, as well as the distorting effects of policies and incentives which favoured obtaining foreign status (Huang, 2002).

Table 3.6 FDI in China, by sector, 1999 (per cent of total)

Sector	Share
Agriculture	1.8
Manufacturing	56.1
Textiles	3.4
Chemicals	4.8
Electronics/telecom equipment	7.8
Construction	2.3
Power, gas and water	9.2
Transport and telecom services	3.8
Wholesale and retail services	2.4
Real estate	13.9
Social services (including hotels)	6.3
Health, sports, education, culture	0.5

Source: SSB, *China Statistical Yearbook* (Beijing, 2000).

7 Structures of foreign invested enterprises

The State Statistic Bureau classifies so-called 'foreign invested enterprises' (FIEs) in China as being an equity Jv, a cooperative Jv, a wholly owned enterprise, a joint exploration or a cooperative development.[19]

Equity and cooperative Jvs tended to dominate in the past, since wholly owned enterprises were restricted to the SEZs until 1986 (Zhou, Delios and Yang, 2002). However, in 1999, equity Jvs and wholly owned enterprises each accounted for around 40 per cent of FDI by value (Table 3.7).

In 1999, there were 8,201 wholly owned foreign enterprises, 7,050 Jvs and 1656 cooperative ventures between Chinese and foreign firms (Chow, 2002). Jvs were the largest group in terms of the value of utilized investment funds.

8 FDI and China's trade and economic development

China's success in opening up to the international economy is reflected in its trade performance (Figure 3.1). Exports grew from USD 26 billion in 1985 to USD 249 billion in 2000. The growth of exports has averaged an annual growth rate of around 10 per cent since the 1980s. In 2001, with 4.3 per cent of world merchandise exports, China was the world's seventh largest trading country with exports as a share of GDP at around 25 per cent.[20] This outward focus has been driven by the activity of FIEs whose exports grew strongly over the 1990s (Figure 3.3). Between 1978 and 2000, China's trade grew four and a half times faster than global trade, at a time when FIEs expanded their share of China's exports from 1 per cent to 45 per cent (Story, 2003).

Table 3.7   FDI in China, by type of enterprise, 1979–99 (USD billion)

Type of enterprise	1979–96	1997	1998	1999
Jv	90.7	19.5	18.4	15.8 (39.2)*
Cooperative Jv	38.0	8.9	9.7	8.2 (20.3)
Wholly foreign-owned	42.5	16.2	16.5	15.6 (38.7)
Joint exploration	0	0.3	0.7	0.3
Cooperative development	5.3	0.4	0.2	0.4
Total	176.6	45.3	45.5	40.3

Note: * Figures in brackets represent percentage are of total investment.

Source: www.chinabusinessreview.com.

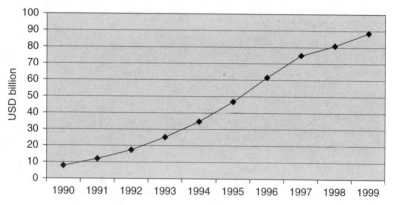

Figure 3.3   Exports by FIEs in China, 1990–9 (USD billion)
Source: SSB, *China Statistical Yearbook* (Beijing, 2000).

China runs large trade surpluses with Europe and the USA and deficits with Asia. China is an assembly base for Asian subsidiaries exporting to western economies and an operations centre for US and EU corporations.

The initial contribution of FIEs to export growth was modest. In 1985 they contributed just 1 per cent of China's exports, but by 1990 the share exceeded 10 per cent. Since 1992 FIEs have become increasingly important, increasing their share to 48 per cent by 2001 (Table 3.8). Currently they account for around 27 per cent of China's industrial output.[21] The output of FIEs grew at four times the rate of local enterprises over the 1990s (Zhang,

Table 3.8 FIEs' share of China's total trade,
1985–2001 (per cent)

	Exports	Imports
1985	1.1	4.9
1990	12.6	23.1
1995	31.5	47.7
1999	45.5	51.8
2000	47.9	52.1
2001	48.0	–

Sources: SSB, *China Statistical Yearbook* (Beijing, 2001); UNCTAD (2002a).

2002). Over 60 per cent of FIE output is exported and this represents about 9 per cent of GDP. Interestingly, FIEs also account for around 52 per cent of imports, reflecting the tariff and duty waivers afforded foreign firms and the import of intermediate goods for processing and assembly as well as capital equipment.[22]

The structure of the export sector generally in China raises issues concerning the extent of positive spillovers in the domestic economy and whether there exists a enclave of foreign exporters. There is concern that given the structure of foreign operations, and the fact that domestic firms involved in export have been predominately engaged in the processing of imported parts and components, there is likely to be limited linkages being established with the local economy despite the dramatic expansion in China's exports. Li (2002) estimates that about 70 per cent of the trade carried out by FIEs constitutes processing and assembling. Given the low level of domestic value added in much of this processing activity, he questions the contribution of FDI in these areas to overall economic development in China. This is compounded by the fact that Chinese domestic enterprises are concentrated in the low-technology export sector, an area which includes toys, travel and sporting goods and yarns and fabrics.

Lardy (2003) observes that foreign firms are responsible for product design, the supply of imported inputs and production equipment and the sale and distribution of the final product on world markets. Wei and Liu (2001) have also called into question the spillover effects of FDI for labour productivity generally in China, and ascribe this to the relatively low share of FDI in overall investment. Various studies, however, have identified the positive impact that FDI has had on the wider Chinese economy (Wu, 1999, 2002; Zhang, 2002). Recent studies also provide increasing evidence that local suppliers are growing and that local content in FIE production is rising (UNCTAD, 2002a).

Table 3.9 Exports of high-technology products from China, value and share by enterprise, 1996–2000

	Total (USD billion)	SOE (%)	FIE (%)
1996	7.7	39	59
1997	16.3		
1998	20.3	25	74
1999	24.7	23	76
2000	37.0	18	81

Source: UNCTAD (2002a).

FIE process trade has been a driving force behind the diversification of China's exports. During the 1980s FDI was concentrated in labour-intensive industries, moving to more technology-intensive industries during the 1990s. Increasingly China has specialized in downstream segments of product assembly in new manufacturing sectors, relying on imports of intermediate goods and components. Exports in consumer electronics, domestic electrical appliances and instruments have risen dramatically. Manufacturers of computers, electronics, telecommunication equipment, pharmaceuticals, petrochemicals and power generating equipment have now established production facilities in China. The 100 leading foreign firms operating in China accounted for 10 per cent of China's exports in 2000 (UNCTAD, 2002a). Most were involved in the electronics and telecoms industries.[23]

This shift is reflected in China's foreign trade, with exports of high and new technology products representing almost 15 per cent of total exports in 2000 (UNCTAD, 2002a).[24] Foreign affiliates accounted for 81 per cent of this trade (Table 3.9). Around one-quarter of exports by FIEs are in high-tech products.

FDI has helped broaden the structure of the economy, facilitated the introduction and adoption of technological advances, increased exports and export competitiveness and provided educational value in respect of a model of the market mechanism. FDI provides managerial skill, labour training and capital, and has led to the establishment of a legal framework to support a private sector and for conducting business. Other institutions necessary for effective working of markets, including the financial system, have also come under increased pressure to adapt and modernize. China is now increasingly using FDI to *acquire* technology rather than relying on doing this through importing capital and equipment, as it has in the past. There has been a rise in investment in technology- and capital-intensive projects. Increasingly large MNCs are strategically locating in China, with nearly 400 of the *Fortune* 500 firms having invested in over 200 projects in China

(UNCTAD, 2002a). China's accession to the WTO is expected to lead to greater investment in capital- and technology-intensive manufacturing areas, with greater opportunity for mergers and acquisitions (M&As).

Foreign firms from the industrialized economies are increasingly locating R&D activities in China because of the need to adapt technology to the local market conditions. The availability of a well-educated pool of researchers, many trained overseas, is supporting this trend. Moreover, as China meets its WTO commitments there will be increasing FDI inflows into services areas such as telecoms, distribution, insurance and banking. Most of the FDI from industrialized countries in these areas will be oriented towards sales into the domestic market, looking for large, fast-growing and developing markets. Such FDI will be better quality, from firms with technical and innovation capabilities, managerial skills and knowledge-based intangible assets.

Over 160,000 FIEs operate in China employing around 20 million people, which represents about 3 per cent of China's non-agricultural personnel (Tseng and Zebregs, 2002). While this is less than 0.8 per cent of the total workforce, in the large eastern provinces FIEs account for around 10 per cent of urban employment (Chow, 2002). In 1999 FIEs accounted for 16 per cent of total industrial and commercial taxes in China, up from 11 per cent in 1995. This trend is likely to continue, with FIEs being one of the fastest-growing revenue sources for government.

9   A theoretical and empirical discussion of firms' FDI decision

A vast literature has emerged seeking to explain why companies engage in production abroad and what determines their choice of location. A good review is provided in UNCTC (1992). Dunning (1993) provides a so-called 'eclectic' view which embraces the concepts expounded in earlier explanations. This suggests that a firm's motivation for FDI depends on the combination of ownership-specific advantages, internalization opportunities and locational advantages in the target market. If a firm cannot exploit each of these three advantages simultaneously, then alternative approaches such as patent, trademark or licensing agreements with domestic producers in the local market or exporting would be more effective foreign market entry strategies.

The ownership and internalization explanations provide a comprehensive rationale for why firms choose ownership of assets as the cross-border form for effecting sales of goods and services. These can be viewed as firm-specific (or supply-side) determinants of FDI. Conversely the locational factors can be viewed as host country (or demand-side) determinants. Ownership-specific advantages are usually conferred by a firm's control of production technology, financial and management resources and marketing techniques, along with other attributes of a proprietary nature. Opportunities arising from internalizing control over production relate to such matters as the costs of quality control and supervision, transport and marketing costs and restrictions on intra-firm transactions.

Dunning (1998) suggests that the location decision has been relatively neglected by researchers, treated as a secondary factor when compared to the focus that exists on the institutional form of a firm's overseas involvement. This aspect is of particular importance for developing countries given the extent of competition between nation states for FDI inflows and the importance of identifying what factors exist that are under the control of governments and can be manipulated to attract FDI. Bende-Nabende *et al.* (2001) argue that firms with similar firm-specific advantages tend to target similar market segments (and adopt similar entry modes) in developing countries. Consequently locational factors are seen as significant in influencing the FDI disparity between specific developing countries and regions.

The list of host country determinants in Box 3.1 provides some indication as to which factors host countries have the power to influence, and to what degree, and how these interact in turn with the motives of firms undertaking the investment (UNCTAD, 1998).

Box 3.1   Host country determinants of FDI

Policy framework for FDI

Economic, political and social stability
Rules regarding entry and operations
Support for a competitive market environment
International agreements on FDI
Trade policy
Tax policy

Economic determinants: classified according to the firms' motivation

Market-seeking
  Market size; market growth; access to regional and global markets; country-specific consumer preferences
Resource/strategic asset-seeking
  Raw materials; low-cost labour; physical infrastructure; skilled labour; technological and other created assets (including brand names) as embodied in local firms and individuals
Efficiency-seeking/cost-reducing
  Cost of resources and assets, adjusted for productivity; transport and communication costs to, from and within host countries; regional integration agreements

Business facilitation

Investment promotion
Investment incentives
Hassle costs: related to corruption and administrative efficiency
'Cultural distance'
Social amenities (for foreign staff, for example)
After-investment services

A study by Nicholas, Gray and Purcell (2001) has concluded that policy factors are relatively less important in the location decision of Japanese firms undertaking FDI in East Asia. Economic fundamentals such as the size and growth performance of the market were deemed most important, along with the political stability issue. Investigation of the motivation of US firms has also found that labour costs and market size were driving forces for FDI choices, with the policy framework being less influential. More generally, Bende-Nabende *et al.* (2002), in a study of the determinants of FDI across East Asia, suggest that the dominant long-run determinants are cost-related factors, followed by the extent of liberalization of investment and trade regimes, political risk, macroeconomic variables and the nature of (outward-looking) development strategies. Real wage rates, human capital and the extent of the liberalization of investment policies are seen as particularly important.

In considering the inflow of FDI into China it is useful to distinguish between the factors motivating firms to move in that direction and factors which cause local enterprises in China to seek foreign participation in their activities.

10 Factors driving FDI inflows to China

China has for a long period been a net exporter of capital, running significant capital account surpluses since 1990 in all years except 1993. Domestic savings have also been traditionally very high. Given that most FDI inflows have traditionally been from East Asia and most capital imports are sourced from OECD countries, FDI does not seem at first glance to be a necessary means for local business to access technology.

Looking at the factors encouraging capital to move into China, market size has been identified as a key influence in attracting investment from the USA and Europe while cheap labour is seen as a significant factor in the export-oriented activities of firms from Hong Kong and Taiwan (Liu *et al.*, 1997; Tseng and Zebregs, 2002). The importance of supporting physical infrastructure has also been important and is reflected in the concentration of investment in the eastern regions of the country.[25] The economic success of the SEZs and coastal cities suggests that the preferential policies for FIEs in respect of taxation, duties, foreign exchange and autonomy have also played a role, although this raises possible problems of regional distortions.[26] Agglomeration effects are also highlighted by Cheng and Kwan (2000), especially in services areas such as law and accounting, as a factor in the location decision of foreign firms.

The role of the overseas Chinese as a source of capital is a factor unique to China. This is likely to have been particularly important at a time when the financial and legal institutions which normally complement foreign activities in a country were an inhibiting factor for many non-Chinese firms. The relative dominance of Hong Kong, Taiwan and Singaporean investment attests to the role of cultural affinity in the early phase (particularly) of FDI in China. Wang (2001) stresses the role informal personal networks in China have played in facilitating the large FDI inflows.

Western companies have tended to be attracted by China's huge market potential and infrastructure needs (Zhou, Delios and Yang, 2002; Story, 2003). European and US corporations direct about two-thirds of their output to the domestic market, whereas the overseas Chinese investors are more geared for export (Tseng and Zebregs, 2002). Notwithstanding this fact, Chinese domestic firms still tend to dominate the local market for industrial goods, with foreign firms managing significant market shares in the highly protected industries.

Cheap labour is no longer a main attraction, with the economy's large and growing demand for infrastructure development and the ability of the local environment to support R&D activities increasingly driving FDI. The availability of hard and soft R&D infrastructure, including increasing numbers of expatriate researchers being lured back to China, has been important since the mid-1990s in attracting investment in high-tech areas (UNCTAD, 2001). The need for foreign companies to adapt technology to the large local market has also caused relocation of R&D activities to China. In terms of *pull* factors bringing FDI into China, it might well be that as a transitional economy, international market experience and exposure to ideas, rather than technology, was an important consideration for producers in China's areas of comparative advantage early in the reform period.

As mentioned earlier, while domestic savings have been maintained at relatively high rates in China (currently around 40 per cent of GDP), the financial system has proved to be inefficient in allocating this to local industry. Efficient firms have found it difficult to access this savings pool; the demand by SOEs for investment funds, and their favoured position through directed lending arrangements, has also limited the availability of capital for other enterprises. These factors have provided a strong motivation to seek a foreign partner to provide capital and has resulted in the concentration of FDI in a vast number of labour-intensive and traditional Chinese enterprises. Together with the weakness in the supporting legal and other market institutions in the early reform period, this provided an opportunity for firms in Hong Kong and Taiwan to shift production to the mainland.[27]

Jvs with foreign firms are a major source of capital and such arrangements also circumvent the many restrictive controls which face domestic firms. Domestic capital also tends to be relatively immobile between regions due to provincial barriers on trade and capital flows. Capital-rich regions, in fact, export capital overseas due to the lack of domestic opportunities while capital-poor provinces import foreign capital. In this sense, therefore, some FDI can be seen to be a result of the intra-regional barriers to capital flows within China.

Many restrictions still exist for foreign companies in China, in concert with an opaque policymaking process. The key issues for investors in China today (Gelb, 2000) include:

- The legal limits to the nature and mode of operation permitted in China, specifically investment structures
- China's implementation of its WTO commitments
- Intellectual property right protection
- Hiring and keeping suitable staff
- Relations with the Chinese authorities.

11   FDI inflows and China's accession to the WTO

In terms of general commitments, these include adherence to the Trade-Related intellectual property and trade-related investment measures agreements (TRIPs and TRIMs, respectively) and the General Agreement on Trade in Services (GATS) (see the appendix, p. 71, for more detail on these WTO agreements as they relate to FDI). The TRIPs agreement will encourage FDI as investors to feel more confident that trademarks and patents will be secure if production proceeds in China. Under the TRIM agreement, requirements for foreign exchange balancing, local content and export performance will be abolished.

Specific sectoral commitments have also been made which will involve significant expansion of market access for foreign firms, particularly in the services areas (Chen, 2002; Li, 2002; Adhikara and Yang, 2002). Areas to be opened up include telecoms, automobiles, insurance and banking. In the automobile sector there will be an elimination of geographic and other restrictions, while increased ownership limits will be phased in for telecoms, life insurance, securities, distribution and retailing. National treatment for foreign banks is also being introduced. FDI is also permitted in urban gas, water supply and heating industries. Restrictions in the audiovisual, tourism and education areas are also in line to be relaxed. For most services there will be a phase-in period of up to six years. It is likely that much of the increased FDI in these areas will be directed to sales for the local market. China's expected export surge following accession is expected to flow from improved market access rather than improved productivity and competitiveness in the traditional labour-intensive sectors. Expanded FDI flows will, however, assist in creating opportunities in these areas. Increased technical-intensive and skill-intensive investment will be needed to stimulate export trade in high-tech areas.

12   Case study: the Chinese automobile industry

The international market for automobiles has been relatively stagnant since the mid-1990s. Multinational car manufacturers are increasingly shifting funds and markets to developing countries. China holds particular promise, with *per capita* income steadily rising to levels around USD 4,000 in Shanghai and other coastal regions (IMF, 2001). By 2010 China is forecast to become the third largest automobile market in the world behind the USA and Japan.[28]

The automobile sector, which historically was one of the first industries opened up to foreigners, is the only area of manufacturing in which China has made specific commitments in investment liberalization in its WTO agreement. A significant expansion in FDI in automobile production and related activities such as consumer financing, distribution, sales and maintenance is expected. More power will also be afforded to the provinces. The automobile industry is one of the authorities' designated key industries in China, seen as an engine for growth over the next decade (SETC, 2001).

In 1984 two joint ventures, the Beijing Jeep Corporation Ltd and the Shanghai VW Automobile Corporation, were established. By 1999 over 400 Jvs had been established in the industry. Five of the country's six key production companies are Jvs, while enterprises producing spare parts are now mainly also Jvs.[29] Wholly owned enterprises are not allowed.

China is currently the eighth largest automobile manufacturer in the world (SETC, 2001). Large local SOEs include the First Automobile Works (FAW) Group, The Dongfeng Group and the Shanghai Automobile Industry Group. Domestically made vehicles account for around 95 per cent of China's sales. Around 2 per cent of production is exported. In 2000, industry output was equal to 4.2 per cent of GDP. The share of imports in sales is down from 10 per cent in 1995, due to expanded assembly operations with foreign Jv arrangements (Xia, 2000).

The Chinese automobile industry is characterized by poor economies of scale, outmoded technology, lack of investment in R&D, inconsistent quality control and inferior management (CAAM, 2002). An automobile made in China is estimated to be 40–50 per cent more expensive than similar products produced abroad (UNCTAD, 2002a). Labour productivity is low and unit labour cost is high.

In 2000, there were 118 car manufacturers, 1,500 auto parts plants, 51 engine manufacturers, 546 refitting enterprises and 136 motorcycle manufacturers. The biggest car plant in China in 2000 (Shanghai VW produced

Table 3.10 Phased tariff reduction on cars, actual rates (per cent), as at 1 January 2000–6

Capacity	Base	2000	2001	2002	2003	2004	2005	2006	2006*
< 300 cc	80	63.5	51.9	43.8	38.2	34.2	30.0	28.0	25
> 3000	100	77.5	61.7	50.7	43.0	37.6	30.0	28.0	25

Note: * July.
Source: Jiang (2002).

about 230,000 sedan vehicles). Total car output nationally was 605,000, less than the output of a medium-size car plant in an advanced economy. Under the current system, every domestic assembler is linked to particular parts suppliers with a strong geographical orientation due to restrictions on internal trade within China. Foreign firms are also constrained as to the models which can be introduced. The import substitution approach and local protectionism has meant that rents in the industry are high. Further, foreign participants have been required to meet requirements which include minority shareholdings, foreign exchange balancing (limiting imports), local content and technology transfer. Scale economies are hard to achieve as a result (there is also overcapacity estimated at around 46 per cent) and little local R&D is encouraged.

China's TRIMs commitment will be a boost for foreign players in the automobile market, while specific measures in respect of tariffs and quotas will be instituted under WTO accession.

China will substantially reduce its customs duty on automobiles from the current levels (based on motor capacity) to 25 per cent and on auto parts from 18–45 per cent to 10 per cent by 2006 (Table 3.10). The currently prohibitive import quota has been raised to USD 6 billion following accession and will rise 15 per cent annually until eliminated (WTO, 2002). Zhong (2002) estimates that imports will rise to about 10 per cent of sales in sedans by the end of the transition period, with prices falling by around 30 per cent. An issue for foreign producers will be to determine the extent to which they wish to import and compete with their local production. An influx of imports and a restructuring of the industry will result in lower retail prices, stimulating demand for cars. At the same time private purchase will be assisted by the increasing availability of auto-financing services which are stipulated as part of China's accession agreement to the WTO. Private consumption has been a stumbling block to development of this industry.[30] Imported prices are high for cars and local product is also expensive and seen as a status symbol rather than a means of general transport by most households. Marketing has not been directed towards a mass market. The government will need to address this issue of the demand side of the market for the industry to develop to its full potential. Currently there are a range of local taxes and charges facing private consumers, beyond the trade-related barriers for imports.[31] Purchase finance initiatives will help in this regard.

The market for repair and maintenance is also expected to grow, stimulating demand for auto parts and accessories. All services related to automobiles are to be liberalized and opened up to foreign firms. These include distribution, marketing, after-sales service, financing, dealership, advertising and imports of parts and accessories. Local content requirements are to be abolished, along with industry subsidies, and global sourcing in parts and accessories will result. Increased competition will make foreign partners speed up the technology transfer and the pace of technical innovation in China. The continued restrictions on equity shares and ownership will act as a drag on developments, however. The requirement that import distributors must be capitalized to the extent of USD 100 million will likely work to encourage on-shore production.

UNCTAD (2002a) estimates that industry output will fall 11 per cent by 2005 as a result of tariff reductions alone. Employment for unskilled and skilled labour is expected to fall by around 8 per cent and 12 per cent, respectively. With industry employment of about 1.8 million persons, this translates to around 200,00 job losses.

Li, Zhai and Xu (2000) estimate that the number of enterprises will decline by 27 per cent by 2006. The Tenth Five-Year Plan for the industry, released in 2001 plans to have two–three large conglomerates by 2005 for car production and five–ten for parts.

Ianchovichina *et al.* (2001) expect exports to rise as the industry becomes more efficient. Whether the industry becomes the manufacturing centre for the world's automobile industry remains to be seen. However conditions within China for the industry certainly have the potential for the automobile industry to be a dynamic export force as well as expanding final production to meet a growing local demand. What is likely, perhaps, is that China will specialize in more compact and economic cars, while importing the upper end of the market.

13   Conclusion

China has been the second largest recipient of FDI inflows over the 1990s, behind only the USA. Since the opening up of the economy to the outside world in 1979, certain patterns and characteristics in respect of FDI inflows to the country can be determined. Initially FDI was mainly sourced from East Asian neighbours and was in labour-intensive industries in which China had a comparative advantage and which traditionally had been important in the economy. This provided a solid base for export growth. Smaller levels of FDI, mainly from industrialized countries, through the 1980s and into the 1990s went into some service areas, predominantly real estate (hotels and property development) and natural resource development. All the while China was strictly controlling the modes of entry, the industry access, the geographical spread of permitted FDI and the timing of entry.

One aspect of the regulation and control has been the concentration of FDI in the eastern provinces, adding to the growing internal inequality evident in China today. Following a further liberalization of FDI in 1992, there was a surge of FDI moving into a wider spread of manufacturing industries including more high-technology areas. Although the FIEs have been important in terms of capital formation in the economy since the 1980s, this reflects to some degree the weakness of the Chinese financial system in efficiently channelling domestic savings to business. The concentration of FDI until relatively recent times in more labour-intensive and traditional manufacturing areas raises the question as to precisely what benefits other than capital have been provided at the cost of foreign ownership. Moreover, the apparent dynamic growth of exports by FIEs, while impressive, has not seen exports as a share of GDP rise dramatically. The links of FDI inflow with economic growth and with technological advance and increased productivity in China warrant close attention.

The fact that China was a transitional economy, unfamiliar with international capitalism and with poorly developed internal institutions (financial, legal, etc.) meant that foreign expertise and international links, as well as capital, were an important benefit from FDI. FDI has been important in opening China to the global economy through its impact on trade. FDI has also provided significant spillover effects for other industries and has helped in the development of market institutions (legal, financial, etc.). Its role in transforming the economy, broadening the structure of output and assisting in the transfer of technology and management skills, has only just begun. However it is likely that the new phase of FDI into China will be qualitatively, if not quantitatively, different and will rapidly advance the modernization and dynamism of the economy. With China's WTO commitments allowing a greater access for FDI, it seems that FDI will increasingly be driven by foreign companies seeking access to a much greater degree than previously to the large domestic Chinese market, particularly in services areas; Chinese authorities and firms will also want to encourage greater technology and productivity transfers. Increased R&D activity by foreign firms in China is also growing in response to the needs of the Chinese market and as a reflection of the increasing availability of research hardware and software.

Appendix

An investment regime can be assessed in terms of the standard of treatment afforded foreign investors, transparency of national laws, national treatment of foreign firms, most favoured nation (MFN) treatment of all source economies and a strict code of conduct for host governments. The WTO does not address the right of establishment for foreign firms. It avoids many issues of host government conduct such as fiscal incentives, capital transfers and dispute settlement. The agreements which impact indirectly on FDI in the WTO agreements are the following:

The General Agreement on Trade in Services (GATS)

This agreement does not explicitly refer to investment; rather, it impacts on investment through reference to the supply of a service from one country to another through a commercial presence in the territory of another country, one of the four identified modes of service delivery defined in the GATS (the others being movement of suppliers, movement of natural persons and cross-border trade). National treatment is provided to foreign suppliers of services.

Under the GATS, countries are required to schedule their commitments to liberalize in particular sectors (i.e. in respect of market access, national treatment and MFN) in terms of the four identified modes of supply. China has listed a number of service industries under this agreement including, telecoms, finance, retail, distribution and insurance.

Agreement on Trade Related Intellectual Property (TRIPs)

These provisions cover copyright and related rights, trademarks, geographical indications, industrial designs, patents, etc. Minimum standards of protection for each category and the procedures and remedies to ensure enforcement of intellectual property (IP) rights in international law are provided. These rights form an important part of the FDI environment, particularly for those products or processes with significant IP content or involving technology transfer. Investment in R&D activities will be positively encouraged by the protection afforded under the TRIPs.

Agreement on Trade Related Investment Measures (TRIMs)

TRIMS is relatively limited in its provisions. The TRIMs agreement relates only to trade in goods. There is no definition of TRIMs in the agreement, rather there is an illustrative list of what is deemed GATT- (or WTO)-consistent. This includes issues of local content requirements, trade balancing requirements (with respect to export–import ratios linked to output), foreign exchange balancing and export restrictions.

Notes

1. The reliability of domestic output data in China is a problem in view of the difficulty in valuing stocks and non-marketed services and also because of inflated estimates by regional officials. Garnaut (1999) suggests that while trade data provides a reasonable indication of China's external relations, real growth is likely to be overestimated by about 2.5 per cent over the reform period. The size of the economy and average incomes are considered to understate the reality.

2. From the mid-1980s up until 2000, global FDI inflows grew at an average annual rate of around 18 per cent, while world trade and output grew at 11 per cent and 8 per cent, respectively.

3. Whereas flows to the USA have varied from three to five times those going to China, the US economy is seven times as large. See below for a discussion of the relative importance of FDI in China.

4. Mexico, France, China, South Africa and Singapore were the countries which had the most significant increases in FDI inflows in 2001. Western Europe, the USA, Canada and Hong Kong were the biggest losers in 2001 (UNCTAD, 2002a).

5. The upswing is expected following China's entry to the WTO (in December 2001) and the impact this will have on new investment, along with an increase in the reinvested earnings of foreign affiliates in China. In 2000–1 this latter source accounted for one-third of total inflows (UNCTAD, 2002a).

6. Concessions included tax holidays along with reduced import duties and tax rates. Companies (foreign and local) operating in the zones were also given greater managerial control, including flexibility in terms of labour market operations. Entry and exit formalities were eased and vast tracts of land were allocated for commercial uses and greenfield establishments (Zhou, Delios and Yang, 2002).

7. ETDZs tend to focus on specific industries and prioritize local infrastructure development (Zhou, Delios and Yang, 2002).

8. The 'gradualist' approach to market reform in China generally, contrasts with the 'big bang' shock therapy adopted by many of the countries in the former Soviet Union (FSU).

9. The Pudong area of Shanghai was created as a development zone in 1990.

10. Round-tripping and mis-reporting may inflate some of the figures for FDI, particularly investment viewed as emanating from Hong Kong. This reflects efforts by mainland enterprises seeking to take advantage of various tax and other benefits which are afforded only to foreign enterprises in China. Nevertheless, the magnitudes are such as to be significant, in both an absolute and relative sense.

11. Compared to Japan, Korea and Taiwan at comparable stages of their development, China has been very open to FDI.

12. FDI as a share of GFCF as an average over the period 1985–95 was 4 per cent for the world, 6.4 per cent for China and 35.3 per cent for Singapore (UNCTAD, 2001). The ratio is still high for Singapore, but has steadily risen for developing countries generally.

13. By the mid-1990s China was the largest outward investor among developing countries and the eighth largest among all countries (Lardy, 2003).

14. Lardy (2003) contrasts this situation with Thailand and Malaysia where the rate of investment rose about 20 per cent over the 1990s as a result of FDI inflows.

15. China, in fact, runs a trade deficit with East Asian economies (except for Hong Kong). The trade deficit with Taiwan and with Korea was USD 2.08 billion and USD 0.79 billion, respectively. In 2001 China had a trade surplus with the USA and the EU of USD 2.58 billion and USD 0.73 billion, respectively. There was a slight surplus of USD 0.11 billion with Japan and a surplus of USD 3.22 billion with Hong Kong (World Bank, 2002).

16. These restrictions also encouraged round-tripping, primarily through Hong Kong (as noted earlier).

17. All the SEZs, the development zones and ten of the fourteen open coastal cities are considered to be in the south-east of China (Gao, 2002).
18. When China initiated its 'open door' policy in 1979, four SEZs were instituted: Shenzhen, Shantou, Zhuhai (all in Guangdong Province) and Xiamen in Fujian province. Hainan was added in 1988. The SEZs enjoyed special policy treatment including a range of incentives for FIEs such as tax and tariff concessions. Provincial governments could also provide a range of inducements in respect of infrastructure support for FIEs. In 1984, fourteen coastal cities were also opened up to foreign investment. Around these coastal cities various technology development zones have been established (e.g. in Pudong in 1990) aimed at attracting investment in high-tech industries.
19. In an equity Jv, the relative equity shares of the local and foreign partners are agreed to and the investors operate the venture and share the risks, profits and losses accordingly. In a cooperative Jv, the Chinese partner provides land, natural resources, labour and other infrastructure support, while the foreign partner provides capital, technology and materials. The distribution of products and profits is subject to negotiation.
20. Canada had 4.2 per cent and the UK 4.4 per cent, respectively, of world merchandise exports in 2001; the USA was the largest trader, with 11.9 per cent.
21. With FIEs accounting for around half of all China's trade, SOEs account for most of the remainder as private firms have a negligible share.
22. China's trade surplus predominantly therefore represents the activity, of SOEs rather than foreign firms. Given that FIEs are a major source of imports, and that when exports alone are considered, China's ratio of exports relative to GDP has not grown markedly over the past decade, it might suggest some export diversion. The rapid growth in exports by FIEs, particularly in the traditional and labour intensive sectors, might reflect shifts in ownership rather than a stimulus to exports *per se*.
23. The companies included: Samsung, IBM, Nokia, Motorola, Seiko, Philips Electronics and Sanyo.
24. In 1985, almost half of China's exports were primary products or resource-based manufactures; by 2000 the share was 12 per cent, with non-resource-based manufactures accounting for 87 per cent of all exports (UNCTAD, 2002a). Just over 22 per cent of exports were in high-technology areas.
25. The eastern coastal regions have had the geographic advantage of being close to ports, particularly Hong Kong, and the dynamic East Asian region as well as the benefit of the loosening of regulation and controls on business activity and trade by the central authorities.
26. There is considerable evidence of the resource mis-allocation effects stemming from rivalry between regions for foreign investment and in seeking to protect their regional markets against products from FIEs (Hoong, 2001; Panitchpakdi and Clifford, 2002).
27. Hong Kong currently accounts for 55 per cent of all foreign invested projects in China (Winn, 2002). Most of this funding is in the light industrial export sector, managed from Hong Kong-based firms.
28. The environmental and social problems this is likely to present is an issue that does not seem to have received a great deal of attention.
29. The largest are Shanghai-VW, Shanghai-GM, First Automobile Works-VW (Changchun), Dongfeng-Citroen and Tianjin Xiali (Toyota).

30. Taxi fleets, companies and government were the sole market until private purchase was permitted in 1985. In 1999 the share of privately owned vehicles was 37 per cent (SETC, 2001). Over the 1990s, private sales grew at an annual average rate of 23.2 per cent. Since 1998 sales to individuals have accounted for around half of all sales.
31. Current indications are that consumption taxes on cars will be increasingly linked to emissions as an effort to address pollution problems. Various other taxes could be directed to curbing usage.

References

Adhikara, R. and Y.Z. Yang, 'China's Increasing Openness: Threat or Opportunity?', www.adb.org/documents/events/2002/trade policy/PRCIO paper.pdf (2002).

Asia Development Bank (ADB), *Asia Development Outlook* (various years).

Bende-Nabende, A., J.L. Ford, J. Slater and S. Sen, 'Foreign Direct Investment in East Asia: Trends and Determinants', *Asia Pacific Journal of Economics and Business*, 6(1) (2001): 4–25.

CAAM (China Association of Automobile Manufacturers) www.caam.org.cn (2002).

Chen Chunlai, 'The Impact of WTO Accession on FDI', in R. Garnaut and L. Song, *China 2002: WTO Entry and World Recession* (Canberra: Asia Pacific Press; ANU, 2002).

Cheng, L.K. and Y.K. Kwan, 'What are the Determinants of the Location of Foreign Direct Investment? The Chinese Experience', *Journal of International Economics*, 51, (2000): 379–400.

Chow, G. *China's Economic Transformation* (Oxford: Blackwell, 2002).

Dunning, J.H. *The Theory of Transnational Corporations* London and New York: (Routledge, 1993).

Dunning, J.H. 'Location and the Multinational Enterprise: A Neglected Factor?' *Journal of International Business Studies*, 29(1) (1998): 45–66.

Economist, The, 10 March 2001: 15.

Economist, The, 10 April 2003: 21.

Gao, T. 'The Impact of Foreign Trade and Investment Reform on Industry Location: The Case of China', *Journal of International Trade and Economic Development*, 11(4) (2002): 367–86.

Garnaut, R. 'Twenty Years of Economic Reform and Structural Change in the Chinese Economy', in R. Garnaut and L. Song (eds), *China: Twenty Years of Reform* (Canberra: Asia Pacific Press, ANU, 1999).

Gelb, C. 'Foreign Investors Wise Up', *The China Business Review 2000*, Chinabusinessreview.com/0011/gelb.html, 2000 (2000).

Hoong Yik Luan, *New China Rising: A Social Economic Assessment of WTO Entry*, (Singapore: Hoong, 2001).

Huang, Y. *Selling China: Foreign Direct Investment During the Reform Era* (New York: Cambridge University Press, 2002).

Ianchorichina, E. and W. Martin, 'Assessing the Implications of Merchandise Trade Liberalization in China's Accession to the WTO'; paper presented to conference, *China and the WTO* (Australian National Universities, Canberra, 16–17 March 2001).

International Monetary Fund (IMF), *World Economic Outlook* (Washington, DC: IMF, December 2001).

Jiang, H. (ed.), *Compilation of the Legal Instruments on China's Accession to the World Trade Organization* (Beijing: Law Press, 2002).

Lardy, N. *Integrating China into the Global Economy* (Washington, DC: Brookings Institution Press, 2003).

Li, S., F. Zhai and L. Xu, 'Impact of WTO Accession on China's Economy', in *Research Report on China's Entry to the WTO* (Beijing: Social Science Documentation Publishing House, 2000): 35–88.

Li, Y. 'China's Accession to WTO: Exaggerated Fears?', Discussion Papers, 165 (New York: UNCTAD, November 2002).

Liu, X., H. Song, Y. Wei and P. Romilly, 'Country Characteristics and FDI in China: A Panel Data Analysis', *Weltwirtschaftliches Archiv*, 133(2) (1997): 313–29.

Nicholas, S., S.J. Gray and W.R. Purcell, 'Do Incentives Attract Japanese Investment to Singapore and the Region?', in S.J. Gray, S.L. McGaughey and W.R. Purcell, *Asia Pacific Issues in International Business* (Cheltenham, Edward Elgar: UK 2001).

Nolan, P. *China and the Global Economy* (London: Palgrave, 2001).

Panitchpakdi S. and M.L. Clifford (2002), *China and the WTO, Changing China, Changing World Trade* (Singapore: J. Wiley, Asia, 2002).

State Statistical Bureau (SSB), *China Statistical Yearbook* (Zhongguo Tongji Chubanshe, Beijing, 2000).

State Statistical Bureau (SSB), *China Statistical Yearbook* (Beijing, 2001).

SETC (State Economic and Trade Commission), *Tenth Five-Year Plan for the Automobile Industry*, www.setc.gov.cn (2001).

Story, J. *China: The Race to Market* (Englewood Chtts: Prentice-Hall, 2003).

Tseng, W. and H. Zebregs, *Foreign Direct Investment in China: Some Lessons for Other Countries*, IMF Discussion Paper, PDP/02/03 (2002).

United Nations Conference on Trade and Development (UNCTAD), *World Investment Report 1998: Trends and Determinants* (New York: UNCTAD, 1998).

United Nations Conference on Trade and Development (UNCTAD), *World Investment Report* (New York: UNCTAD, 2002a).

United Nations Conference on Trade and Development (UNCTAD), 'UNCTAD Predicts 27% Drop in FDI Inflows this Year', Press Release, 24 October (New York: UNCTAD, 2002b).

United Nations Conference on Trade and Development (UNCTAD), *Trade and Development Report* (New York: UNCTAD, 2002c).

United Nations Conference on Trade and Development (UNCTAD), *World Investment Report* (New York: UNCTAD, 2001).

United Nations Centre on Transnational Corporations (UNCTC), *The Determinants of Foreign Direct Investment, A Survey of the Evidence*, Division of Transnational Corporations and Investment (New York: United Nations, 1992).

Wang, H. *Weak State, Strong Networks: The Institutional Dynamics of Foreign Direct Investment in China* (Hong Kong: Oxford University Press, 2001).

Wei, Y. and X. Liu, *Foreign Direct Investment in China: Determinants and Impact* (Cheltenham: Edward Elgar, 2001).

Winn, H. 'China Needs Hong Kong', *Hong Kong Mail*, 4 May 2002: 14.

World Bank, *World Development Report* (Washington, DC: World Bank, 2002).

WTO www.wto.org (2002).

Wu, Y. 'The Determinants of Economic Growth: Evidence from a Panel of Chinese Provinces', in L. Song (ed.), *Dilemmas of China's Growth in the Twenty First Century* (Canberra: Asia Pacific Press, ANU, 2002).

Wu, Y. (ed.), *Foreign Direct Investment and Economic Growth in China* (Cheltenham: Edward Elgar, 1999).

Xia, N. 'China's Automobile Industry to Take the Brunt of Impact of WTO Entry', www.tdctrade.com/report/indprof/001006.htm (2000).

Zhang, Q. 'Regional Developments in China: The Role of FDI, Exports and Spillover Effects', in L. Song (ed.), *Dilemmas of China's Growth in the Twenty First Century* (Canberra: Asia Pacific Press, ANU, 2002).

Zhong, H. 'Domestic Industries Face to Face with WTO Accession', www.tdctrade.com/report/indprof/020101.htm (7 January 2002).

Zhou, C., A. Delios and J.Y. Yang, 'Locational Determinants of Japanese Foreign Direct Investment in China', *Asia Pacific Journal of Management*, 19(1) (2002): 63–86.

4
Maximizing Benefits from Foreign Direct Investment and Minimizing its Costs: What Can We Learn from China?

Kevin Honglin Zhang

Foreign direct investment (FDI) by multinational corporations (MNCs) has been viewed as a major catalyst to economic growth in developing countries. Yet the benefits of FDI do not automatically accrue and evenly across countries. It is possible for some countries even to be worse off with inward FDI flows. National policies and the host government's bargaining power against MNCs matters for attracting FDI and for reaping the full benefits. This study attempts to shed light on the question of how a developing country can maximize the benefits from FDI and minimize its cost, based on China's experiences in the 1980s and 1990s.

China has been the most dynamic FDI host country in the world since the late 1970s. In the twenty-five since economic reforms were initiated in 1978, China has become the largest recipient of FDI in the developing world and globally the second largest (next to only the USA) since 1993. In 2002, China received $ 52.7 billion of FDI inflows; surpassing the USA and becoming the largest host country in the world. By the end of 2003, the accumulated FDI in China was $ 500 billion. The contributions of inward FDI to the Chinese economy have burgeoned in ways that no one anticipated. In 2001, FDI inflows constituted over 10 per cent of gross fixed capital formation (GFCF); 28.5 per cent of industrial output was produced by the foreign-invested enterprises (FIEs); and half of China's exports were created by FIEs (SSB, 2003; UNCTAD, 2003).[1]

As much by luck as by design, China seemed to stumble onto a FDI strategy that has proved remarkably successful, enhancing economic growth and helping the country move quickly to a market-based system. But can the Chinese experience serve as a model for other countries? This study addresses two groups of questions. First, what benefits and opportunities can FDI bring to the development process, and what risks and dangers accompany it? When are the benefits and opportunities likely to predominate, and when are the risks and dangers likely to prevail? Second, do host authorities have a larger role to play to enhance the use of FDI in the development process? If so, what policies should host governments adopt to capture the benefits, avoid the dangers and maximize the contributions of FDI?

Countries seek FDI to help them grow and develop, and host government policies seem to be a key to attract FDI and increase the benefits from it. China's experience shows that the best way of attracting FDI and drawing more benefits from it is not passive liberalization alone. Liberalization and incentive polices can help get more FDI, but they are certainly not enough for the purpose of using FDI as an engine of economic growth. Attracting types of FDI with greater potential for benefiting host countries, such as FDI in technologically advanced or export-oriented activities, is more demanding task than just liberalizing FDI entry and operations. Once countries succeed in attracting foreign investors, government policies are crucial to ensure more benefits and avoid dangers from FDI. Well-designed strategies and policies can induce faster upgrading of technologies and skills, promote exports, raise local procurement and secure more reinvestment of profits. They can also counter the potential dangers related to FDI through performing anticompetitive practices and preventing foreign affiliates from crowding out viable local firms in strategic industries.

The chapter is organized as follows. Section 1 depicts overall patterns of FDI in China, highlighting important characteristics of multinational firms in the country. Section 2 provides an analytical framework of the potential impact of FDI on host economies and policies of host governments. How FDI affects the Chinese economy, and the relevant government policies, are addressed in Sections 3 and 4. Section 5 discusses the challenges China faces after accession to the World Trade Organization (WTO) and summarizes conclusions.

1 Patterns of FDI in China

Three prominent features about FDI into China may be identified: Hong Kong and overseas Chinese are dominant investors; the explosive growth of FDI flows in the 1990s; and the concentration of FDI in China's coastal regions (Zhang, 2001b).

Unlike other host countries, most of FDI into China did not come from worldwide FDI sources (such as the USA, EU, Japan and other industrial countries) but from Hong Kong and the overseas Chinese in Asia.[2] During the period 1979–99, half of total FDI received in China (50.32 per cent) was made by Hong Kong investors. Other major Asian investors in the top fifteen FDI sources of China include Taiwan (ranked fourth), Singapore (fifth), South Korea (seventh), Macao (tenth) and Thailand (fourteenth). Together with Hong Kong, they contributed 71 per cent of the total FDI flows in China. With a share of 19 per cent, the USA, Japan and EU together played a minor role (Zhang, 2000b).[3] The unique FDI sources are a result of China's export-oriented strategy and the special links of Hong Kong Taiwan and overseas Chinese in Asia with China in culture and history (Zhang, 2003).

China experienced a FDI boom during the 1990s relative to the moderate growth in the 1980s. In 1992 China seemed to have reached its critical threshold of attracting FDI on a large scale. The single-year FDI flow in 1993 ($ 26 billion) exceeded the cumulative flows ($ 23 billion) of the previous thirteen years (1979–91). FDI fell in 1999 and 2000 due to the Asian financial crisis, but soon recovered in 2001 and 2002. China's FDI boom seems not merely a part of the global expansion of multinationals, the share of China's FDI in developing countries rose from 7.7 per cent in 1984 to 33 per cent in 1994, and the share in the world increased from 2 per cent to 14 per cent during the same period. The FDI boom and growth shares resulted from China's unique advantages over other host countries in attracting foreign investors, including a large domestic market, cheap labour and land costs, rapid economic growth and a liberalized FDI regime (Zhang, 2001b, 2001c).

The regional distribution of FDI within China has been highly concentrated in the coastal area, which account for about 86 per cent of total FDI in China. In particular, the top three provinces (Guangdong, Jiangsu and Fujian) attracted half of the total FDI in China. The uneven regional distribution of FDI in China is a result of a variety of factors, including the biased FDI policies toward the coastal region, regional differences in development levels and regional cultural and historical connections to foreign investors.

In addition to the three features, the following characteristics should not be ignored: (a) the majority of FDI (about 60 per cent) went to the manufacturing sector, in contrast to the lions share of service FDI in many countries; (b) investment by large MNCs grew rapidly, with nearly 80 per cent of all *Fortune* 500 companies already in China (UNCTAD, 2003); (c) unlike FDI in many host countries, almost all of foreign affiliates were established with greenfield investment, rather than M&A; (d) the dominant entry mode of MNCs into China has been Jv, but wholly foreign-owned projects rose rapidly and its importance is now close to Jv; and (e) while small-scale, labour-intensive and export-oriented FDI projects were dominant in the 1980s and the early 1990s, large scale, capital and technology-intensive, and local market-oriented FDI activities have increased substantially.

2   An analytical framework: the impact of FDI and the host government

Few areas in the economics arouse so much controversy and are subject to such varying interpretations as the issue of dangers and benefits of FDI. Theoretically, one point of view suggests that inward FDI is likely to be detrimental to the host country's economic growth because: (a) FDI may lead to shrinking of indigenous industries through intense competition due to the strong economic power of MNCs; (b) FDI may lower domestic savings; (c) FDI may reduce the host country's welfare when MNCs manipulate market power and transfer pricing; (d) FDI may create enclave economies within a host country, widen the income gap and bias the host economy toward an inappropriate technology and product mix.[4] At the other extreme, one could argue that FDI is likely to be an engine of host economic growth. The arguments on which this point of view is based include, beside others: (a) inward FDI may enhance capital formation and employment opportunities; (b) FDI may promote manufacturing exports; (c) FDI may by its very nature, bring into host economies special resources such as management know-how, skilled labour access to international production networks and established brand names; and most important; (d) FDI may result in technology transfers and spillover effects.[5]

Given the potential positive and negative effects of FDI on host economies, the outcome of FDI depends largely on a host country's capacity to influence and control MNC activities. Studies of the host country's influence and control over FDI suggest that the capacity may depend on its bargaining power and the possibilities for increasing it. A country's ability to bargain with MNCs, in turn, depends in large part on attributes of the industries of FDI and the nature of the host country. Three aspects of industrial structure may be crucial in determining the bargaining power of a host country: (a) the extent of competition in the industry; (b) the nature of the technology; (c) the importance of marketing and product differentiation (Moran, 1985). The bargaining power for the host country is high relative to MNCs if competition is high, if technology is stable and if marketing is of little importance.

The nature of the host country also has a large influence on its bargaining power. If a developing country is large and is seen as an important market for the MNC, if it would be costly for the MNC to relocate and if the government is well informed about the MNC's costs, then the country's bargaining position will be relatively strong. It may be able to get away with relatively high taxes on the MNC's profits and tight regulation of its behaviour (e.g. its employment practices and its care for the environment). If, however, the country is economically weak and MNCs are footloose, then the deal it can negotiate is unlikely to be very favourable.

3 Benefits from FDI

Table 4.1 provides some indicators that suggest the importance and contribution of FDI to the Chinese economy. In 2002 the ratio of FDI stock to GDP was 36 per cent; the share of FDI flows in gross capital formation was 10 per cent; FIEs produced 28.5 per cent of total industrial output and also contributed 15 per cent of the total tax revenue. The most obvious benefits from FDI are perhaps its role in exports and its spillover effects on China's market-oriented

Table 4.1   Importance of FDI in the Chinese economy, 1992–2002

Item	1992	1997	2002
FDI flows (billion US dollars)	11.2	45.3	52.7
Share of China's FDI flows, developing countries (%)	22.5	26.2	25.0
Share of China's FDI flows, world (%)	6.6	10.8	12.0
FDI flows as a ratio of China's gross domestic investment (%)	7.4	14.6	10.5*
FDI stock (billion US dollars)	34.4	220.1	446.2
Share of China's FDI stock, developing countries (%)	5.1	20.5	19.1
Share of China's FDI stock, world (%)	1.1	6.3	6.3
FDI stock as a ratio of China's GDP (%)	7.1	29.4	36.2
Exports by foreign affiliates (billion US dollars)	17.4	75.0	166.0
Share of exports by foreign affiliates, total exports (%)	20.4	41.0	51.0
Industrial output by foreign affiliates (billions US dollars)	37.7	174.7	329.2*
Share of industrial output by foreign affiliates, total industrial output (%)	6.0	12.7	28.5*
Number of employees in foreign affiliates (million)	6.0	17.5	20.0*
Tax contributions from foreign affiliates as share of total tax revenue (%)	4.1	13.2	14.6*

Note: * Figures are for 2001 due to the unavailability of data for 2002.

Sources: Computed from SSB, *China Statistical Yearbook* (Beijing, various years); UNCTAD, *World Investment Report* (1998 and 2003); SSB, *China Foreign Economic Statistics Yearbook* (Bejiing, various years).

reforms. Exports by FIEs in 2002 were $ 166 billion, 51 per cent of China's total exports in that year. FDI has brought extra gains to China in facilitating its transition toward a market system that began in the late 1970s, and which in turn enhanced income growth.

Benefits from FDI in China may be assessed in the light of two aspects: (a) the traditional contribution in capital formation, technology and management know-how transfers, human capital development, employment opportunities and export promotion; and (b) a special contribution in facilitating China's market-oriented reforms through diversifying the ownership structure, establishing market-oriented institutions and reforming SOEs (Zhang, 2001a, 2001d).

FDI contributed China's exports in both augmenting export volume and upgrading export structure. While China's exports totalled $ 18 billion with 47 per cent in manufactured goods in 1980, the corresponding numbers in 2001 were $ 266 billion and 90 per cent, respectively. Exports by foreign affiliates in China rose 57 per cent annually in 1980–2002, and the value of their exports in 2002 were $ 166 billion, comprising 51 per cent of China's total exports in that year (SSB, 2003). Export products by FIEs are mainly labour-intensive manufacturing goods (such as electronics, machinery, footwear, toys, travel goods, textiles and clothing). Export promotion through foreign affiliates is one of major reasons that China is open to foreign investors. FDI helped to channel capital into industries that had the potential to compete internationally, and the global linkages of MNCs facilitated their access to foreign markets. FDI also promoted exports through the teaching of modern marketing strategies, methods, procedures and channels of distribution (Lardy, 1995; Zhang and Song, 2000).

FDI contributes to China's capital formation not only through providing additional capital supply, but also by facilitating structural transformation and the upgrading of domestic industries. Overall, FDI inflows constituted about 10 per cent of gross domestic investment during the 1990s. In addition, FDI has contributed to domestic capital formation by mobilizing domestic investment, especially in infrastructure (e.g. the supply of electricity, transportation and telecoms). In the case of Jvs, Chinese partners usually provide existing plants and production facilities, and additional financial resources through FDI help them to upgrade old plants that would otherwise have required a substantial amount of domestic capital investment. The automobile industry is such an example. Over the 1990s, world major auto makers such as Volkswagen, GM, Ford, Toyota, Honda and so on, established affiliates in the form of Jvs in automobile manufacturing. The Jvs have played a prominent role in restructuring and upgrading China's automobile industry, transforming it from an infant to an almost mature industry.

MNCs brought China modern technologies, some of them not available in absence of FDI, and raised the efficiency with which existing technologies are used (Zhang, 2001d). A central objective of China's FDI strategy is to obtain advanced technology through MNCs. China provides special preferences and incentives to MNCs for the transfer of advanced technology in areas such as transportation communications, energy, metals, construction materials, machinery, chemicals, electronics, pharmaceuticals and medical equipment. However, technology transfer in these industries was very limited before the early 1990s, because of the export-promotion FDI policy, in which market-seeking FDI was not allowed (Zhang, 2001b). After realizing that FDI with modern technologies usually targets domestic markets, rather than exports, China adopted a new FDI policy of an 'exchange market for technology', gradually opening domestic markets to MNCs.

FDI also has significantly reduced China's unemployment pressure and made a vital contribution to government revenues. By the end of 2001, over 20 million local workers were employed in foreign affiliates in China, comprising 11 per cent of total manufacturing employment. Tax contributions from foreign affiliates rose with FDI flows, and the FDI share in China's total tax revenue increased from 4 per cent in 1992 to 14.6 per cent in 2001 (SSB, 2002).

FDI has had important spillover effects on China's transition toward market economic systems, which in turn enhanced income growth, because markets are viewed as a better way to organize economic activities than centrally planned economies. Three particular benefits may be identified (Zhang, 2001d).

Diversifying the ownership structure

China's reforms involved changes a system with predominantly state ownership towards a more desirable mix of state-owned, collective and private ownership. In 1992 SOEs accounted for 48 per cent of total domestic output, collective enterprises for 38 per cent and private enterprises (including FIEs) for 13 per cent, rising from a negligible share in earlier years. By the end of 2001, the share of industrial output by SOEs had fallen to 18 per cent and that of private sector risen to 38 per cent (28.5 per cent by FIEs) (SSB, 2002).

Establishing market-oriented institutions

FDI in China has stimulated the transition through introducing a market-oriented institutional framework. In order to effectively attract and utilize foreign capital, China liberalized its FDI regime in the 1980s by establishing SEZs and coastal open cities. This liberalization exerted a constant pressure in the direction of introducing market mechanisms in other sectors. The legal framework specifically pertaining to FDI, has for example, prompted numerous laws and regulations governing domestic economic activities as well. This is especially true in relaxing foreign exchange restrictions, establishing a regulatory framework for the protection of IP rights and reforming accounting systems.

Facilitating reforms of SOEs

FDI in China has played a unique role in rejuvenating and reforming SOEs, either directly through Jvs with SOEs or indirectly through demonstration effects from the operations of FIEs. Foreign investors are expected to introduce market-oriented management systems, such as incentive schemes, production organization systems, advanced accounting methods and risk management, in line with those practised in market-based economies. Since many FIEs in China are Jvs with SOEs, their potential impact on SOE reforms should be considerable.

In addition, FDI seems to be conducive to the transition by stimulating competition and fostering China's integration into the world economy. The entry and rise of FIEs is expected to break China's state monopolies and oligopolistic structure. With forward and backward linkages between domestic firms and FIEs, China's integration with the world economy has been deepened.

4 China's FDI strategy and policies

China's opening to FDI was symbolized by the promulgation of the 'Chinese–Foreign Joint Venture Law' on 1 July 1979. While permitting entry of foreign firms, the law did not create a legal framework that permitted currency convertibility and reduced red tape. In 1986, new provisions including preferential tax policies were established to encourage foreign investment. However, FDI was invited exclusively for exports, except offshore oil exploration and the real estate sector. Under such an export-promotion FDI regime, many export-processing and export-assembling plants (mainly from Hong Kong and Taiwan) were established in the SEZs, the open coastal cities and the ETDZs. At the same time, foreign investors that aimed at domestic markets encountered many difficulties and their investment was relatively small (Zhang, 2000a).

The 'export-promotion' FDI strategy did not change much until 1992, when China began gradually to open its domestic market to MNCs in certain sectors, including telecoms, transportation, banking and insurance. The gradual shift from an 'export-promotion' to a 'technology promotion' FDI regime was largely due to pressures from the USA and West European countries that had increasing trade deficits with China due to China's FDI-led export boom. Moreover, China realized that technology transfers from industrial countries might not be possible if the market-oriented FDI was not allowed.

Many observers view China's success in attracting FDI as a puzzle, noting its obvious disadvantages relative to other host countries: China had little legal security so that property rights were not well defined; China's currency was not convertible so that foreign investors had no insured sources of hard currency earnings; corruption was severe and growing so that foreign investors incurred additional costs. These disadvantages, however, were offset by China's huge market, large FDI flows from Hong Kong and other overseas Chinese and the liberalized FDI regime (Zhang and Markusen, 1999).

Domestic market and cheap labour

The huge domestic market and cheap labour made China a highly desirable location for FDI by MNCs, and hence China was an extremely strong positive lure for foreign investors. The advantage of market size was enhanced by China's rapid economic growth after 1980. China's real GDP grew at average annual rate of over 9 per cent in 1979–2002, the highest in the world in that period.

Overseas Chinese

China has a special asset of overseas Chinese, particularly in Hong Kong and Taiwan, who provide most of the FDI received in China. This can be explained by 'Chinese connections' based on the fact that overseas Chinese share the same language, culture and family tradition; and that they also have relatives, friends, and former business ties in China. These connections make overseas Chinese much easier to negotiate with and operate Jvs in China relative to investors elsewhere.

Liberal regime

China has systematically liberalized its FDI regime and created a variety of incentives polices since 1979. The attitude of the Chinese government toward MNCs is far more liberal than most other developing counties, especially those in the East Asia such as Japan, South Korea and Taiwan.

While market size, overseas Chinese connections and the FDI regime played a critical role in the FDI boom, the contributions of other factors should not be ignored. These factors included China's cheap resources, such as land and raw materials, improving infrastructure conditions due to rapid economic growth and the overall expansion of multinationals in the developing world in the 1990s.

Why did China benefit more from FDI? Four main reasons may be identified: (a) China's effective FDI strategy, (b) FDI from Hong Kong and Taiwan (c) a strong central government, and (d) China's rapid economic growth.

FDI regime

China singled out and encouraged two categories of FDI: export-oriented FDI and technologically advanced FDI, for which many incentives were offered. China's demands clustered around performance requirements in two categories: pressuring the MNCs to produce more value added domestically, provide more local content in their finished product and expand the linkages into the indigenous economy; and encouraging the MNCs to use their worldwide marketing networks to export more products and components out of China.

Hong Kong and Taiwan

The benefits from Hong Kong–Taiwan FDI are many: they present more opportunity for local control, their technology is more labour intensive and consistent with China's comparative advantages, their focus is primarily on cost reduction and price competitiveness, the majority of their output is exported and the overall expense to the local economy is less.

Government

China's competent government lends credibility to its bargains and thus contributes to a stable investment environment. The government's monopoly over Jv approvals allows it to determine the range of terms for FDI contracts. The central government also is positioned to supervise individual bargaining sessions at the firm level and the state organs and personnel subject to central supervision can control the negotiating process.

Rapid economic growth

Other strengths may have also contributed to China's success in utilizing FDI. Growing market size due to rapid economic growth after 1980, for example, was perhaps the greatest strength China had in bargaining with MNCs, particularly in industries in which international competition to enter the huge market is fierce (Zhang, 1999). The strength gives China the ability to utilize competition among MNCs to play one off against another for better terms.

The Chinese government has been considering three objectives as key elements of its FDI strategy: (a) attracting FDI, (b) benefiting more from it and (c) reducing its dangers. The Chinese leaders understood that attracting FDI might not be enough to ensure that its full economic benefit were derived, since foreign investors might not transfer enough new technology or transfer it effectively and at the desired depth. Policies have thus been designed to induce investors to act in ways that enhance the development impact – by building local capacities, using local suppliers and upgrading local skills, technological capabilities and infrastructure.

The main polices and measures used by China to achieve its goal include: (a) Increasing the contribution of foreign affiliates to the host country through mandatory measures: the objective is to prescribe what foreign affiliates should do to raise exports, train local workers or transfer technology. The key issue here relates to the use of performance requirements. (b) Increasing the contribution of foreign affiliates to the host country by encouraging them to act in a desired way: the key issue here, as in attracting FDI, is using incentives to influence the behaviour of foreign affiliates (incentives may be tied to performance requirements). Particularly important here is enticing foreign affiliates to transfer technology to domestic firms and to create local R&D capacity. According to the Chinese government (*Business Times*, 6 October 2003), over 400 centres for R&D have been established by MNCs in China, with $ 3 billion of investment for R&D mainly in electronics, telecoms, transportation, pharmacies, chemical materials and chemicals.

China has been learning that foreign affiliate activities can be influenced to create enhanced benefits from FDI only if the country strengthens its capabilities. New technologies can be diffused in China only if the skill base is adequate or if domestic suppliers and competitors can meet MNCs' needs and learn from them. Export activities can grow only if the quality of infrastructure permits. What China did was to build domestic capacities, drawing on foreign affiliates and their parent firms in this effort.

Conflicts still exist between China and MNCs. China may desire large investment with export orientation, but MNCs may prefer small investment aiming at the domestic market; China may want high-technology and high value added projects, which may not be what MNCs are willing to offer; MNCs may desire wholly owned affiliates, rather than Chinese preferred majority Jv structure. While China's commitments to entry to the WTO (liberalized ownership structures and opening up more sectors including services) may help attract more FDI flows from western MNCs, the benefits China can draw from the investment depend on China's bargaining power relative to MNCs and China may develop a regulatory system to manage and control MNC behaviour.

To reduce the dangers from FDI and minimize the costs, China has paid special attention to seven key aspects: (a) anticompetitive practices by foreign affiliates; (b) volatile FDI flows and related payments deleterious to the balance of payments; (c) tax avoidance and abusive transfer pricing by foreign affiliates; (d) crowding out of local firms and suppressing domestic entrepreneurial development; (e) crowding out of local products, technologies, networks and business practices with harmful socio-cultural effects; (f) concessions to MNCs, especially in export-processing zones (EPZs), allowing them to exploit labour; (g) excessive influence on economic affairs and decisionmaking, with possible negative effects on industrial development and national security.

5   Concluding remarks: challenges after China's entry to the WTO

China's accession to the WTO in 2001 has created not only opportunities of attracting more foreign investors but also challenges of how to avoid the dangers of FDI. It is estimated that over $ 60 billion of FDI will flow into China in 2003 and China could attract about $ 100 billion of FDI annually after 2007 due to a further liberalized FDI regime under China's commitment to the WTO and potential rapid economic growth. More favourable FDI measures have been introduced in the services as well as the manufacturing sector.[6] China will allow 100 per cent foreign equity ownership in such industries as leasing, storage and warehousing and wholesale and retail trade by 2004, advertising and multimodal transport services by 2005, insurance brokerage by 2006 and transportation of goods (railroad) by 2007. With more FDI in services, China's investment environment should in turn be further enhanced.

While this success is impressive, the challenges China faces in using FDI to enhance growth are severe, particularly after WTO accession. China's FDI regime and relevant policies will have to adjust to be consistent with WTO rules, resulting in a growing share of FDI by western MNCs. Large western MNCs have great bargaining power relative to developing host countries, including China, this power is greatly strengthened by their predominantly oligopolistic positions in worldwide product markets. MNCs thus enjoy the ability to manipulate prices and profits, to collude with other firms in determining areas of control and generally to restrict the entry of potential competition.

FDI may be detrimental to the Chinese economy, because (a) rather than enhancing China's economic growth, FDI might actually slow down growth by making the Chinese economy dependent or controlled by large MNCs; (b) in the long run FDI may reduce China's foreign exchange earnings on both current and capital accounts; (c) the contributions of FIEs' public revenue may be considerably less than it should be as a result of transfer pricing and the variety of investment allowances provided by the Chinese government; (d) the management know-how and technology provided by MNCs may in fact inhibit developing local sources of these scarce skills and resources due to the foreign dominance in Chinese markets.

The true dangers from FDI may be on more fundamental levels of long-term national welfare: (a) MNCs may suppress domestic firms and use their advantages in technology to drive out local competitors; (b) MNC activities may reinforce China's dualistic economic structure and exacerbate income inequalities due to their uneven impact on development (Zhang and Zhang, 2003); (c) MNCs may influence government policies in directions unfavourable to China's development by gaining excessive protection, tax rebates, investment allowances and cheap factory sites and social services; and (d) powerful MNCs may gain control over Chinese assets and jobs and exert considerable influence on political as well as economic decisions at all levels.

Whether or not China will benefit more from FDI and reduce its dangers in the long term (the next two or three decades) depends largely on how China strikes the balance between technology transfers and domestic market protection. China may take advantage of its large size in forming its strategy to shape MNC activities. In particular, China may adopt well-defined measures of investment promotion to choose the right FDI projects; to design realistic domestic content requirements to upgrade domestic industries; and to set up optimal export-performance requirements to create advanced comparative advantages in global markets.

Notes

1. An example of the popular views on the impact of inward FDI on the Chinese economy is the article in *Foreign Affairs*, 'China Takes Off' (Hale and Hale, 2003). However, in his recent book, Huang (2003) made a provocative counter-claim: the large absorption of FDI by China is a sign of some substantial weaknesses in the Chinese economy.
2. Although Hong Kong was returned to China from the UK on 1 July 1997 its capital flows into China are still viewed as 'foreign' investment under the policy of 'one country and two systems'. It should be noted that a part of the reported Hong Kong FDI is actually either western industrial countries' investment going through their subsidiaries based in Hong Kong, or Taiwanese investment under the name of Hong Kong for political reasons. The latter was especially true before 1992 when the Taiwanese government officially permitted FDI into China. Moreover, in the early 1990s a small part of the reported Hong Kong FDI was carried out by subsidiaries located in Hong Kong but owned by Chinese central or local governments to take advantage of preferential treatment under the name of FDI (UNCTAD, 1996).

3. In comparison with other host countries, Wei (1995) found that China attracted less FDI from major investing countries in terms of both flows and stock measurements. He pointed out, for example, that US investment in China falls short of its 'potential' by almost 89 per cent.
4. For more discussions of the issue, see surveys by Helleiner (1989) and Caves (1996).
5. It has been recognized that the positive externality or spillover effects of FDI in host economies may be more critical than its direct impact mentioned above (UNCTAD, 1992). The spillover efficiency occurs when advanced technologies and managerial skills embodied in FDI are transmitted to domestic plants simply because of the presence of MNCs. The technology and productivity of local firms may improve as FDI creates backward and forward linkages and foreign firms provide technical assistance to their local suppliers and customers. The competitive pressure exerted by the foreign affiliates may also force local firms to operate more efficiently and introduce new technologies earlier than what would otherwise have been the case.
6. For example, China has already opened up in retail trade and attracted FDI from nearly all the big-name department stores and supermarkets such as Auchan, Carrefour, Diary Farm, Ito Yokado, Jusco, Makro, Metro, Pricesmart, 7-Eleven and Wal-Mart (UNCTAD, 2003).

References

Caves, R., *Multinational Enterprises and Economic Analysis*, 2nd edn (New York: Cambridge University Press, 1996).

Hale, D., and L.H. Hale, 'China Takes Off', *Foreign Affairs*, 82(6) (November/ December 2003).

Helleiner, G., 'Transnational Corporations and Direct Foreign Investment', in H. Chenery and T.N. Srinivasan (eds), *Handbook of Development Economics*, (New York: Elsevier Science, 1989): 1441–80.

Huang, Y., *Selling China: Foreign Direct Investment during the Reform Era* (New York: Cambridge University Press, 2003).

Lardy, N.R., 'The Role of Foreign Trade and Investment in China's Economic Transformation', *The China Quarterly*, 144 (1995): 1065–82.

Moran, T.H., *Multinational Corporations: The Political Economy of Foreign Direct Investment* (Lexington, MD: Lexington Books, 1985).

State Statistical Bureau (SSB), *China Statistical Yearbook* (1992–2003) (Beijing: China Statistics Press).

United Nations Conference on Trade and Development (UNCTAD), *World Investment Report* (various years, 1991–2003) (New York: United Nations).

Wei, S., 'Attracting Foreign Direct Investment: Has China Reached its Potential?' *China Economic Review*, 6(2) (1995): 187–200.

Zhang, K.H., 'How Does FDI Interact with Economic Growth in a Large Developing Country? The Case of China', *Economic Systems*, 23(4) (1999): 291–303.

Zhang, K.H., 'Human Capital, Country Size, and North–South Manufacturing Multinational Enterprises', *Economia Internazionale/International Economics*, 53(2) (2000): 237–260.

Zhang, K.H., 'Why is US Direct Investment in China so Small?', *Contemporary Economic Policy*, 18(1) (2000b): 82–94.

Zhang, K.H., 'Roads to Prosperity: Assessing the Impact of FDI on Economic Growth in China', *Economia Internazionale/International Economics*, 54(1) (2001a): 113–25.

Zhang, K.H., 'What Explains the Boom of Foreign Direct Investment in China', *Economia Internazionale/International Economics*, 54(2) (2001b): 1–24.

Zhang, K.H., 'What Attracts Multinational Corporations to Developing Countries? Evidence from China', *Contemporary Economic Policy*, 19(3) (2001c): 336–46.

Zhang, K.H., 'How Does FDI Affect Economic Growth in China?', *Economics of Transition*, 9(3) (2001d): 679–93.

Zhang, K.H., 'Why does China Receive so much FDI from Hong Kong and Taiwan?', *China Economic Review*, forthcoming (2004).

Zhang, K.H. and J. Markusen, 'Vertical Multinationals and Host-Country Characteristics', *Journal of Development Economics*, 59 (1999): 233–52.

Zhang, K.H. and S. Song, 'Promoting Exports: The Role of Inward FDI in China', *China Economic Review*, 11(4) (2000): 385–96.

Zhang, X. and K.H. Zhang, 'How does Globalization Affect Regional Inequality within a Developing Country? Evidence from China', *Journal of Development Studies*, 39(4) (2003): 47–67.

5
Foreign Investment in India: Riding the Wave

Ashima Goyal

A careful examination of the potential impact of different categories of foreign investments allows implications to be drawn for actions of governments and of investors, which have the potential to increase the amount and maximize welfare from such investment. Conceptual issues are emphasized, illustrated by the Indian experience, and some international comparisons made.

At the micro level, a large literature demonstrates that rising financial intermediation contributes to development, by improving the allocation of risk and the accessibility of finance. Macro work, in the endogenous growth genre, echoes this theme. Foreign inflows contribute to financial deepening, to learning and knowledge spillovers, and allow resources to move where their productivity is higher. But the 1990s also saw the highest incidence of currency crises compounded by banking crises. Moreover, short-term capital flows place limitations on monetary policy. It will be argued, however, that appropriate regulatory and macroeconomic policy will help to reduce the probability of crises lower risk and allow a closer alignment of developing country interest rates to world levels. The latter will further stimulate the domestic economy, and attract foreign direct investment (FDI). Regulation should be designed to boost learning, to use and multiply the effects of new technology and social movements. Thus, appropriate policies and institutions can mitigate the dangers and allow potential benefits to be realized.

Section 1 examines the trends in different categories of foreign investment after entry into India was liberalized in the 1990s. In Section 2, analytical issues pertaining to foreign portfolio investment (FPI), and FDI are taken up and policy resolutions suggested. Future trends are considered in Section 3, and finally some implications of new technology and social innovations are drawn out in Section 4.

1   Background: trends in different categories of foreign investment in India

Changes in the technology of communication and liberalizing reform in many parts of the globe saw a large expansion of global capital flows in the 1990s. There was both a *push* and a *pull* effect. India provides a good example of these changes. Tables 5.1 and 5.2 show the magnitudes and the composition of different types of flows. Thus foreign investment (FI) comprises FDI and FPI. These together are regarded as non-debt creating inflows. Table 5.2 shows the percentage share of the various components of debt-creating inflows and their decline over these years. The share of short-term debt in particular has been falling. The category 'Other Capital' includes lagged export receipts, which are very sensitive to expected depreciation, and showed large fluctuations in periods of high rupee volatility.

FDI is the most stable of the various categories; its coefficient of variation is lower than that of both FPI and Non-resident Indian (NRI) deposits (Table 5.1). FPI is sensitive to exchange rate volatility and NRI flows to this and to the gap between Indian and foreign interest rates. The quantum jump in FI flows occurred in 1993–4; therefore the coefficient of variation is calculated for the period after that date.

India was underestimating its FDI, by as much as 81 per cent. The Reserve Bank of India (RBI) has released estimates for the period 2000–3 more in line with international norms.[1] In the column of corrected FDI an average percentage correction has been made for the earlier years.

Table 5.3 demonstrates the push factor – the fall in the share of FDI going to developed countries – in the 1990s, and therefore its greater availability for developing countries. Of these, Asia, and especially China, gained the largest share. India's share, although growing, remains small. The years 1999 and 2000 showed dips in FDI flows to developing countries, which were subsequently reversed. These dips were therefore due to global, not country-specific factors.

What about the pull factor? Why, for example, has India done so poorly compared to China? Table 5.4 suggests that the difference may not be as large as it is commonly thought to be. The lack of transparency in China and the possibility of large-scale round tripping which occurs to take advantage of concessions offered,[2] suggests that FDI into China is probably over-estimated, while as we saw, it is underestimated in India. Some corrections are called for. As a first step we deduct inflows from China's three neighbours in column (5). Next a 50 per cent decrease gives a possible lower limit for the Chinese figure, to be compared with the corrected upper limit for India. Also remembering that China had opened out to FDI since 1978, while Indian reforms lagged by a decade, India is not doing so badly and may hope by the mid-2020s, to reach the peak inflows China received in the mid-1990s.

94

Table 5.1 Foreign investment in India, 1990–2003 ($ million)

Years	FDI	Corrected FDI	Corrected FDI as % of FI	FPI	Total FI	NRI deposits	Reserves (increase − / decrease +)
1990–1	97	164.9	96.5	6	170.9	2,136	1,278
1991–2	129	219.3	98.2	4	223.3	577	−3,385
1992–3	315	535.5	68.7	244	779.5	2,163	−698
1993–4	586	996.2	21.8	3,567	4,563.2	1,171	−8,724
1994–5	1,314	2,233.8	36.9	3,824	6,057.8	986	−4,644
1995–6	2,144	3,644.8	57.0	2,748	6,392.8	948	2,936
1996–7	2,821	4,795.7	59.1	3,312	8,107.7	3,305	−5,818
1997–8	3,557	6,046.9	76.8	1,828	7,874.9	1,153	−3,893
1998–9	2,462	4,185.4	1,01.5	−61	4,124.4	960	−3,829
1999–2000	2,155	3,663.5	54.8	3,026	6,689.5	1,540	−6,142
2000–1	2,342	4,029	59.3	2,760	6,789	2,317	−5,830
2001–2	3,905	6,131	75.2	2,021	8,152	2,728	−11,757
2002–3	2,574	4,660					−23,943
Mean*		4,376.68		2,432.25		1,742.13	
Std. dev.		1,150.69		1,119.21		862.19	
Coeff. of var.		0.26		0.46		0.49	

Note: * The mean, standard deviation and coefficient of variation, for FDI, FPI and NRI deposits, are calculated from 1994–5 to 2001–2.

Table 5.2 Capital inflows in India, 1990–2002

Variable	2001–2	2000–1	1999–2000	1998–9	1997–8	1996–7	1995–6	1994–5	1993–4	1992–3	1991–2	1990–1
Total capital inflows (net) ($ billion) of which (in per cent):	9.6	9.0	10.5	8.4	9.9	12.0	4.1	8.5	8.9	3.9	3.9	7.1
Non-debt-creating inflows (FDI + FPI)	62.1	56.6	49.7	28.6	54.8	51.3	117.5	57.9	47.6	14.3	3.4	1.5
Debt-creating inflows	14.8	69.3	23.1	54.4	52.4	61.7	57.7	25.0	21.3	39.9	77.5	83.3
(a) External assistance	12.6	4.7	8.6	9.7	9.2	9.2	21.6	17.9	21.4	48.0	77.7	31.3
(b) Ext. com. borrowings*	−12.0	44.5	3.0	51.7	40.6	23.7	31.2	12.1	6.8	−9.2	37.2	31.9
(c) Short-term credits	−9.3	1.2	3.6	−8.9	−1.0	7.0	1.2	4.6	−8.6	−27.8	−13.1	15.2
(d) NRI deposits**	28.9	25.7	14.7	11.4	11.4	27.9	27.0	2.0	13.5	51.6	7.4	21.8
(e) Rupee debt service	−5.4	−6.8	−6.8	−9.5	−7.8	−6.1	−23.3	−11.6	−11.8	−22.7	−31.7	−16.9
Other capital***	23.1	−25.9	27.2	17.0	−7.2	−13.0	−75.2	17.1	31.1	45.8	19.1	15.2

Notes

* Refers to medium- and long-term external commercial borrowings.

** Including non-resident (non-repatriable) rupee (NRNR) deposits.

*** Includes delayed export receipts, advance payments against imports, loans to non-residents by residents and banking capital.

Source: Reserve Bank of India, *Annual Report 2001–2*, Appendix Table VI. 7.

Table 5.3 World FDI, 1980–2001

	1980	1990	1995	1996	1997	1998	1999	2000	2001
World ($ billion)	54.0	202.8	330.5	386.1	478.1	694.5	1088.3	1491.9	735.2
Developed countries (%)	84.7	81.2	61.5	57.0	56.1	69.7	77.0	82.3	68.4
Africa (%)	0.7	1.2	1.7	1.5	2.3	1.3	1.2	0.6	2.3
Latin America and Caribbean (%)	13.6	5.1	9.3	13.7	15.5	11.8	10.0	6.4	11.6
Asia (%)	0.7	12	22.8	24.2	22.1	13.8	9.4	9.0	13.9
China (%)	0.1	1.7	10.9	10.4	9.3	6.3	3.7	2.7	6.4
India (%)	0.1	0.1	0.7	0.7	0.8	0.4	0.2	0.2	0.5
Central and Eastern Europe (%)	0.1	0.3	4.5	3.5	4.0	3.3	2.3	1.8	3.7

Note: There are three components in FDI: equity capital, reinvested earnings and intra-company loans.

Source: http://stats.unctad.org.

Table 5.4 FDI comparisons for China and India, 1987–97

$ billion (1)	India FDI (2)	India Corrected upper limit (3)	China FDI (4)	China FDI 23 neighbours (5)	China Corrected lower limit (6)
1987	0.2	0.4	2.7	0.8	0.4
1988	0.1	0.2	3.7	1.3	0.7
1989	0.3	0.4	3.8	1.4	0.7
1990	0.2	0.3	3.8	1.6	0.8
1991	0.1	0.1	4.7	1.5	0.8
1992	0.3	0.5	11.3	2.3	1.2
1993	0.6	0.9	27.8	6.6	3.3
1994	1.0	1.7	34.0	10.2	5.1
1995	2.1	3.6	37.8	4.0	2.0
1996	2.4	4.1	42.1	17.2	8.6
1997	3.6	6.1	52.4	27.1	13.5

Note: In column (5), the FDI flow to China subtracts that from Hong Kong, Macao and Taiwan.

Sources: Chinese data from SSB, *China Statistical Yearbook* (Beijing 1998); Indian data from IMF-CD ROM 2002.

Finally, the distribution of FDI over Indian industrial sectors is also illuminating (Table 5.5). While engineering (including infrastructure) has taken the major share, finance was booming in the early years as foreign banks and financial service firms entered. But the currently dominating sectors are services, electronics and computers. This reflects the boom in software, information technology enabled services (ITES), and business process outsourcing (BPO).

2   Issues and potential solutions

Foreign portfolio investment

Together with short-term debt, this is one of the most mobile categories of foreign inflows. It helps to deepen and modernize capital markets, but policies that assure macroeconomic stability are necessary complements to such capital flows.

The workhorse framework to analyse the effect of capital flows on the domestic economy is the Mundell–Fleming (M–F) model.[3] Because interactions are complex, the simplest version, which assumes perfect capital mobility, and static exchange rate expectations, is the one that influences understanding of policy effectiveness. If domestic and foreign assets are perfect substitutes, then capital arbitrage would equate the domestic to the world interest rate. Then if the exchange rate is flexible, monetary policy is effective in influencing output. A rise in money supply reduces domestic

Table 5.5 Distribution of FDI over industry, 1992–2002

Industry	1992–3	1993–4	1994–5	1995–6	1996–7	1997–8	1998–9	1999–2000	2000–1	2001–2**
Chemicals and allied products	16.8	17.7	16.2	8.9	14.8	8.7	18.8	7.6	7.2	2.2
Engineering	24.9	8.2	15.1	17.8	35.5	19.6	21.4	20.6	14.3	7.7
Finance	1.3	10.5	11.2	19.0	10.5	5.0	9.2	1.3	2.1	0.7
Services	0.9	5.0	10.7	7.1	0.7	10.9	18.4	7.3	11.8	37.8
Electronics and electrical equipment	11.7	14.2	6.5	9.1	7.5	21.8	11.4	10.9	11.2	22.1
Food and dairy products	10.0	10.8	7.0	6.0	11.5	3.8	0.9	7.7	3.9	1.6
Computers	3.0	1.9	1.2	3.7	2.9	4.7	5.3	6.3	16.0	12.3
Pharmaceuticals	1.1	12.3	1.2	3.9	2.3	1.1	1.4	3.4	3.2	2.3
Others*	30.4	19.5	31.0	24.5	14.3	24.3	13.1	35.0	30.3	13.3
Total ($ billion)	0.3	0.4	0.9	1.4	2.1	3.0	2.0	1.6	1.9	3.0

Notes

* Domestic appliances is added in 'others' category from 1998–9 data.
** Provisional.

Source: RBI Annual Report (various issues).

interest rates below world rates leading to a capital outflow. The exchange rate depreciates, until the consequent rise in exports and demand raise both output and interest rates. Fiscal policy is ineffective. The rise in interest rates following a fiscal stimulus has the opposite effect of lowering demand until the equilibrium earlier interest rate is re-established.

If the exchange rate is fixed, the opposite result holds. Monetary policy loses any impact. Foreign inflows resulting from the rise in interest rates neutralize any reduction in money supply. Fiscal policy is effective. The sequence is that a demand stimulus leads to a rise in interest rates, foreign inflows, money supply and output. Policymakers often refer to monetary independence, a fixed exchange rate and free capital flows as 'the impossible trinity', and use it to justify the inability of monetary policy to respond to the domestic cycle. Since there are long leads and lags and political constraints on fiscal policy the 'impossible trinity' implies the emasculation of macroeconomic policy as a whole.

But a potential policy triangle due to Frankel (1999) shows the 'impossible trinity' to be only one corner of the triangle. There is actually a whole range of policy options available in moving across exchange rate regimes from the fixed to the float, under varying degrees of capital mobility. The M–F model does suggest, however, that a domestic interest rate that far exceeds the international rate, under large foreign inflows, may have adverse effects. If sterilization policies are adopted to reverse the monetary consequences of foreign inflows, and interest rates rise, this just attracts more inflows. The costs of swapping forex assets for government bonds can be high in thin capital markets. If banks and financial institutions hold more government debt, the liquidity available for other purposes is reduced. The decrease in credit to the private sector is then due more to the policy of preventing exchange rate appreciation and accumulating reserves than just because of high government borrowing.

With less than full capital mobility, and a fixed exchange rate, monetary policy can be used to stimulate the domestic economy and lower interest rates to the point where reserves would start falling below the desired level (Romer, 2000).

The discussion so far assumed has static exchange rate expectations, but problems are further compounded by the role of expectations. International arbitrage equates the world interest rate to the domestic interest rate adjusted for country risk, expected depreciation of the country's exchange rate and its expected rate of inflation. Under a managed exchange rate, a higher interest gap may lead to an equilibrating rise in expected depreciation or a rise in country risk. A monetary–fiscal policy coordination that lowers this gap and smoothes domestic interest rates can lower real interest rates, stimulate the real sector and improve real fundamentals, in an economy with wage–price rigidities (Goyal, 2002). Risk arises from an excessively loose as well as an excessively tight monetary policy.

Since monetary policy in developing countries largely just reacts to foreign inflows, it tends to neglect the domestic cycle. Foreign capital movements tend to be pro-cyclical, so money supply expands in a boom and contracts in a slump. But by choosing an appropriate exchange rate policy and finding a sustainable point in Frankel's triangle it is possible for monetary policy, even in the presence of foreign inflows, to be attuned to the requirements of the domestic cycle. This will make both the economy and the inflows it attracts more stable.

The early fix price Keynesian models with unemployed resources showed that domestic expenditure reduction was not sufficient to achieve internal and external balance. Equilibrium on the trade account required changes in the nominal exchange rate – that is, expenditure switching policies. For example, devaluation would stimulate exports and compress imports, thus improving the trade deficit and reducing the need for domestic output compression. The model can be extended to allow for foreign inflows (Corden, 2002). If there is excess capacity, a monetary–fiscal stimulus would be sufficient to absorb the inflows. The current account deficit would be balanced over time as exports rose with productivity (Obstfeld and Rogoff, 1995). Without slack in the economy, a real appreciation may be required.

Central banks need to calculate liquidity requirements over a wide range of possible shocks. Reserves must cover the potential external drain (mobile short-term debt), and the internal one (flight from domestic currency). Borrowing abroad, to meet foreign currency demand should not be necessary for at least a year. Therefore reserves must cover some percentage (about 20 per cent) of broad money that could be mobilized against reserves. But in India the short-term foreign debt was always low and has fallen further. Second, domestic residents do not have full capital account convertibility, so that there are limits on a potential domestic drain. Estimates of optimal foreign exchange reserves for India are much below the 2003 levels of above $ 80 billion.

Reserves do function as signal variables, giving confidence to volatile components of capital inflows. But unutilized resources represent a forgone opportunity in a capital-scarce country. Too much foreign investment has fed reserves accumulation (Table 5.1). Developed countries keep minimum reserves since they have easy access to liquid international capital markets. Asian countries hold maximum reserves; informal swap agreements will lower the need for precautionary holdings, allowing productive utilization of reserves, such as through a current account deficit that directly and indirectly makes more capital available for investment.

Foreign direct investment

FDI comes in for investment purposes and is the most stable category of foreign inflows, as the East Asian crisis demonstrated. It can contribute to technology transfer, and has helped exports to expand in China. But what is its contribution to growth? In a neoclassical growth model, with smooth substitution between labour and capital, the contribution of capital to growth is small, so that of foreign capital, itself a fraction of capital, would be even smaller. But foreign capital does contribute to relaxing a foreign exchange constraint, smoothing consumption over time and allowing investment to differ from domestic savings.

Modern macro theories, based on rigorous micro foundations, demonstrate that a concerted rise in investment could have permanent effects on growth, because of multiple Pareto-ranked equilibria. A variety of models generate these (see, e.g., Goyal, 1999). An economy could be stuck in a 'bad' state, with higher underutilisation of resources and lower growth, because of a lack of coordination among firms. It might not be profitable for one firm to invest alone, but where a number of them are doing so, expected profitability rises for an individual firm. Strategic externalities occur where the decisions of one firm depend on those of others. Spillovers arise where the actions of one firm affect the profits of another. Then public policy, and stimuli for investment, could help start a cumulative movement leading to a better outcome. These theories resurrect old development ideas of the 'big push' and 'critical mass'.

Endogenous growth models emphasize the role of externalities on the supply side. Knowledge incorporated in human or physical capital can raise marginal products of other factors. These spillovers are not taken into account in making private decisions. Private investment can be less than the social optimum. More openness, trade and foreign inflows can cause increasing returns to capital and higher growth. Then growth can be investment- rather than savings-constrained; potential contributions of FDI are large; foreign and domestic investment can be complementary. These theories also allow us to derive conditions under which FDI contributions could be maximized.

Preconditions for foreign inflows to have beneficial effects in both sets of models are first, that foreign investment must not substitute for domestic investment. The two must be rising together. Second, the push effects, whereby a larger share of FDI goes to developing countries, must be sustained. In Goyal (1995), analysing the situation just after the jump in foreign inflows to India, these arguments were made. In retrospect, we can see that the beneficial multiplier did not set in because public investment, which had averaged about 10 per cent of GDP before reforms, fell to about 7 per cent, average domestic private investment did not rise to compensate and it fluctuated severely. The push factor for FDI slowed towards the end of the 1990s (Table 5.4). Macro policy did not sustain the stimulus. Improvements in this respect in 2003 include a major national highway project and falling interest rates. Industry has revived, and so have global push factors.

102   *Foreign Investment in India*

Explanations for multinational FDI include profit differentials, portfolio diversification, micro and macro imperfection-based theories that highlight transaction costs, product cycles and the strength of currencies (Dunning, 1993). FDI makes the spatial optimization of an inter-related set of the firms' activities possible. Factors that originally attracted FDI to developing countries were political stability, government policies and cheap labour. But market size, expected growth and skilled labour now dominate (Chakrabarti, 1998).

India shares with China the advantage of a large domestic market. But FDI that came in to exploit tariff protection and the domestic market, such as in the production of cars, found it more economical to produce for exports; competitive entry has reduced costs and improved efficiencies. This also happened in China. India's skilled labour is attracting a large amount of FDI in ITES, and this will facilitate a process of development where labour is absorbed in higher-productivity activities. A Networked Readiness Index, prepared by Harvard University and the World Economic Forum, which gives the e-preparedness of 82 nations, gives India the rank of 37, ahead of China and Russia. A.T. Kearney (2002), in their FDI confidence index, note that India is ninth among countries with the most positive outlook improvement compared to 2002. India's skills in the ICT sector are contributing to this.

If there are increasing returns to knowledge, then returns would be highest in the developed countries, and the latter continue to attract the major share of FDI. But ICT reduces risk, information and transaction costs, and makes competitive high-quality clusters feasible in developing countries.

3   Future trends

The role of information and communication technology

ICT industries are important themselves and are a major source of FDI. Knowledge spillovers dominate in such industries and ICT intensifies such effects in other areas, raising the overall productivity of FDI.

Since the early 1990s, the Indian software industry has grown at annual rates of over 50 per cent. In 2001–2 it accounted for 2.87 per cent of Indian GDP, 16.5 per cent of its exports and 500,000 direct jobs. Every direct job created 2.5 indirect jobs. As software exports slowed due to the American recession, ITES export boomed at 59 per cent, with MNCs looking for cheaper outsourcing. Such captive units showed 90 per cent growth. ITES is projected to reach $ 21–$ 24 billion, or 12 per cent of the world market, and create 1.1 million jobs by 2008 (Kogut and Metiu, 2001, pp. 261–2; Nasscom, 2003). A.T. Kearney (2003) gives India the top slot as a potential location for ITES.

Although the industry is still not very large relative to total GDP or employment, the high growth rates and the industry's adaptability and dynamism are promising. When software slowed ITES took over. It has regularly been forecast that the industry would collapse and die. First it was thought to be a fluke caused by Y2K outsourcing, but contacts developed during such work allowed the industry to move on to other areas. These contacts also increase business in other industries and services.

The major share of innovation and high-value added products continues to be with the North. But it does not follow, although it is often said,[4] that the ICT industry cannot contribute substantially in the South unless it produces higher-value added products. It may be possible to leapfrog, but most progress occurs as steady steps up a ladder. Small new entrants have to negotiate for survival, to keep options open, to think strategically and combine with those who can gain. Developing countries often have a range of labour skills. Low-wage outsourcing gives new opportunities and enables learning-by-doing for labour with lower skills, allowing their managers to interact closely with customers, and understand their requirements. Some may then migrate from simple job completion to designing customized software for business processes, and finally develop their own branded products for niche markets. Other employees of large firms may set up their own startups. ITES businesses are not mere enclaves in a sea of poverty; there are other spread effects through the employment multiplier. Mushrooming cyber cafes in urban and community centres in rural areas are closing the digital divide. An initial stage for developing countries is about learning international norms and standards, and ICT aids this process. It is then possible to 'appear in public without shame' (Amartya Sen, quoting from Adam Smith in Sen, 1999, p. 71): to speak the same language; to understand what international markets require; to translate local concerns into the new language.

ICTs are subject to *network externalities*. The key defining feature of the latter is that the returns rise with the number of users; therefore expectations are important and lock-in occurs (Farrell and Klemperer, 2002). Since one consumer's utility depends on another's use, a product succeeds that many expect to succeed, and it is difficult for any one consumer to stop using it. The benefits of standardization grow with the size of the network. Compatibility across products allows consumers to benefit from larger markets, migrate across products, mix and match components and removes the fear of being stranded with losers. Firms benefit as production costs fall due to economies of scale, learning and technological spillovers. Compatibility reduces a sudden shift from one network to the other, so that competition is reduced in the early stages of the product life cycle, but since a number of firms compete with similar components competition becomes more intense in the later stages.

There are negative features that enhance inequality under network effects. Standards help specialists who want to compete globally, but incompatibility helps sustain local protection. Network externalities normally destroy smaller networks, which cannot compete with the larger ones. Therefore, standardization and open sources are important for the even spread of the ICT industry, and the success of FDI.

Standards

Two ways of achieving compatibility or standardization are through communication and negotiation, or unilateral action (market leadership). Industry or government-sponsored standards development organizations (SDOs) have proliferated since market players may have strategic interests to promote lock-in to their standards. Public and quasi-public SDOs ensure interoperability and open standards. They have safeguards built in to ensure the public interest. In order to preserve incentives for innovation even with open standards, any propriety technology or Intellectual property rights (IPR) made part of a formal standard is made available for non-exclusive licensing on fair terms, including reasonable fees. International standards committees are being set up across a variety of products and processes because of the example of ICTs (David and Shurmer, 1996).

When standardization conversion costs are small relative to network effects all countries gain from accepting common standards (Gandal and Shy, 2001). Open standards enhance competition and innovation, but are especially valuable when they apply to inputs. Such interoperability turns competitors into complementors. Conversion costs to common standards should be lowered, and IPRs should be limited to facilitate interoperability between competing products.

In intermediate products, for example, the source code wired into products or required to write the software, must be in the open domain, either on payment of a licence fee, or free. An alternative to open source is free software. The free software foundation believes that the fastest way to make something the standard is to give it away free. A well-known example is Linux versus Microsoft. The voluntary contributions of thousands of users are developing Linux at speeds comparable to Microsoft's more directed and protected approach. These arguments overturn the well-accepted ones about patent rights and protection to innovation as necessary to stimulate further research.

The issue of standards has a broader scope, and although ICT has given a fillip to open standards, the latter are by no means the established practice. Since the Uruguay Round of GATT left open the option of setting individual country health and safety standards, standardization policy is a key instrument used to erect non-trade barriers (NTBs). These conflicts continue in the new WTO regime.

Innovation

Recent survey results have demonstrated that in the USA patents are used more for blocking and defensive purposes, and are not very important as a means to appropriate returns from innovation, except in pharmaceuticals. Superior sales and service, lead time and secrecy are more important for appropriation (Hall, 2002).

Openness benefits the technological laggards, and ICT lowers the costs of accessing information and of catching up with the frontier. But openness benefits technological change and innovation and thus carries beneficial externalities for all. A survey by Encaoua and Hollander (2002) reports that high knowledge diffusion is a precondition for competitive pressure to increase the speed of technological progress.

Modern research also emphasizes the contribution of learning-by-doing and human capital formation to the innovation process. Acemoglu (2002) argues that high British unemployment in the nineteenth century lowered learning-by-doing, since fewer people were working. In contrast, in the US, under labour shortage, rapid labour-using technological progress occurred. We should see technology advance in bursts as large volumes of labour are matched with higher-productivity work. A 'virtuous cycle' can occur if technology develops to use the new volumes of cheaper and skilled workers that become available.[5] Many developing countries have the advantage of a large number of young people that can more easily acquire the new skills in demand.[6]

These complementarities make FDI beneficial for the majority. Open standards allow competitors and induce innovation, but an open interface is even better. It encourages *complementors*. If productivity rises, developed countries specialize more in the production of digital tools and developing countries in using them, and the price of these tools falls factor price equalization will work more by raising wages in developing countries than by lowering wages in developed countries (Mansell, 2001).

Politics

Politics enters as soon distributional issues are involved. It is helpful, where feasible, to separate the political and technological issues[7], and focus on concessions where the loss is minor compared to the potential gains. Factoring in the returns of network expansion makes the costs of greater openness and market access minor. Policies that boost education and innovation in both the North and the South would further reduce these costs.

Therefore far-seeing policies should lock-in the large Southern populations to the network of development, even at the cost of some minor concessions. Migration of educated individuals will fall as their share of knowledge work goes up, yet their contribution to the world can continue, with a fall in the tensions associated with migration and a preservation of local diversity. When network effects dominate, it pays to expand the market. Many service jobs are immobile so there will always be jobs available for the unskilled in the North. Cheap education and training facilities will also prevent adverse effects of such policies on low-skill Northern workers. De Long (2002) argues that a major reason for the rapid rise in inequality in America in the 1990s was the decline in the quality of primary education and the affordability of secondary education; there is clearly a role here for government policy. Both FDI and ICT are most effective when they induce more innovation and learning.

Regulation

Before the 1970s, worldwide competition policy was influenced by the Harvard School Structure–Conduct–Performance (SCP) paradigm, in which high industry concentration led to high profits. Policy aimed at lowering concentration and preventing mergers. But the Chicago School pointed out that profits may arise from a decrease in costs which is good for the consumer. It is efficient firms which grow larger. Profits may fall over time, making profits is what all firms try to do, perfect competition with zero profits is actually never found. The focus should therefore be on the firms' action and what regulations make it do. In contrast to the SCP paradigm, conduct affects structure. Regulators should aim to encourage efficiency, and prevent only price or antientry collusion. The transaction costs perspective adds that the tendency towards opportunism should be minimized but vertical integration may be necessary to save transaction costs under asset specificity. The Austrian School emphasizes that dynamic monopoly profits may be necessary for innovation. Waves of creative destruction monopoly profit these in time, a perspective particularly relevant for the ICT industry and FDI.

A country keen to use FDI to further development should have a regulatory structure that encourages innovation. If the major contribution of FDI comes from learning, and developing human capital, transparent, non-discretionary, rule-based regulation must seek ways to maximize these aspects. Entry of new firms should enhance competitiveness, together with efficient restructuring. Entry contests and mergers can build world-class scale. But in the context of changes in international patent regimes, safeguards must be built in to encourage knowledge spillovers. Kumar (2003) suggests incorporating provisions for compulsory licensing, building in a relaxation of patent restrictions for pure research purposes in international legislation and introducing utility models and industrial design patents which have been very effective in encouraging adaptive innovations and healthy rivalry among domestic firms in East Asian countries.

Reforms have improved the environment for FDI, but misperceptions remain. India has one of the most liberal technology agreements, but even China has some restrictions. Institutional structures make initial entry smooth. There is automatic approval in India through the Foreign Investment Promotion Board (FIPB) of the Department of Industrial Promotion and Policy (DIPP), or through the RBI, subject to a small number of restrictions that a steering committee (GOI, 2002) has suggested should be largely scrapped. It has also made recommendations to remove other small irritants. Local and state-level clearances still account for large delays but here an expected major beneficial reform is that states are being encouraged to adopt legislation such as the Andhra Pradesh Infrastructure Act which sets up an overriding authority for local clearances.[8]

Specific issues arise in regulating ICT industries, but some of them have more general application in encouraging a rapid innovation-driven growth process.

Under network externalities competition policy has to consider dynamic aspects. Concessions may be required to make a market initially; they are not necessarily aimed at destroying competition. Policies that improve one's product need to be distinguished from those that block a competitor. Open standards are an example of the first case; these need to be encouraged. Competition policy should give rivals rights such as reverse engineering that allow them to insist on compatibility, notwithstanding patent rights (Farrell and Klemperer, 2002).

IPRs, by turning the initial choices of a small user group into *de facto* standards, may confer monopoly rights without any significant innovation. There should be only limited copyright protection for interfaces when a firm improves an interface to allow products of different manufacturers to work together in a computer system. Reproduction and translation of copyright code is essential for this (Gandal, 2002). In markets where incompatibility is a strategic choice for inefficient firms with large installed bases, regulation is required, along with measures to enhance the role of public and quasi-public SDOs, their speed and conflict-resolution capabilities.

Social innovation

Important among new trends are innovative ways in which firms are developing both their own markets and the societies of which they are a part. This is one way that FDI can contribute directly to maximizing welfare. Corporate social responsibility is finding many takers. Corporates are adopting villages, sponsoring education and training and improving the environment and infrastructure. Such activities contribute to social capital, a higher stock of which raises a firm's productivity. But a firm may free-ride on others' contributions; if everyone attempts that, social capital will be undersupplied, and all will be worse off. This is an example of a *collective action failure*. A longer-term perspective, with more weight on the future, can prevent such a failure. So can rising personal rewards from social responsibility, and loss from its absence. All three are at work in the Indian situation, but the first two dominate.

First, as the government retreats from the commanding heights, civil society and corporates are slowly coming in to fill the leadership vacuum, and seeing a future that they can help to make. As business is given more respect it is willing to take up more responsibility. There is a sense that only social progress will guarantee sustained personal progress. Moreover, as brands and reputation become important, companies are developing a longer-term perspective. Worldwide firms have often contributed to local communities; this improves labour relations and expands their customer base. Over time, it improves the quality of the resources they can draw upon, and therefore contributes directly to their competitive edge. Sharing management practices with the community helps them improve local efficiency and spread better standards. They gain directly also, since alliances with NGOs and community associations expand the resources they can command to meet their own targets. It is not possible to continue long as an island of quality in polluted surroundings: IT companies, for example, know that the spread of high-quality education is essential to fulfil their future labour force needs, and they are willing to contribute to ensure it. A survey in 2001 found Indian IT companies at the top in the social responsibility charts.

Second, the green movement has made consumers more conscious of what firms do to the environment. In developed countries more than half the consumers avoid the products of companies that are not socially responsible. Professionals are more willing to work for companies that contribute to the community, and are happier and more productive in such companies. There is a 'feel good' factor. Market capitalization is higher for such firms, suggesting that even shareholders reward such activities. All these features increase direct rewards for a social conscience; missing out on these rewards is an indirect punishment for the lack of one.

Even if only a minority contributes, social responsibility serves as a signalling device and identifies this minority with the rewards outlined above. Since social capital increases with the number of contributing firms, as more firms undertake such activities the rewards to these activities rise. There could be a 'critical mass' beyond which the majority becomes socially responsible. Such arguments apply with equal force to foreign firms, especially as new firms enter with FDI. Expenditure on the local community also signals a long-term perspective; it allays fears that FDI firms want to exploit resources and poor environmental standards.

Such expenditure, however, is not a substitute for corporate ethics and governance. Bribes and handouts cannot create the same goodwill. In order to prevent any misuse accounts for social activities must be transparent, fully audited and reported in the balance sheet. This will also aid public awareness of such activities.

Active community association helps a firm leverage its assets and identify business opportunities, turning social responsibility into social innovation. The Ford Foundation (2002) has catalogued many case studies where partnership with low-income communities has moved beyond philanthropy to yield mutually profitable new businesses. An American retail chain, for example, helped in the celebration of local festivals and expanded its sales. The OECD has also issued guidelines for social responsibility.

4   Conclusion

The message of the chapter is that policy to boost activity and learning spillovers, with some safety-enhancing regulation, will be most successful in harnessing the flood of foreign inflows. Macroeconomic policy should thus aim for a competitive exchange rate and low interest rates, rather than high interest rates and an appreciating currency in the face of foreign inflows. An appropriate exchange rate policy would allow counter-cyclical macroeconomic policy suited to the domestic cycle. Stimulating activity rather than appreciating the exchange rate should be used to prevent reserve accumulation above a desirable level. The exchange rate should appreciate only if productivity rises, not just with a rise in inflows.

It is high growth and labour skills that attract FDI; regulation should enhance innovation and knowledge spillovers from FDI, thus setting off a 'virtuous cycle'. Apart from direct contributions to such spillovers, ICT contributes concepts such as network externalities and standards that help to appreciate the elements of such a cycle. ICTs' spread has underlined the value of education, and made firms more willing to contribute to education and undertake more social responsibility. Enhancing education is also the way to make workers in the North move up the value chain and reduce political resistance to outsourcing jobs.

Notes

1. The revisions have been made under equity capital, reinvested earnings and inter-corporate debt transactions. The latter two had been neglected earlier. Steps are also being taken to expand the coverage of FDI statistics. Out of fourteen items listed under these heads, six items comprising non-cash acquisitions, reinvested earnings of indirectly held FDI enterprises, short-term trade credit, financial derivatives, debt securities and land and buildings will be added in the future (RBI, 2003). It should be noted that a lack of uniformity persists even among international agencies. UNCTAD excludes external commercial borrowings from the definition of FDI, while the IMF includes this category, together with reinvested earnings and subordinated debt.
2. Global Development Finance estimated in 2002 that round-tripping accounted for 50 per cent of total FDI inflows into China in 1999 and 2000. Guy Pfeifferman, Chief Economist of IFC, at a presentation in Washington, DC (April 2002), estimated India's actual FDI inflow to be between US$ 5–$ 8 billion, assuming a 40 per cent return on equity (see GOI, 2002).
3. The general theories covered here would be discussed in any text on open economy macroeconomics. A recent one is Sarno and Taylor (2002). Some of this material is also covered in Goyal (1995).
4. Kogut and Metiu (2001) and Mansell (2001) take this position. Professor Sadagopalan, Director of IIIT, Bangalore, argued that all kinds of work add value in their own way.
5. Acemoglu (2002) builds up a more complete case that technological advance has, in the past, responded positively to profit motives and better factor availability.
6. India produces 70,000–85,000 software engineers annually, along with about 45,000 other IT graduates, and there are plans to double the capacity (Kogut and Metiu 2001).
7. David and Shurmer (1996), point out that this is the practice in SDOs for the telecoms sector.
8. The report on FDI, GOI (2002) makes a copy of this Act available in one of its Appendices.

References

Acemoglu, D., 'Technical Change, Inequality, and the Labour Market', *Journal of Economic Literature*, 40(1) (2002): 7–72.

Chakrabarti, A., 'Foreign Direct Investment and Host Country Interaction: A Strategic Approach', unpublished PhD dissertation (University of Michigan, 1998).

Corden, W.M., *Too Sensational: On the Choice of Exchange Rate Regimes* (Cambridge, MA: MIT Press, 2002).

David, P.A. and M. Shurmer, 'Formal Standards-Setting for Global Telecommunications and Information Services', *Telecommunications Policy*, 20 (1996): 789–815.

De Long, B., 'New US Paradigm for the Times', *Economic Times*, Mumbai edition, 30 July, 2002.

Dunning, J.H., *Multinational Enterprises and the Global Economy* (New York: Addison-Wesley, 1993).

Encaoua, D. and A. Hollander, 'Competition Policy and Innovation', *Oxford Review of Economic Policy*, 18 (2002): 63–79.

Farrell, J. and P. Klemperer, 'Coordination and Lock-In: Competition with Switching Costs and Network Effects', *Handbook of Industrial Organization*, 3, www.paulklemperer.org (2002).

Ford Foundation, *Win Win* (17 October 2002), available at http://www.fordfound.org/publications/recent_articles/docs/winwin_brochure.pdf.

Frankel, J., 'No Single Currency Regime is Right for all Countries or at all Times', NBER Working Paper, 7338 (Cambridge, MA: NBER 1999).

Gandal, N., 'Compatibility, Standardization, and Network Effects: Some Policy Implications', *Oxford Review of Economic Policy*, 18 (2002): 80–91.

Gandal, N. and O. Shy, 'Standardization Policy and International Trade', *Journal of International Economics*, 53 (2001): 363–83.

GOI (Government of India), 'Report of the Steering Group on Foreign Direct Investment' (New Delhi: Planning Commission, 2002).

Goyal, A. 'Foreign Inflows: Evil, Blessing or Opportunity?' in K.S. Parikh (ed.), *Mid-Year Review of the Indian Economy, 1994–95* (New Delhi: Konark Publishers Pvt Ltd, 1995).

Goyal, A., *Developing Economy Macroeconomics: Fresh Perspectives* (New Delhi: Allied Publishers, 1999).

Goyal, A., 'Coordinating Monetary and Fiscal Policies: A Role for Rules?', in Kirit S. Parikh and R. Radhakrishna (eds) *India Development Report 2002* (New Delhi: IGIDR and Oxford University Press, 2002).

Hall, B., 'The Assessment: Technology Policy', *Oxford Review of Economic Policy*, 18 (2002): 1–9.

Kearney, A.T., 'FDI Confidence Index' (A.T. Kearney, 2002), available at www.atkearney.com.

Kearney, A.T., 'Where to Locate' (A.T. Kearney, 2003), available at www.atkearney.com.

Kogut, B. and A. Metiu, 'Open-Source Software Development and Distributed Innovation', *Oxford Review of Economic Policy*, 17(2) (2001): 248–62.

Kumar, N., 'Intellectual Property Rights, Technology and Economic Development: Experiences of Asian Countries', *Economic and Political Weekly*, 38 (18 January 2003): 209–26.

Mansell, R., 'Digital Opportunities and the Missing Link for Developing Countries', *Oxford Review of Economic Policy*, 17 (2001): 282–95.

Nasscom, 'ITES-BPO Sector' (2003), available at www.nasscom.org.

Obstfeld, M. and K. Rogoff, 'The Intertemporal Approach to the Current Account', in G.M. Grossman and K. Rogoff (eds), *Handbook of International Economics*, III (Amsterdam: North-Holland, 1995).

RBI (Reserve Bank of India), 'Revised Data on Foreign Direct Investment', Press Release (Mumbai: RBI, June 30 2003), available at www.rbi.org.in.

RBI (Reserve Bank of India), *Report on Currency and Finance, Annual Report* and *Handbook of Economic Statistics* (Mumbai: RBI, various issues).

Romer, D., 'Keynesian Macroeconomics without the LM Curve', *Journal of Economic Perspectives*, 14(2) (2000): 149–69.

Sarno, L. and M.P. Taylor, *The Economics of Exchange Rates* (Cambridge: Cambridge University Press, 2002).

Sen, A., *Development as Freedom* (New Delhi: Oxford University Press, 1999).

United Nations Conference on Trade and Development (UNCTAD), *World Investment Report* (Geneva: UNCTAD, various issues).

6
Foreign Direct Investment, Resource Availability and Efficiency in India

Veena Keshav Pailwar[1]

1 Introduction

The balance of payment crisis of 1991 necessitated the implemention of various liberalization and structural reform measures in India. Since then, India has followed a policy of opening up of the economy to FDI and other types of capital flows. Not only has the total flow of private foreign capital increased sharply in the post-liberalized years but the composition of these flows has also shifted in favour of FDI. Data available from the *Economic Survey of India* (2002–3) indicates that FDI flows were 1.1 per cent of total capital inflows in 1990–1; this share had increased to 31.4 per cent in 2001–2. Various issues of the *World Investment Report* also show that India's share in total FDI flows moving to the developing countries has significantly improved.

In spite of the large increase in FDI flows to India these still form only a small proportion of India's GNP (Table 6A3.7) (see the appendixes on pp. 127–31). Many FDI flows are also at the expense of various fiscal and financial incentives that place a heavy burden on the government exchequer. It is therefore pertinent to assess impact of foreign capital, especially FDI flows, on the Indian economy.

The impact of FDI flows has been analysed in terms of investment performance, productivity, market concentration, competitive pressures and export/trade performance in numerous studies in both the pre- and the post-liberalized era in India. Though the FDI companies have been found to be more profitable (Kumar, 1994) the contribution of FDI flows in filling the resource gap of the country has been doubted (Athreye and Kapur, 2001). Similarly FDI companies have been criticized for low export intensity, growing import intensity of exports and net negative foreign exchange earnings (Goldar and Ishigami, 1999; Pailwar, 2001). However the phenomenon of low export intensity is not peculiar only to FDI companies but domestic companies also suffer from the problem (Kumar, 1994; Athreye and Kapur, 2001). Conversely, industries with high foreign shares are more export-intensive (Lall and Mohammad, 1985; Majumadar and Chibber, 1998).

This chapter analyses these issues for the post-liberalized era in India. Section 2 analyses the impact of FDI flows on domestic savings and investment behavior. Section 3 examines the impact of FDI on the foreign exchange gap. Section 4 draws inferences about the contribution of FDI on improving profitability and efficiency in Indian industries and also analyzes the strategies pursued by FDI and non-FDI companies to counteract competition. Section 5 summarizes the findings and draws policy implications.

Appendix 1 is a brief note on the data sources, coverage of data and computation of various key ratios used in the study. Appendix 2 elaborates on the definition and measurement of key ratios. Appendix 3 provides the values of the various computed key ratios and other data tables referred to in the study.

2 FDI and the resource gap

FDI, saving and investment: theoretical arguments and empirical evidence

Proponents of the free flow of foreign capital argue that such flows can break the 'vicious circle' of poverty of the developing countries by filling the resource gap (domestic saving – required domestic investment).

Among the various types of foreign capital flows, FDI flows are preferred because these are non-debt creating flows, adding directly to the capital stock, benefiting the host country by inducing larger competition and providing modern technology and managerial skills, which increases the productivity of capital.

On the other hand, the critics point out that increased FDI flows enhance the wealth of individuals and motivate them to spend on consumption goods, and thus rather than adding to total available surplus funds may merely replace the domestic savings of the host countries. Similarly it is feared that these flows may even also replace the existing investment in the host countries.

Empirical studies provide mixed results and point out that the impact of FDI on the resource gap largely depends on the structure of the economy and the policies pursued by the host country (Agosin, 1994; Fry, 1995; Dhar and Roy, 1996; Bosworth and Collins, 1999). Using the outcome of these studies, Athreye and Kapur (2001) have also conjectured that as India has relatively high saving rate it is quite possible that FDI may merely be substituting domestic saving.

One of the latest studies carried out for India and other neighbouring countries is that by Agrawal (2000). This econometric study, using panel data from five South Asian countries (India, Pakistan, Sri Lanka, Bangladesh and Nepal) for the period 1965–96 finds that FDI is a significant explanatory factor in explaining the behaviour of investment in the sample South Asian countries.

Most of the above studies are based on a pre-1991 dataset for empirical validation of the relationship between FDI, saving and investment behaviour in the host countries. The results obtained on the basis of study of other countries may often not be applicable for India because of the differing structure of the economies. Many changes have also taken place in India since 1991, due to the vigorous liberalization measures pursued. It is thus pertinent to examine the relationship between FDI, saving and investment behaviour using more recent data. A modest attempt has been made below by observing the overall trends in saving, investment and FDI flows and then by carrying out a simple statistical and economic analysis.

The impact of FDI on saving and investment behaviour in india

In order to assess the relationship between FDI and saving and FDI and investment, the correlation coefficient between gross domestic saving and net FDI and between gross fixed capital formation (GFCF) and FDI inflows were estimated using data for the post-liberalized period. To estimate the correlation coefficient all the variables were expressed as a percentage of GNP (Table 6A3.7).

Estimated correlation coefficients show that there is no significant correlation between saving and net foreign direct inflows (correlation coefficient of 0.303018) and the investment and FDI inflows (correlation coefficient of −0.04647) in the post-1991 period.

A positive correlation coefficient between domestic saving and net FDI flows during the period may even be emerging due to the economic policies pursued. Even in the pre-1991 era domestic saving in India was quite high, and there was a growing trend in the saving rate because of the saving rate-promoting policies pursued by the government. These policies have continued in the post-1991 era. India has also adopted FDI-promoting polices in the post-1991 era, and a positive relation ship may be emerging as a result.

However, a positive impact of FDI on domestic saving, whatever its level of significance, cannot be ruled out completely and cannot simply be attributed to the saving-promoting economic policies. Quite possibly the form in which these FDI flows are entering the country may result in the development of the financial market, especially the equity market. Various issues of *World Development Indicators* (WDI) show that a larger and larger amount of FDI is entering India in the form of mergers and acquisitions (M&As). The larger acquisition of shares of domestic companies by foreigners is adding liquidity in the equity market, attracting additional resources from investors and may thus be boosting overall domestic saving in the economy in a scenario where financial markets are still suffering from the problem of asymmetric information. The corelation coefficient between investment and FDI inflows is not only insignificant, it also has a negative sign. Thus, it may be that FDI inflows, at the margin, are crowding out domestic investment.

One possible explanation for this behaviour may be the tax concessions available for FDI flows. To take the benefit of the favourable tax treatments attached to FDI, a larger amount of domestic funds may be simply be being re-routed to India without adding to the country's capital stock. As has been indicated above, in the recent past much FDI has entered the country in the form of M&As rather than as greenfield investment. FDI is thus possibly taking the form of technology transfer rather than investment in plant and machinery and thus the total investment rate is not increasing even in the presence of larger flows of FDI.

The absence of a significant correlation between domestic saving and FDI flows and investment and FDI flows may also be due to the very low proportion of these flows in India's GNP.

3   FDI and the foreign exchange gap

The contribution of FDI in filling the foreign exchange gap

Apart from the resources gap, FDI inflows are also expected to bridge the foreign exchange gap directly, by bringing in foreign currency in the form of FDI, and indirectly, by enhancing export competitiveness and boosting the exports. However, the critics argue that FDI inflows can actually deteriorate the current account and the overall balance of payments (BOP), as these flows are often associated with increased purchases of raw materials, intermediate goods and capital goods and also the repatriation of profits, dividends, royalties, technical and licence fees. It has also been pointed out that the restrictive environment, with limits on foreign equity participation, a weak patent regime, restrictions on dividend payments and outflow of foreign currency, often deters the entry of FDI and the most productive technology to the host economies. A limited inflow of FDI with outdated technology can contribute only little to export competitiveness.

Referring to the ambiguity in the role of MNCs in export promotion in developing countries, Dunning (1993) pointed out that the impact is likely to vary according to the degree of their multinationality, their size and the stage of development of the countries in which they operate, the age, extent and pattern of the investment, the structure of competition facing the MNEs and the motive behind the investment. Resource-seeking FDI promotes vertical FDI, whereby MNCs separate different production stages geographically across countries, to take advantage of lower factor prices (Helpman, 1984), and should increase exports from the host country. An open and liberal trade regime attracts export-oriented FDI. On the other hand, a restrictive economic environment, manifested in the form of high tariff barriers and an artificially fixed exchange rate regime have often been found to attract

FDI of a market-seeking variety or import substituting horizontal FDI (Markusen, 1998), which is unlikely to result in better host-country export performance.

Empirical studies provide mixed results, which vary widely for developed and developing countries. A number of studies point out the positive impact of FDI inflows on the trade and overall BOP of the developed host countries (Pain and Wakelin, 1997, for OECD countries; Greenaway, Sousa and Wakelin, 2002, for the UK).

However the empirical studies carried out for developing countries do not paint a very promising picture. Lall and Streeten's (1977) study for six developing countries found that, on average, MNE affiliates recorded a net deficit on their external transactions mainly on account of outflow of profits, dividends and royalties.

Most of the empirical studies carried out exclusively for India also do not find that FDI or MNCs contributed much to export intensity and overall BOP current account (Kumar, 1990; Chandra, 1993; Sharma, 2000; Aggarwal, 2001). However, Lall and Mohammad (1985), and Majumdar and Chibber (1998) found export intensity to be positively related to the extent of foreign ownership.

Foreign exchange earnings and expenditure of companies in India

It emerges from the theoretical arguments and empirical studies referred above that the opening up of an economy and the creation of a level playing field, irrespective of the ownership structure of the companies, encourages vertical, efficiency-seeking and export-oriented FDI into the host countries and brings an overall improvement in the export and other foreign exchange earnings of both FDI and non-FDI companies.

Hence it is pertinent to examine whether the post-liberalized era in India has brought desirable changes in this direction. Though there are some studies available for India for the post-liberalized era the coverage of these studies is basically restricted to export behaviour (Sharma, 2000; Aggarwal, 2001). The results of Sharma's (2000) study have largely been affected by the pre-1991 restrictive regime. Because of the large-scale liberalization and globalization measures a significant structural break has taken place in the economy, and hence it is essential that any study takes this fact into account, either analysing the data for the post-1991 period separately or else introducing a structural break in the aggregate dataset that includes the data of the pre-1991 period as well.

As the foreign exchange gap of a country is not only the outcome of the export performance but also of the other variables affecting trade and the invisible account of the BOP, it is equally essential to analyse the performance of FDI companies *vis-à-vis* non-FDI domestic companies on these various accounts as well. Below, an assessment of the impact of FDI on the

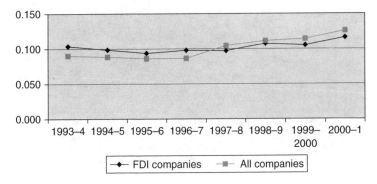

Figure 6.1 Trend in export intensity, 1993–2001

current account has been made for the post-reform period by comparing the performance of the FDI companies with that of 'all companies' in India, using various key ratios. Inferences about the performance of non-FDI domestic companies have been drawn on the basis of the performance of all companies given the performance of FDI companies (see Appendixes 1–3).

FDI companies have been criticized for the declining export intensity and increasing import intensity of exports in India (Pailwar, 2001) in the early years of reform period. However, the results of this study, based on the decadal data for the post-reform period, indicate that the export intensity of these companies is not very different from overall export intensity in India. Along with the FDI companies, the non-FDI companies also faced a declining trend in the first half of the 1990s. In the second half of the 1990s, the average export intensity in India increased. It also emerges than on average FDI companies performed better than non-FDI companies during the post-reform period (Figure 6.1 and Table 6A3.3, p. 130).

One more positive feature is that in the second half of the 1990s both FDI and non-FDI companies recorded a declining trend in the import intensity of sales and, hence, in the import intensity of exports. In fact in the late 1990s FDI companies were able to record positive net foreign exchange earning on trade account, as reflected in a value of import intensity of exports of less than 1. However, the net contribution of non-FDI companies to the trade account is still negative. As a result of the lower import intensity of sales, the FDI companies have performed much better than the non-FDI companies in India in the import intensity of exports (Figure 6.2, Table 6A3.3).

The performance of non-FDI companies compared to the FDI companies is also poor on account of invisibles. As a result, non-FDI companies have registered lower net foreign exchange earning intensity than FDI companies (Figure 6.3, Table 6A3.3). However, some respite is visible, as indicated in the

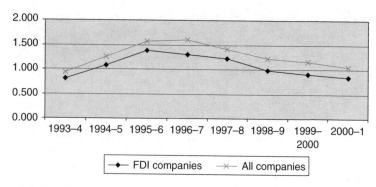

Figure 6.2   Trend in import intensity of exports, 1993–2001

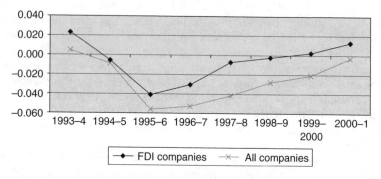

Figure 6.3   Trend in net foreign exchange inflow intensity, 1993–2001

continuous improvement in the net foreign exchange earnings of all types of companies in India during the second half of the 1990s. FDI companies, in fact, even recorded positive foreign exchange earnings in 1998–9.

It emerges from the above analysis that the performance of the FDI companies is comparatively better than the non-FDI companies on current account. However, differences in the performance are only marginal except in the case of import intensity of exports (Table 6A3.3).

4   Profitability, productivity and efficiency of FDI

Some theoretical underpinnings

FDI inflows and the entry and existence of MNCs are also expected to improve the productivity and profitability of the host countries, either directly or indirectly, on three accounts.

First, MNCs are firms intensive in the use of knowledge capital – reflected in human capital in the form of scientific and technical workers – proprietary assets in the form of patents and blueprints and marketing assets in the form of trademarks and brand names (Markusen, 1998, 2000). FDI inflows – associated with knowledge capital – are expected to enhance directly the productivity of companies with an FDI component and hence boost the overall productivity and profitability levels in the host countries, especially the developing countries where technological advancements are limited.

Second, besides the direct impact, the presence of highly efficient MNCs or FDI companies generates competitive pressures for domestic firms, motivating them to incur higher expenditure in R&D activities, leading to better allocative efficiency and increasing the overall productivity and profitability in the host economies (Caves, 1974).

Third, improvement in the level of performance of non-FDI companies in the host economies can also be expected from the spillover of knowledge from FDI inflows from various channels, such as vertical integration between FDI companies and firms without any FDI component arising out of input supplies, mobility of human capital and observation and copying activities of FDI companies by non-FDI companies.

However the above arguments related to productivity, efficiency and profitability are based on number of assumptions.

Direct benefits from the entry of MNC affiliates may be constrained by the type of FDI they bring in and the macroeconomic policies pursued by the host countries. Export-promoting FDI, without any restriction on the size of the plants, is most likely to reduce unit cost and enhance productivity of the MNCs' subsidiaries. On the other hand, import substituting FDI, with restrictions on plant size, which prohibits installation of optimum plants, may not be productivity-enhancing in the host countries (Moosa, 2002).

It has also been argued that the absorption of the latest or advanced technology requires some threshold level of technological development and human capital in the host economy. De Mello (1997) has indicated that developing countries are less efficient in the use of new technologies embodied in FDI. Foreign investors, realizing this, rather than transferring the new technology may simply pass on the technology suiting the specific production and institutional characteristics of the host economies. In such a scenario FDI, may not be an important vehicle for cross-border transfer of knowledge.

Counteracting the arguments related to the improvements in market structure it has been pointed out that these benefits depend to a large extent on initial market conditions. If initial market conditions are characterized by the dominance of small firms and large technological gaps between local firms and MNC affiliates, then the entry of MNCs' subsidiaries, rather than promoting competition in the economy may create a monopolistic or oligopolist market structure (Lall and Streeten, 1977). Foreign firms may drive domestic firms to the fringes in such a situation by virtue of economies of scale, predatory pricing and even dumping.

Empirical studies show that in large industrial economies such as the UK and the USA, spillover through vertical linkages is positive and in some cases substantial (Girma and Wakelin, 2001; Haskel, Pererira and Slaughter, 2002). On the other hand, in the developing countries the spillover effects have been found to be more varied, and dependent on whether or not the host country has obtained the minimum threshold of absorptive capacity (Borensztein, Gregorio and Lee, 1998, for sixty-nine developing countries; Aitken and Harrison, 1999, for Venezuela; Djankov and Hoekman, 2000, for the Czech Republic; Smarzynska, 2002, for Lithuania).

A number of studies addressing the issue of productivity, efficiency and profitability of MNCs or FDI companies and domestic enterprises without a FDI component have been carried out for India for the pre- and post-liberalized era. The findings of some of the recent studies in this area are now summarized.

Using detailed (unpublished) firm-level data from 1984–5 to 1988–9, Kathuria (1996) examined the relationship between foreign investment in a sector and the productivity of domestic firms in the same sector. The results indicated that Jvs or firms having foreign equity participation exhibited less deviation from the most efficient productivity levels than domestic firms. The dispersion of productivity is smaller in sectors with more foreign firms. However, the spillovers are positive only for the firms belonging to low-technology sectors (where the technology gap between domestic and foreign firms is not high). Kathuria argued that the increased competition caused by the entry of MNCs forces the local inefficient firms either to be more productive by investing in physical or human capital, or to leave the industry. Some of the post-reform studies for India provide interesting but conflicting results. Kathuria's (2002) study for post-liberalized India showed that after liberalization the productivity of Indian industry, especially the foreign-owned firms improved. However the improvement on the domestic non-FDI firms is limited to scientific firms. Firms with R&D expenditure could also benefit from spillover effects.

Murali's (2002) study reports that, contrary to expectations, there is no evidence that foreign investment is directly more productive than domestic investment. However, local firms benefit from spillover effects arising from copying from multinational operations these benefits are higher for larger firms and those that do more business domestically.

A comparative performance evaluation of companies in India

A modest attempt has been made below to compare the efficiency and profitability level of FDI companies with the overall performance of all the companies operating in India during the post-liberalized period, using

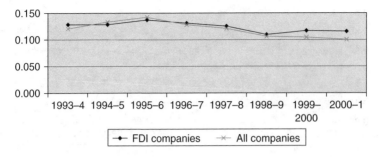

Figure 6.4 Trends in profitability, 1993–2001

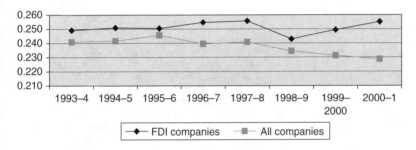

Figure 6.5 Trends in overall cost efficiency, 1993–2001

various key ratios (see Appendixes 1–3 for the data). We then examine the strategies pursued by the two types of companies to combat competitive pressures.

The FDI companies in India, on average, have been able to maintain higher profitability than the overall profitability level of the companies operating in India, though the difference is not very significant (Table 6A3.6, p. 131). Contrary to expectations, the overall level of profitability in India is declining. However, the extent of decline in profitability is lower for FDI companies. It can be hence, ascertained that the domestic non-FDI companies have faced a larger decline in their profitability (Figure 6.4).

The higher profitability of the FDI companies is a result of better cost efficiency. Though the difference in the cost efficiency of FDI companies and overall cost efficiency in India is marginal (Table 6A3.6), there was a continuous decline in the average cost efficiency in India in the second half of the 1990s (Figure 6.5).

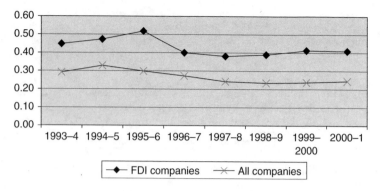

Figure 6.6   Trends in capital cost efficiency, 1993–2001

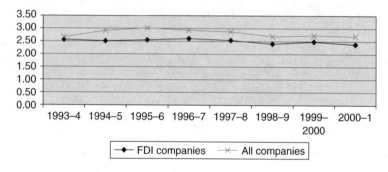

Figure 6.7   Labour cost efficiency, 1993–2001

Overall higher cost efficiency in the FDI companies is achieved by higher capital cost efficiency (Figure 6.6).

On the other hand, non-FDI companies are trying to maintain their profitability levels through higher labour cost efficiency. Contrary to expectations, overall labour cost efficiency in India is much higher than that of the FDI companies (Figure 6.7, Table 6A3.6).

However, both FDI companies as well non-FDI companies faced a declining trend in labour and capital cost efficiency in the second half of the 1990s, although it seems to have been averted after 1995 (Figures 6.6, 6.7). This finding is contrary to the findings of Kathuria (2002), whereby after liberalization companies operating in India during the period 1989–90 to 1996–7 registered higher productivity also reflecting cost efficiency. This trend does not seem to have been sustained in the second half of the 1990s, and to a certain extent can also be attributed to the overall global slowdown.

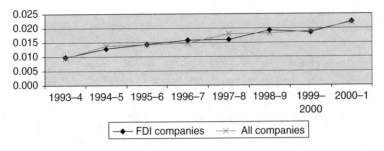

Figure 6.8 Trends in skill intensity, 1993–2001

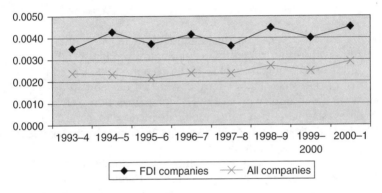

Figure 6.9 Trends in R&D intensity, 1993–2001

Though FDI and non-FDI companies widely differ in labour cost efficiency, the skill intensity in both types of companies is more or less same (Figure 6.8, Table 6A3.6). It seems that the pressures to retain highly skilled and qualified personnel have increased in the post-reform era and both types of companies are trying to retain their best-qualified personnel by paying higher and competitive salaries. This may reflect the high mobility of human capital in India, and possibly could become an important conduit of spillover effects.

Competitive pressures and strategies

The FDI and non-FDI companies in India are pursuing similar strategies to combat competitive pressures and to retain their profitability and market shares. FDI companies are spending a marginally higher proportion of their sales revenue on R&D activities than the overall level in India (Figure 6.9,

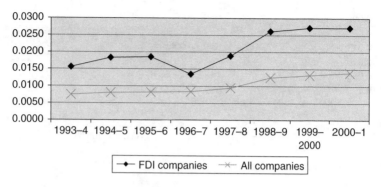

Figure 6.10   Trends in advertisement intensity, 1993–2001

Table 6A3.6). However, even this marginally higher R&D intensity of FDI companies will further widen the technological gap between both types of companies, as FDI companies have better recourse to advanced technology which is an outcome of R&D activities carried out abroad. Average R&D intensity in India, along with that of FDI companies, however, has remained more or less stagnant, with only a moderate increase towards the end of the 1990s. Thus R&D activities do not seem to be the main strategic focus for the companies operating in India.

FDI companies are also trying to compete with domestic non-FDI companies for the existing market via higher advertisement intensity. The past presence of non-FDI companies in the local market and familiarity of the consumers with their product helps these companies to maintain a low level of advertisement intensity. However, this advantage may be eroded by the large advertisement campaigns of the FDI companies. Threatened by the increasing reach of FDI companies in the local mass, the domestic companies are now trying to retain their market share and local presence by increasing their advertisement intensity (Figure 6.10).

Non-FDI companies in India have traditionally tried to compete for a share of the domestic market for their product by providing a larger selling commission to traders. Though FDI companies provide less selling commission, the selling intensity of these companies is not significantly different from that of the non-FDI domestic companies (Figure 6.11, Table 6A3.6). Selling commission intensity for both types of companies during the 1990s remained more or less stagnant, and is also not the main strategic focus for both types of companies in India in the post-reform period.

Thus it seems that in the post-liberalized scenario Indian FDI and non-FDI companies are competing with each other via larger advertisement expenditure rather than via higher R&D expenditure or selling commission.

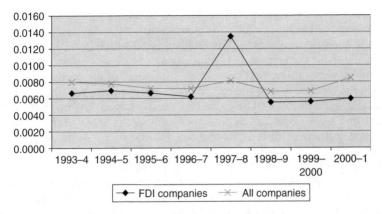

Figure 6.11 Trends in selling commission intensity, 1993–2001

5 Conclusion and policy implications

Even after a decade of globalization and liberalization, India has so far not been able to attract a significant amount of FDI and hence these flows do not have much of an impact on domestic and saving behavior. There has also been no substantial improvement in the performance level of companies operating in India due to opening up of the economy to the FDI inflows. Profitability and efficiency levels in India seem to be more affected by cyclical fluctuations. The marginal improvement in the export and import intensity of sales and of exports in the second half of the 1990s can largely be attributed to the various tax and non-tax incentives granted by the government to the companies engaged in export activities and are not the result of FDI flows *per se*.

Higher investment is definitely needed to infuse a sense of efficiency and productivity and to improve the competitiveness of Indian products in international markets. However, to boost overall investment level in the economy it is not sufficient only to generate higher surplus funds but also to create an investor-friendly environment so that the higher saving is channelled to higher investment, irrespective of the source of origin. Investors and companies operating in India have often cited the poor infrastructure, bureaucratic and procedural hurdles, complicated legal system, discriminatory and cumbersome taxation system, high transaction cost, inflexible and strict labour laws and so on as major obstacles to a large inflow of FDI and also a larger level of domestic investment. Poor infrastructure not only deters potential entrants but is also one of the important reasons for the low level of export intensity of sales of companies operating in India. Poor roads, insufficient storage facilities, low capacity of ports, insufficient power supply and communication facilities increase operational costs and reduce the competitiveness of Indian products in international markets.

Several reform measures have been introduced which have simplified the tax structure of the economy by reducing its complexity. However, as these reform measures do not yet cover the entire range of the economy, certain anomalies have crept into the tax structure. For example, VAT, in a modified form, has been introduced in India, but it is still largely VAT up to the manufacturing level; disparities in tax rates for different players in the economy generate feelings of discrimination and also deter the entry of potential players.

The disparity in the levels of various types of duties for the major competing countries should also be minimized for Indian goods to be competitive in international markets. In spite of the reduction in the peak rate of custom duties from 150 per cent in 1990–1 to 35 per cent in 2001–2, India has one of the highest customs tariff rates in the world.

It is essential not only to boost the level of investment but also the efficiency in its utilization. Indian companies in general are highly capital cost inefficient; domestic non-FDI companies can effectively counteract competition from the MNCs only by improving productivity and capital cost efficiency (long-run competitiveness), which require higher R&D, and not simply higher levels of advertisement expenditure (short-term measures), the strategy at present pursued by the non-FDI companies in India. To improve the technology level in Indian companies higher incremental tax incentives may need to be granted for cutting back the dividend, interest and royalty income in R&D activities. These measures would not only improve the quality and competitiveness of Indian products but also reduce the outflow of foreign exchange from the country. It is also essential to reform the patent regime in line with WTO guidelines. Replacement of process patents by a product patent regime would motivate foreign investors not only to bring in new and most efficient technology but also to carry out more R&D activities in India. An integrated approach, simultaneously addressing the various inefficiencies in the system, is needed to create an investor-friendly environment in India, to infuse a fair amount of competition, and to boost overall investment in the economy.

Appendix 1:   note on data sources, coverage and construction

Data for FDI companies (both public and private limited companies) used in this study is based on the RBI studies on the Finances of Foreign Direct Investment Companies, published in the various issues of the *RBI Bulletin*. Several revisions have been made in by the RBI in the definition of FDI companies. Prior to 1993, FDI companies were those companies for which 40 per cent or more of the equity capital was held outside India in any one country, or 25 per cent or more equity capital was held by one company abroad. Since 1993, a company in which 10 per cent or more equity capital is held by a single non-resident investor is defined as a Foreign Direct Investment Company. With this change in the definition, the data prior to 1993–4 is not comparable with that of post 1993–4. 2000–1 is the latest year for which data is available from the above sources. Hence the dataset in this study is limited to the period of 1993–4 to 2000–1.

The performance of FDI companies has been compared in this study with the overall performance of all the companies operating in India. To assess the overall performance, the aggregate data has been generated here by adding the separately available data for public limited and private limited companies from the RBI studies on Finances of Non-Government, Non-Financial Public/Private Limited Companies. As the data for FDI companies is available separately, the inferences about the performance of the non-FDI companies are drawn on the basis of performance of all companies operating in India.

128

Appendix 2: estimation of variables and key ratios

Table 6A2.1 Foreign exchange earnings and expenditure efficiency ratios

Variable	Measurement	Notations
1 Foreign exchange earnings (FEE) intensity	FEE/sales	*EAR*
2 Exports intensity	Exports/sales	*EXP*
3 FEE other than exports (OFEE) intensity	OFEE/sales	*OEAR*
4 Foreign exchange expenditure (FED) intensity	FED/sales	*EXPD*
5 Import intensity	Imports/sales	*IMP*
6 FED other than imports (OFED) intensity	OFED/sales	*OEXPD*
7 Net foreign exchange earnings (NFEE) intensity	NFEE/sales	*NFLOW*
8 Import intensity of exports	Imports/exports	*IMPEXP*

Table 6A2.2 Profitability and efficiency ratios

Variable	Measurement (ratio)	Notations
Profitability	Profits after tax/sales	*PROF*
Overall cost efficiency or productivity	Gross value added/sales	*OPROD*
Capital cost efficiency or productivity	Gross value added/gross fixed assets	*KPROD*
Labour cost efficiency or productivity	Gross value added/total compensation to employees	*LPROD*
Skill intensity	Managerial compensation/total compensation to employees	*SKINT*

Table 6A2.3 Measurement of competitive pressures

Variable	Measurement (ratio)	Notations
R&D intensity	R&D/sales	*RDINT*
Advertisement intensity	Advertisement expenditure/sales	*ADINT*
Selling commission intensity	Selling commission/sales	*SCINT*

Appendix 3: values of key ratio and other data tables

Table 6A3.1 Ratios related to foreign exchange earnings and expenditure: FDI companies, 1993–2001

Ratio	EAR	EXP	OEAR	EXPD	IMP	OEXPD	NFLOW	IMPEXP
1993–4	0.122	0.104	0.018	0.099	0.084	0.016	0.023	0.806
1994–5	0.122	0.099	0.023	0.128	0.106	0.022	−0.006	1.072
1995–6	0.113	0.094	0.019	0.153	0.130	0.023	−0.041	1.386
1996–7	0.123	0.098	0.025	0.153	0.128	0.026	−0.030	1.306
1997–8	0.135	0.097	0.037	0.142	0.119	0.023	−0.008	1.223
1998–9	0.133	0.107	0.026	0.135	0.106	0.029	−0.002	0.989
1999–2000	0.134	0.105	0.029	0.132	0.096	0.036	0.003	0.911
2000–1	0.149	0.116	0.032	0.136	0.097	0.039	0.013	0.834

Table 6A3.2 Ratios related to foreign exchange earnings and expenditure: all companies, 1993–2001

Ratio	EAR	EXP	OEAR	EXPD	IMP	OEXPD	NFLOW	IMPEXP
1993–4	0.104	0.090	0.014	0.100	0.084	0.015	0.005	0.935
1994–5	0.105	0.088	0.017	0.114	0.111	0.024	−0.009	1.253
1995–6	0.102	0.086	0.016	0.158	0.135	0.023	−0.056	1.568
1996–7	0.110	0.086	0.024	0.163	0.139	0.024	−0.053	1.606
1997–8	0.135	0.105	0.030	0.176	0.147	0.029	−0.041	1.410
1998–9	0.141	0.111	0.029	0.169	0.136	0.033	−0.028	1.221
1999–2000	0.144	0.114	0.030	0.165	0.132	0.033	−0.021	1.153
2000–1	0.163	0.126	0.037	0.167	0.132	0.035	−0.003	1.045

130

Table 6A3.3 Percentage weighted average ratios related to foreign exchange earnings and expenditure: difference in performance

Companies	EAR	EXP	OEAR	EXPD	IMP	OEXPD	NFLOW	IMPEXP
FDI companies	13.24	10.44	2.80	13.64	10.71	2.93	−0.41	102.60
All companies	13.04	10.39	2.65	15.70	13.04	2.86	−2.66	125.50
% difference	−0.19	−0.05	−0.14	2.06	2.33	−0.07	−2.25	22.90

Note: Ratios are the percentage weighted averages for the period 1993–4 to 2000–1 and computed using the dataset referred to in Appendix 1.

Notations: Refer to Table 6A2.1.

Table 6A3.4 Ratios related to profitability, efficiency and other variables: FDI companies, 1993–2001

Year	PROF	OPROD	KPROD	LPROD	SKINT	RDINT	ADINT	SCINT
1993–4	0.129	0.249	0.449	2.562	0.010	0.0035	0.0156	0.0067
1994–5	0.129	0.251	0.474	2.506	0.013	0.0043	0.0183	0.0069
1995–6	0.137	0.250	0.518	2.547	0.014	0.0037	0.0186	0.0067
1996–7	0.131	0.255	0.400	2.602	0.016	0.0042	0.0135	0.0062
1997–8	0.125	0.256	0.381	2.539	0.016	0.0036	0.0189	0.0135
1998–9	0.110	0.243	0.390	2.407	0.019	0.0045	0.0262	0.0055
1999–2000	0.117	0.249	0.413	2.487	0.019	0.0040	0.0272	0.0056
2000–1	0.116	0.255	0.409	2.382	0.022	0.0045	0.0272	0.0059

Table 6A3.5 Ratios related to profitability, efficiency and other variables: all companies operating in India, 1993–2001

Year	PROF	OPROD	KPROD	LPROD	SKINT	RDINT	ADINT	SCINT
1993–4	0.121	0.241	0.291	2.662	0.010	0.0024	0.0075	0.0080
1994–5	0.134	0.242	0.329	2.908	0.014	0.0023	0.0081	0.0078
1995–6	0.142	0.246	0.299	3.013	0.014	0.0022	0.0082	0.0072
1996–7	0.128	0.240	0.273	2.931	0.015	0.0024	0.0084	0.0072
1997–8	0.121	0.241	0.242	2.874	0.018	0.0024	0.0095	0.0081
1998–9	0.106	0.234	0.235	2.697	0.018	0.0027	0.0126	0.0068
1999–2000	0.105	0.231	0.238	2.732	0.019	0.0025	0.0132	0.0069
2000–1	0.100	0.229	0.245	2.701	0.022	0.0029	0.0139	0.0084

Table 6A3.6 Percentage weighted average ratios related to profitability, efficiency and other variables: difference in performance

Companies	PROF	OPROD	KPROD	LPROD	SKINT	RDINT	ADINT	SCINT
FDI companies	12.12	25.10	41.45	248.09	1.76	0.41	2.25	0.70
All companies	11.72	23.67	25.99	280.54	1.71	0.25	1.07	0.75
% difference	−0.40	−1.43	−15.46	32.45	−0.05	−0.16	−1.17	0.05

Note: Ratios are the percentage weighted averages for the period 1993–4 to 2000–1.

Notations: Refer to Table 6A2.2 and Table 6A2.3.

Table 6A3.7 Trends in saving and investment rates, 1990–2001

Year	Sr	Ir	FDIr	IFDI r
1990–1	23.41	23.24	0.03	0.03
1991–2	22.38	22.37	0.05	0.06
1992–3	22.11	22.80	0.13	0.14
1993–4	22.86	21.75	0.22	0.24
1994–5	25.15	22.23	0.42	0.42
1995–6	25.44	24.64	0.61	0.62
1996–7	23.41	23.01	0.74	0.75
1997–8	23.33	21.89	0.87	0.88
1998–9	21.86	21.69	0.60	0.61
1999–2000	23.36	21.78	0.49	0.49
2000–1	23.58	22.07	0.52	0.52

Notations

Sr (Gross domestic saving at current prices/GNP)*100; *Ir* (GFCF at current prices/GNP)*100; *FDIr* (Net FDI/GNP)*100; (where net FDI 5 FDI inflow 2 FDI outflow); *IFDIr* (FDI inflow/GNP)*100.

Source: Estimated rates in this table are based on the data available from various issues of the *National Accounts Statistics and Economic Survey*.

Note

1. The author is thankful to Ms Vandana Mahajan for research assistance.

References

Aggarwal, A., 'Liberalization, Multinational Enterprises and Export Performance: Evidence from Indian Manufacturing', ICRIER, Working Paper, 69 (June 2001).

Agosin, M.R., 'Saving and Investment in Latin America', UNCTAD Discussion Paper, 90 (1994).

Agrawal, P., 'Economic Impact of Foreign Direct Investment in South Asia', Indira Gandhi Institute of Development Research, Working Paper (January 2000).

Aitken, B.J. and A.E. Harrison, 'Do Domestic Firms Benefit from Direct Foreign Investment? Evidence from Venezuela', *American Economic Review*, 89(3) (1999): 605–18.

Athreye, S. and S. Kapur 'Private Foreign Investment in India: Pain or Panacea?', *The World Economy*, 24(3) (2001): 399–424.

Babu, S.M., 'Trade Liberalization and Export Competitiveness of Indian Manufacturing', *Productivity*, 40(1) (1999).

Borensztein, E.G., J. De Gregorio and J.W. Lee 'How Does Foreign Direct Investment Affect Economic Growth?', *Journal of International Economics*, 45 (1998): 115–35.

Bosworth, B.P. and S.M. Collins, 'Capital Flows to Developing Economies: Implications for Saving and Investment', *Brookings Papers on Economic Activity*, 1 (1999): 143–69.

Caves, R.E., 'Multinational Firms, Competition and Productivity in Host Country Markets', *Economica*, 41 (1974): 176–93.

Chandra, N.K., 'Planning and Foreign Investment in Indian Manufacturing', in Terence Byres (ed.), *The State and Development Planning in India* (Oxford: Oxford University Press, 1993).

De Mello, L.R., 'Foreign Direct Investment in Developing Countries and Growth: A Select Survey', *Journal of Development Studies*, 34(1) (1997): 1–34.

Dhar, B. and S. Roy, 'Foreign Direct Investment and Domestic Savings–Investment Behaviour: Developing Countries' Experience', *Economic and Political Weekly*, 31, Special Number (1996): 2547–51.

Djankov, S. and B. Hoekman, 'Foreign Investment and Productivity Growth in Czech Enterprises', *World Bank Economic Review*, 14 (2000): 49–64.

Dunning, J.H., *Multinational Enterprises and the Global Economy* (Reading, MA: Addition-Wesley).

Economic Survey of India, Government of India Publications (2002–3).

Fry, M., *Money, Interest and Banking in Economic Development*, 2nd edn (Baltimore, MD: Johns Hopkins University Press).

Girma, S. and K. Wakelin, 'Regional Underdevelopment: Is FDI the Solution? A Semi-Parametric analysis', GEP Research Paper, 2001/11, University of Nottingham (2001).

Goldar, B. and E. Ishigami, 'Foreign Direct Investment in Asia', *Economic and Political Weekly*, 34(22) (1999): S. M50–M60.

Greenaway, D., N. Sousa and K. Wakelin, 'Do Domestic Firms Learn to Export from Multinationals?' *GEP Research Paper*, 2002/11, University of Nottingham (2002).

Haskel, J.E., S.C. Pereira and M.J Slaughter, 'Does Inward Foreign Direct Investment Boost the Productivity of Domestic Firms?', NBER Working Paper (January 2002).

Helpman, E., 'A Simple Theory of International Trade with Multinational Corporations', *Journal of Political Economy*, 92 (1984): 451–71.

Kathuria, V. 'Spillover Effects of Technology Transfer to India: An Econometric Study: Some Preliminary Results', Institute for Studies in Industrial Development (ISID), New Delhi, Working Paper (January 2002).

Kumar, N., *Multinational Enterprises in India* (London: Routledge,1990).

Kumar, N., *Multinational Enterprises and Industrial Organization: The Case of India* (Thousand Oaks, CA: Sage, 1994).

Lall, S. and P. Streeten, *Foreign Investment, Transnationals and Developing Countries* (London: Macmillan, 1977).

Lall, S. and S. Mohammad, 'Foreign Ownership and Export Performance in the Large Corporate Sector in India', *Journal of Development Studies*, 20 (1983): 56–7.

Majmudar, S.K. and P. Chibber, 'Are Liberal Foreign Investment Policies Good for India?', *Economic and Political Weekly* (February 1998): 267–70.

Markusen, J.R., 'Multilateral Rules on Foreign Direct Investment: The Developing Countries' Stake', University of Colorado and NBER, Working Paper (October 1998).

Markusen, J.R., 'Foreign Direct Investment and Trade', University of Adelaide, Centre for International Economic Studies, Policy Discussion Paper, 0019 (2000).

Moosa, I.A., *Foreign Direct Investment, Theory, Evidence and Practice* (London: Palgrave, 2002).

Murali, P., 'Foreign Investment and Productivity: A Study of Post Reform Indian Industry', Copenhagen Business School, Department of International Economics and Management, Working Paper (June 2002).

Pailwar, V., 'Foreign Direct Investment Flows to India and Export Competitiveness', *Productivity*, 1 (2001): 115–22.

Pain, N. and K. Wakelin, 'Export Performance and the Role of Foreign Direct Investment', *The Manchester School of Economics and Social Studies*, 66 (1998): 66–8.

Sharma, K., 'Export Growth In India: Has FDI Played A Role?', Yale University, Economic Growth Centre, Discussion Paper, 816 (2000).

Smarzynska, B.K., 'Does Foreign Direct Investment Increase the Productivity of Domestic Firms? In Search of Spillovers through Backward Linkages', World Bank Policy Research Working Paper, 2923 (October 2002).

7
The European Union's Foreign Direct Investment into Indonesia: Determinants and Threats

Bala Ramasamy and Matthew Yeung

1 Introduction

For many developing economies, foreign direct investment (FDI) has been the oil that fired the engine of economic development. Typical examples include Malaysia, Singapore, Taiwan and South Korea. For countries that entered the FDI arena in the 1970s, the early-mover advantage provided them with the necessary flow of investment. Having access to cheap labour and natural resources made these economies a haven for MNCs from developed economies. Over time, however, a greater number of players have entered this FDI tournament. The late-comers, such as Vietnam, China, the Central and East European (CEE) countries as well as several Latin American nations, are now able to compete with the early-movers and in some cases are winning the tournament. At the same time, the proportion of FDI flowing to developing countries has decreased markedly in recent years (UNCTAD, 2002). South-East Asia has been particularly hit as FDI declined from USD 27.7 billion in 1997 to USD 10.7 billion in 2001. This dramatic decline has made the tournament among these countries more intense.

This chapter addresses the case of Indonesia. In particular, we examine the FDI that flows from the EU, the largest foreign investor in Indonesia. The chapter has two main objectives: first, to identify the significant factors that contribute towards the flow of FDI from EU to Indonesia and, second, to compare the strength of these factors *vis-à-vis* other developing countries in the region. The recent emergence of transition economies in Central and Eastern Europe as well as Indochina makes this study relevant as it shows the importance of infrastructure development and productivity if Indonesia wishes to see a continuous flow of FDI from Europe. Failure to do so will result in Indonesia's continuous decline in the FDI tournament, displaced by these transitional economies. Faced by a shattered domestic financial sector and tight public finances, FDI may come as a saviour to the Indonesian economy.

Section 2 provides some stylized facts on FDI in Indonesia. Section 3 considers the determinants of FDI from EU to Indonesia. Indonesia's position in the FDI tournament is discussed in Section 4. The chapter ends with a conclusion (Section 5), which provides some policy implications.

2 FDI in Indonesia

Among ASEAN countries, Indonesia was a major recipient of FDI throughout the twentieth century. Lindblad (1998) reported that Indonesia raked in more than half of the FDI to South-East Asia in 1914 and 1937. Even in 1989, about 46 per cent of FDI to the region settled in Indonesia. Table 7.1 shows the flow of FDI to Indonesia and other ASEAN countries since 1989. Indonesia was the third largest recipient after Singapore and Malaysia, thus edging out Thailand. This was the scenario prior to the 1997 crisis. JETRO (1999) and Gray (2002) report that the financial crisis did not cause any sudden withdrawal of FDI among the East Asian economies, except for Indonesia. The reversals that started in late 1997 continued into 2000. Despite the decline in FDI, in terms of stock, Indonesia accumulated more than USD 60 billion, making it the second most favoured location. Such was its attractiveness in the past. With the right policy mix coupled with a stable and investor friendly government, Indonesia should be able to return to its past glory (US Embassy, 2001). Equally important will be the guarantee of private property rights as Indonesia embarks on its restructuring plan (Gray, 2002).

FDI inflow into Indonesia has not been without its problems. A cursory look at the FDI regulatory regime shows the bumpy ride that the country has had since its independence. The nationalist Sukarno furthered Indonesia's independence by nationalizing Dutch-, British- and American-owned assets. The new Suharto government reversed Sukarno's policies in 1967 through the enactment of Law No. 1. The new law provided some amount of security for investors, it also offered a range of incentives which was becoming a standard feature among ASEAN countries. In the mid-1970s, however, the tide turned. With the oil price hike, Indonesia returned to import substitution policies, especially in the heavy and intermediate industries. The BKPM (Indonesia's Investment Coordinating Board) was established in 1973 with a mandate of issuing investment licences but the proviso was that foreign equity be reduced to a minority share within a span of ten years. When oil prices declined in the mid-1980s, Indonesia started to return to its pro-FDI policies. Domestic markets were gradually opened up and foreign equity participation increased. In order to develop its non-oil sector further, deeper liberalization was undertaken in 1992, 1994 and 1996. Felker and Jomo (1999) claim that by 1997, Indonesia's FDI regime was on a par with its ASEAN neighbours.

136

Table 7.1 Inward FDI into ASEAN, flows and stock, 1989–2000 (US$ million)

	FDI flow							FDI stock		
	1989–94*	1995	1996	1997	1998	1999	2000	1980	1990	2000
Brunei	6	13	(69)	2	(20)	(38)	(19)	19	30	–
Cambodia	52	151	294	204	121	135	153	191	191	758
Indonesia	**1,524**	**4,346**	**6,194**	**4,677**	**(356)**	**(2,745)**	**(4,550)**	**10,274**	**38,883**	**60,638**
Lao PDR	19	95	160	91	46	79	72	2	13	659
Malaysia	3,964	5,816	7,296	6,513	2,700	3,532	5,542	5,169	10,318	54,315
Myanmar	135	277	310	387	314	253	240	5	173	2,408
Philippines	879	1,459	1,520	1,249	1,752	737	1,489	1,281	3,268	12,688
Singapore	4,798	8,788	10,372	12,967	6,316	7,197	6,390	6,203	28,565	89,250
Thailand	1,927	2,004	2,271	3,627	5,143	3,562	2,448	981	8,209	24,165
Vietnam	651	2,336	2,519	2,824	2,254	1,991	2,081	7	230	17,956
ASEAN	13,955	25,285	30,867	32,541	18,270	14,703	13,846	24,132	89,880	26,2837

Note: *Annual average.

Sources: ASEAN FDI Database and *World Investment Report 2001*, www.aseansec.org/6546.htm.

Under the tutelage of the IMF, a drastic liberalization of FDI was under-taken. The Indonesian government was forced to open up the banking, oil and gas, mining, oil palm and other sectors to foreign investment. Divesture by foreign investors to local citizens (usually 1 per cent–5 per cent) is still in effect although there is pressure to eliminate this as well (US Embassy, 2001).

The EU has been a principal source of FDI for Indonesia. Lindblad (1998) shows that more than 70 per cent of Indonesia's FDI in the colonial period was from the Netherlands. More recently, more than a third of FDI between 1996 and 2000 originated from the EU, as shown in Figure 7.1. Among the EU countries, the UK, Germany, the Netherlands and France account for between 90 and 95 per cent of FDI (EU, 1999–2001). From the EU's stand-point, Indonesia has emerged as an important location since the outflow to Indonesia as a proportion of total FDI increased gradually after the early 1990s (see Table 7.2). As with most other sources of FDI, the flows to Indonesia declined with the advent of the 1997 financial crisis.

Table 7.2 also explains the motivation for this study. The 1990s saw a gen-eral decline in intra-EU FDI. Among the beneficiaries were the Latin American countries and the Pre-Accession Countries (PAC). Several Asian countries like China were also important recipients. With the emergence of these newcomers, how would Indonesia as an FDI location be affected? How do the locational factors of Indonesia compare to those of other competing nations? These issues are dealt with in the following sections.

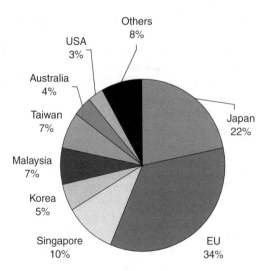

Figure 7.1   Indonesia: major sources of FDI, 1996–2000
Source: US Embassy (2001).

Table 7.2   EU FDI to selected countries/regions, 1992–9 (per cent)

	1992	1993	1994	1995	1996	1997	1998	1999
India	−0.08	0.40	0.30	0.26	0.30	0.39	0.23	0.16
Thailand	0.37	0.25	0.34	0.57	0.58	0.32	0.14	0.31
Malaysia	0.60	0.88	0.55	−0.19	0.25	0.27	1.18	0.03
Indonesia	**−0.11**	**0.29**	**0.41**	**0.58**	**0.63**	**0.30**	**0.06**	**0.02**
Singapore	0.35	−0.10	0.51	0.66	0.40	1.34	−0.61	−1.38
Philippines	0.13	0.10	0.69	0.01	0.25	0.25	0.31	0.24
China	0.17	0.28	0.70	0.75	1.44	1.03	0.29	0.17
S. Korea	0.30	0.25	0.36	0.29	0.30	0.39	0.74	0.27
Japan	0.66	−1.91	0.36	0.86	1.96	0.32	0.33	1.49
Taiwan	−0.03	0.12	0.09	−0.03	0.33	−0.41	0.04	0.02
Hong Kong	−0.45	0.20	−0.45	0.68	0.41	0.06	−0.39	0.62
EU15	73.43	62.47	67.37	54.02	56.65	44.26	40.06	53.38
Extra EU15	26.57	37.53	32.31	45.97	42.94	55.47	59.89	46.62
NAFTA	11.13	21.31	11.05	26.53	15.93	24.37	36.59	32.65
Asia	2.37	1.45	4.58	5.06	7.36	5.27	2.97	2.42
ASEAN	1.33	1.47	2.51	1.70	2.17	2.53	1.11	−0.72
PAC	–	–	3.78	5.54	4.96	4.29	2.96	2.20
Lat America	1.31	0.93	4.48	3.50	5.55	9.58	8.42	6.75

Source: EUROSTAT.

3   Determinants of EU FDI to Indonesia

This section attempts to isolate significant factors which affect EU FDI to Indonesia. We limit these factors to locational aspects because, unlike other studies (e.g. Kimura and Lee, 1998), our study focuses on FDI from a recipient country perspective. Isolating the locational aspects of FDI is possible as these are factors within the control of governments. Providing a conducive investment environment, for instance, through good infrastructure, skilled labour, etc., is strategic and policy-related. Thus, this study follows a similar framework used by Tatoglu and Glaister (1998), Chandraprapalert (2000), Love and Lage-Hidalgo (2000), Manaenkov (2000), Zhao and Zhu (2000) and Thomas and Grosse (2001). Due to limited time series available for the EU's investment to Indonesia, we consider the determinants of EU FDI to the ASEAN countries. This allows us to set up the data in a panel setting and thus increase the degrees of freedom. Our assumption here is that the determinants found significant in the EU–ASEAN investment relationship should hold true for Indonesia. As explained in Section 2, Indonesia is among the more important destinations in the ASEAN region. Hence, our assumption may not be too limiting.

Since the upsurge of world FDI after the Second World War several lines of thought have attempted to explain the motives for international production. These include Macdougal (1960), who used the concept of capital arbitrage in a perfectly competitive environment. Hymer (1960) then suggested that MNCs were oligopolistic firms which needed to produce in various countries to compete against rivals. Later, Vernon (1966, 1979) introduced the product life cycle concept that attempts to explains the movement of production operations from one country to another in search of markets and lower cost production bases. Buckley and Casson (1976) and Rugman (1981) then brought on board the importance of tangible assets which an MNC possesses and explained international production as a means through which ownership of assets was internalized. Dunning's (1977, 1981, 1993) eclectic paradigm is probably by far the most comprehensive framework that explains the reasons for FDI, especially when seen from a developing recipient country perspective. Dunning (1993, p. 76) has himself admitted that the eclectic paradigm is not a theory of FDI but 'general framework for determining the extent and pattern of both foreign owned production undertaken by a country's own enterprises and also that of domestic production owned by foreign enterprises'. Nevertheless, the advantage of a paradigm is that it is able to include newer findings as and when they arise. The eclectic paradigm envelops different theories of FDI and is dynamic in nature (Dunning, 2000). Dunning's OLI framework has been explained in detail in most FDI literature.[1] Briefly, the Ownership advantage (O) explains who will undertake FDI; the Location advantage (L) explains where will FDI flow to; and the Internalisation advantage (I) explains the 'how' of FDI, or the mode in which international production will take place. When put together, it explains the 'why' of FDI as well.

This chapter seeks to isolate the locational advantages that Indonesia possesses which make it an attractive off-shore production base among EU investors. It has been argued that in the process of globalization developing countries are converging in terms of competitiveness. However, Narula and Wakelin (1998) found that country-specific variables, especially technological factors, are the most important factors explaining competitiveness among developing countries. O'Donnele and Blumentritt (1999) also found that more holistic improvements in the investment climate of a host country can improve its competitiveness, rather than strategies directed at particular industries. Hence, it is worthwhile to consider Indonesia's strengths *vis-à-vis* its competitors in the region.

Variable selection

Following Dunning (2000) and Mallampally and Sauvant (1999), we categorize the determinants of FDI into four motivations – market-seeking, resource-seeking, efficiency-seeking and strategic asset-seeking. These determinants and their expected relationship with FDI are shown in Table 7.3.

MNCs which are *market-seeking* emphasize the size of the market and the buying power of the domestic market as well as its growth potential. Most

Table 7.3   Determinants of FDI

Types of FDI	Determinants	Variables	Acronym	Expected sign
Market-seeking	Market size	Population density	**POPD**	+
	Market purchasing power	GDP per capita	**GDPCAP**	+
	Market potential	Annual consumption growth	**CONSG**	+
	Availability of raw materials	Exports of raw materials and petroleum products	**EXPORT**	+
	Availability of unskilled labour	No. of available workers in ISIC division 1, 2 and 3	**UNSKILL**	+
Resource-seeking	Availability of labour	No. of available skilled workers in ISIC division 6, 7, 8 and 9	**SKILL**	+
		per cent of paved roads	**ROAD**	+
	Physical infrastructure	No. of telephone lines per capita	**PHONE**	+
Efficiency-seeking	Cost of resources	Productivity (GDP per worker)	**PROD**	+
		Difference in interest rates between EU and ASEAN	**INTEREST**	+
Strategic reasons	Agglomeration	Income payment	**AIP**	+
	Export base	Exports to ASEAN	**EXINTRA**	+
	Technology acceptance	No. of mobile phones per 1,000 people	**MOBILE**	+

studies have used some variable to depict the role of these factors (Scaperlanda and Balough, 1983; Lucas, 1993; Love and Lage-Hidalgo, 2000; Yang, Groenewold and Tcha, 2000). It is logical to assume that larger market size, increased purchasing power and high growth potential will attract greater amounts of FDI. The rational for the positive relationship is that a reduction in the cost of entry and economies of scale can be exploited in larger markets. At the same time, an increase in purchasing power allows

greater product differentiation to take place that may result in the localiza-
tion of the product/service. As FDI is a long-term commitment, a promising
future for the host country naturally attracts MNCs to invest. In analyzing
the motives for FDI into Turkey, for example, Tatoglu and Glaister (1998)
found 'gaining ... new markets' as the most important reason. We have used
population density as a proxy for market size, GDP per capita for market purchasing power and annual consumption growth to measure the market
potential.

MNCs which are *resource-seeking* tend to locate their investment in countries which are able to provide them with relatively cheap and abundant
scarce resources. The concept of 'resources' here does not imply only
unskilled labour, important as it may be, but also other resources including
raw materials and physical infrastructure. Some survey studies have tested
the unit cost of labour to depict the cheap labour hypothesis but with limited success (Dunning, 1986; El-Haddad, 1988). In this study we test the
quantity of unskilled labour and its effect on EU FDI into the ASEAN countries. Since the 1970s Indonesia has been able to attract investment by utilizing its large pool of cheap labour resources (Spar, 1996); the availability of
educated but unskilled workers was an important attracting feature. The
question as to whether this has continued to be important will be answered
based on our statistical analysis. The quantity of unskilled labour is proxied
by the number of workers employed in ISIC Divisions 1–3.[2] While the proportion of the labour force which does not have post-secondary qualifica-
tion may have been a better proxy, data limitation forces us to make an
assumption that the size of the labour force in these ISIC divisions reflects
the extent of available unskilled labour in the respective economy. The
number of workers in ISIC divisions 6–9, on the other hand, measures skilled
labour.[3] These divisions represent the services sector where more qualified
workers (white-collar) are demanded. The availability of skilled labour
allows MNCs to strengthen their ownership advantage by adapting it to the
local environment. This allows them to expand their market not only in the
host country but in the region as well. We expect a positive relationship
between FDI and both these proxies for labour.

Some EU MNCs may have possessed ownership advantage in resource-
based sectors but due to depleting resources in their home countries, their
comparative advantage may be declining. Relocating their plants or expanding into greenfield areas such as Indonesia may strengthen their comparative advantage. The hypothesis is that Indonesia's abundance of resources
suitable for these sectors is an attracting feature for EU FDI. In this study we
employ the exports of raw materials and petroleum-related products to
measure the extent of Indonesia's ownership of raw materials. A positive
relationship is expected. It must be pointed out that previous studies as sur-
veyed by UNCTC (1992) find only limited importance for the 'availability
of raw materials' determinant.

The availability of resources alone does not guarantee an influx of FDI. The necessary infrastructure needs to be in place to allow the movement of these resources from source to plant to port (Porter, 1990). Several studies have found a significant positive relationship between the level of infrastructure and inward FDI. These include Terza and Arromdee (1991); Cheng and Kwan (2000) and Zhao and Zhu (2000). In our study, this is tested using the length of paved roads and telephone lines per capita as proxies.

Efficiency-seeking FDI tends to locate itself in countries that can give it cost advantages. Based on Hymer's (1960) hypothesis that MNCs operate in an oligopolistic market structure where competition is intense, locating production and service operations at lower-cost locations may provide the firm with the advantage it needs. This type of FDI may cater not only for the domestic market but increasingly for the region as well. The labour cost difference between the host and the home country is a determinant that has been tested in various studies (Yang, Groenewold and Tcha, 2000; Love and Lage-Hidalgo, 2000; Thomas and Grosse, 2001).[4] These studies have found a significant relationship between the wage differential and inward FDI. However, the nature of the relationship has been mixed. Love and Lage-Hidalgo (2000) found a positive relationship in the wage differential between Mexico and the USA and FDI inflows to Mexico. Thomas and Grosse (2001) found this relationship only for efficiency-seeking FDI. However, Yang, Groenewold and Tcha (2000) and Lucas (1993) found that an increase in wage cost increases FDI inflow. The explanation here is that increasing wages raises the tendency for labour to be substituted with capital, which results in an increase in FDI. Since both explanations are plausible, we utilize a measure of labour productivity to consider the extent to which cost of resources determines the level of EU FDI into Indonesia. The inclusion of labour productivity is seen as a broader measure of cost of production (Caves, Porter and Spence, 1980). Australia and Singapore, for instance, are able to attract large amounts of FDI although their wage levels are higher than those in many other East Asian countries. This may imply that cost factors alone do not attract FDI. Hence, our measure of labour productivity could also reflects the real returns of investing in a low-wage country. In this study we measure labour productivity using GDP per worker.

Another variable included under the 'cost of resources category' was the difference between the interest rates of the EU countries and the respective ASEAN country. Petrochilas (1989), in his study of Greece, found a negative relationship between FDI and the country's discount rate. It was explained that a higher discount rate reflects the cost of local capital which complements foreign capital. We would expect that a wider positive gap between the interest rates of EU and ASEAN countries would increase the amount of FDI, and vice versa.

FDI may flow into a country not only for its own market nor to capture the locational advantage of the country *per se*, but rather to use it as a springboard into other countries in the region. Investment could also flow purely to follow competitors or to follow customers. These are considered to be the *strategic reasons* for investing in a host economy. In the USA, for example, it has been found that MNCs tend to base their location decisions on the actions of previous foreign investors (Kotabe, 1993; Wilkinson and Brouthers, 2000). New MNCs are able to slide down the learning curve of first-movers, and so reduce the risk factor. In this sense, locating their investment in a country that already hosts other MNCs can be seen as a strategic move or what is known as 'agglomeration' (Mallampally and Sauvant, 1999). Indonesia could thus be used as an export base. Another factor which needs to be considered in the strategy category is the degree of openness of countries to new technology. The acceptance of new technology by the labour force, the government and business is crucial in a technology-savvy world. We employ intra-ASEAN trade as a proxy for the export base argument. We include accumulated income payment (which includes employee compensation paid to non-residents and investment income payments on direct investment, portfolio investment and other investment) to depict the agglomeration phenomenon. Acceptance of new technology is proxied by the number of available mobile phones per 1,000 population.

The dependent variable used in this study is EU's FDI stock in the selected ASEAN countries in year *t*. The selection of a stock variable was to avoid any bias towards any particular period of observation (Coughlin and Sergev, 2000). It can further be argued that since our independent variables are also stock variables, FDI stock may be a better measurement than FDI inflows.

Data and model

A balanced panel dataset spanning 1992–9 for the five major ASEAN countries – Indonesia, Malaysia, the Philippines, Singapore and Thailand[5] – was used in this study. Following Larrain, Reisen and Maltzan (1997), the panel estimation was performed by estimating (1) with the usual assumptions of a fixed-effect model in a one-way error component regression (Baltagi, 1995):

$$\begin{aligned}
\text{FDI}_{it} = \alpha &+ \beta_1\text{AIP}_{it} + \beta_2\text{CONSG}_{it} + \beta_3\text{EXINTRA}_{it} + \beta_4\text{EXPORT}_{it} \\
&+ \beta_5\text{GDPCAP}_{it} + \beta_6\text{INTEREST}_{it} + \beta_7\text{MOBILE}_{it} + \beta_8\text{POPD}_{it} \\
&+ \beta_9\text{PROD}_{it} + \beta_{10}\text{ROAD}_{it} + \beta_{11}\text{PHONE}_{it} + \beta_{12}\text{SKILL}_{it} \\
&+ \beta_{13}\text{UNSKILL}_{it} + \varepsilon_{it}
\end{aligned} \tag{1}$$

where subscripts *i* and *t* denote countries and years, respectively, while α is country-specific intercept (fixed effects) and ε is the error term. FDI_{it} is the FDI stock from the EU to an ASEAN country in year *t*. Independent variables are as explained in Table 7.3.

Results of regression

Results from the panel estimation of the regression, as shown in Table 7.4, suggests that seven out of twelve variables are statistically significant at the 10 per cent level or better. All variables followed the expected sign, except one (**UNSKILL**). Although some insignificant variables have unexpected sign, there is no evidence to suggest that their corresponding beta coefficient has a value other than zero. In summary, **GDPCAP, MOBILE, PHONE, POPD, PROD, ROAD** and **UNSKILL** are found to be important factors that determine inward FDI from EU to ASEAN. As stated earlier, we assume that these same factors also determine the flow of FDI from EU to Indonesia.

Market- and resource-seeking reasons stand out as motivations for EU FDI to ASEAN. Population density and GDP per capita, which are proxies for market size and purchasing power respectively, are significant. Having the largest population size among the ASEAN countries is a relative strength for Indonesia, but having the lowest GDP per capita among the five founding members reduces that attraction. As mentioned earlier, the variable representing unskilled labour carries a negative sign. This would mean that an increase in the number of unskilled workers decreases the stock of FDI from the EU. This result seems to contradict the cheap labour argument. Hence, promoting the availability of cheap labour alone would not attract greater amounts of FDI from the EU. Productivity, which we found to be significant, needs to be emphasized. Our results concur with those of Bartels and Freeman (2000) whose micro-level study points to the need to increase the emphasis on human capital. However, our **SKILL** variable produces insignificant results.

Table 7.4   Panel estimation of the determinants of FDI

Variable	Beta coefficient	t-statistics	p-value
ALG	−0.005	−0.443	0.661
CONSG	−11.232	−0.543	0.591
EXINTRA	−0.059	−1.412	0.169
EXPORT	54.103	1.028	0.313
GDPCAP	0.436	1.727	0.096*
INTEREST	−12.994	−0.299	0.767
MOBILE	14.840	4.903	0.000*
PHONE	21.693	2.763	0.010*
POPD	1.798	1.901	0.068*
PROD	71.696	1.904	0.068*
ROAD	65.488	2.155	0.040*
SKILL	−0.344	−1.273	0.214
UNSKILL	−0.339	−1.768	0.088*

Notes: Overall fit of the model: F-statistics = 25.5 (p-value = 0.001); adjusted R^2 = 0.91.

* Significant at the 10 per cent level.

What stands out clearly in our analysis is the importance of physical infrastructure in attracting FDI from the EU. Both **ROAD** and **PHONE** produce very strong positive results. This may explain why countries such as Malaysia and Singapore tend to attract a large portion of EU FDI to ASEAN. For Indonesia to compete with its ASEAN partners, infrastructural development may hold the key. As most efforts in infrastructure among the ASEAN countries are government-initiated, the need for a stable regime with a long-term vision becomes imperative. Surprisingly, the availability of raw materials does not seem to matter to EU investors. On the strategy aspect, openness to technology as proxied by number of mobile phones, comes out very strongly. In this aspect, too, Indonesia lags behind its neighbours. ITU (2002), for example, report that the number of mobile phone subscribers per 100 inhabitants was 2.47 in Indonesia, compared to, say, Malaysia which was 29.95 in the same year. Both the agglomeration variable and the intra-ASEAN trade variable do not produce significant results. Hence, the notion that investment in ASEAN is used as a springboard for export to other ASEAN countries is not supported by our analysis. It is likely that the EU investor views each ASEAN country as a separate entity. The benefits of the Asian Free Trade Area (AFTA) have not yet been realized, possibly due to the early stage of the liberalization process.

Indonesia's competitive advantage

Now that the determinants that matter in EU's FDI into ASEAN has been identified, this section compares Indonesia's competitive advantage *vis-à-vis* other major recipients of FDI from EU sources. In our analysis, we have included other ASEAN countries, selected CEE countries and major Latin American nations. Apart from Indonesia, fourteen other nations have been included in the analysis.

The method of analysis used in this study is based on a *data visualization approach*. 'Visualization' simply means presenting information in pictorial form and using human recognition capabilities to detect patterns (Eick and Fyock, 1996). Data visualization is a visual interpretation of complex relationships of multidimensional data. It is defined as the process of applying automation technology and a discovery process to datasets in an effort to discover underlying information from the data (Nicholas and Meinke, 1999). It is a process that relies heavily on graphical tools, computer generated visuals and animations to determine and illustrate data relationships. In recent years, data visualization techniques have been attracting considerable attention and gaining widespread acceptance due to the availability of software and hardware technology that has the capability to facilitate the practical use of applications with interactive three-dimensional graphics. The importance and advantages of data visualization have been comprehensively discussed by Brown *et al.* (1995), Youngsworth (1999) and Nicholas and Meinke (1999).

There are a number of statistical methods for transforming data into a geo-metric representation. These include the principal component analysis (PCA), corresponding analysis and multidimensional scaling. Given their multivariate nature, employing these methods enables a treatment of multiple-attribute data simultaneously. The multivariate nature of the data can reveal relationships that would not be detected in a series of pairwise comparisons of variables. These graphical representations are usually inter-preted as perceptual maps in marketing science. Perceptual mapping, or preference mapping, is a statistical technique that is frequently employed by marketers to create a geometric representation of customer's perceptions of the qualities possessed by products/brands comprising a previously defined product market. The maps greatly improve understanding of the competi-tive structure (Day, Shocker and Srivastava, 1979). In our analysis, prod-ucts/brands are replaced with countries, represented by locations in space. The dimensions of this space distinguish the competitive alternatives and present benefits or costs important to the choice of investment. Countries are thus located in such a space according to a set of coordinates that rep-resents the extent to which the country possesses each benefit or cost attribute. Attributes are often used to mean choice criteria.[6] In our case, the set of benefit and cost attributes was derived from the regressions in Section 3.

The conventional PCA is adopted to create a geometric representation of a country's strengths in attracting FDI. PCA is a statistical procedure that allows the researcher to find a reduced number of dimensions that account for the maximum possible amount of variance in the data matrix and is capable of analysing numerical variables so they can be represented on a lower dimensionality space. The substitutability among countries based on a single determinant or multiple determinants can be clearly identified from inspecting the resulting map. This technique is useful for exploratory analy-sis of multivariate data because the new dimensions can be represented graphically and admits a more succinct interpretation than the original data matrix (Young and Valero, 1999). Xlstat 4 handled the computational pro-cedures. PCA tries to satisfy all of the relationships including those between countries, between attributes and between countries and attributes simulta-neously, and projects both attributes and countries onto a bi-plot. Two maps were generated and these are presented in Figures 7.2 and 7.3. Figure 7.2 depicts the comparative advantage of countries in 1999 while Figure 7.3 shows the movement of these advantages from 1992 to 1999. To determine the dimensionality of the final result, the cumulative percentage of inertia is examined. The statistics suggest that a two-dimensional solution in our case explains at least 80 per cent of the variation, whereas increasing to a three-dimensional solution increases the attainable amount of variation only marginally (by an additional 8 per cent). Thus, the two-dimensional solu-tion seems comparable with the three-dimensional solution in term of varia-tion explained, but has more interpretability. Our interpretation therefore is based on the two-dimensional solution. These maps transform countries into a position in space according to a set of coordinates which represents the extent to which the country possesses each benefit or cost attribute. They enable us to investigate intra-relationships among attributes and the relative positioning of competitors to the attributes. The FDI tournament is presented in two dimensions where relative 'distances' between country alternatives may be loosely interpreted as measures of substitutability of each alternative for any other (see Day, Shocker and Srivastava, 1979). Hence, one might expect that there would not be a great deal of difference in terms of returns by placing investment in two countries that are situated close to each other.

Young and Valero's (1999) interpretation of PCA is used to interpret Figures 7.2 and 7.3:

Vectors point away from the origin in some direction. Vectors pointing in the same direction correspond to variables that have similar response profiles and can be interpreted as having similar meaning in the context set out by the data. Vectors pointing in opposite directions correspond to variables with similar but reversed response profiles, such as when there are negative correlations. Long vectors are more strongly related to the components being displayed than are short vectors. Long vectors are more important in interpreting the meaning of the components. Points that are close together correspond to observations that have similar scores on the components displayed in the plot.

In addition, the angles between vectors on the same panel[7] represent the strength of the relationship between attributes. The wider the angle, the weaker the relationship between the variables. Interaction between variables is beyond the scope of this study, as our primary interest is to identify countries that have similar attributes, and hence are substitutable. Each vector represents one FDI determinant and the head of the vector is the one away from coordinate (0,0). If the vector is pointing to the right of the y-axis, then countries that are located to the right of the vertical axis can be interpreted as those countries that have the relative advantage in that attribute. The opposite is true if the vector is pointed to the left. Using the normal y-axis, countries that are positioned to the extreme right possess the best relative combination of the six determinants as identified in Section 3.

In Figure 7.2, it is evident that Singapore is a clear winner in this locational tournament. Singapore possesses all the ingredients that EU investors are looking for, relative to the other fourteen countries. The position of Indonesia towards the left of the figure reveals its weakness when compared to Singapore and Malaysia. Indonesia's closest ASEAN competitors seem to be Vietnam and the Philippines. However, the fact that these countries are clustered in the bottom left-hand corner of the map indicates the lack of the

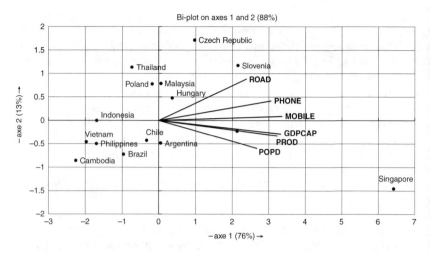

Figure 7.2   Competitive advantage of selected countries, 1999

required attributes. Outside the ASEAN region, Indonesia is in competition with the South American NICs such as Brazil and Chile. More importantly, the threat posed by the CEE countries is clear from the map in Figure 7.2. Slovenia, the Czech Republic and Hungary are in a far better position compared to Malaysia, let alone Indonesia. The CEE countries are closer in terms of geographic distance and culture to the EU countries, which further increases the threat they pose to Indonesia and other ASEAN countries.

It must be noted that the position of these countries in the map indicates their attractiveness *vis-à-vis* other countries. To consider the relative position of countries for each individual factor, one needs to rotate the *x*-axis to the bold line of the respective factor. Countries that are positioned at the right most are relatively well positioned. For example, when **ROAD** is considered, Singapore, Slovenia and the Czech Republic are relatively well positioned compared to other countries. Indonesia is still better positioned than Vietnam but the South American NICs are again a major threat. When other determinants are considered, the results do not change dramatically.

Figure 7.3 shows the movements of competitive advantage between 1992 and 1999. All countries have seen improvements in their relative positions in this period. Countries such as Singapore and Slovenia experienced major improvements in their competitive advantage while Vietnam and Laos had minor changes in their positions. There was a moderate improvement for Malaysia. The point that is obvious is the improvement experienced by the CEE countries. Abandoning socialist regimes seem to have paid for these countries, as all four considered in our analysis experienced dramatic improvements in their positions. Hungary, for example, was marginally to the left of Malaysia (indicating that Malaysia was in a slightly better

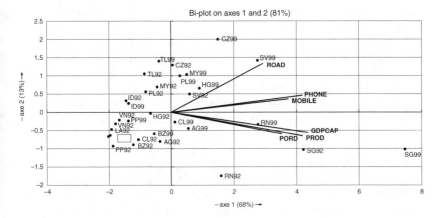

Figure 7.3 Competitive advantage of selective countries, 1992–9

position) in 1992. However, by 1999, it had overtaken Malaysia in its locational advantage. Figure 7.3 further supports the argument that the competition faced by Indonesia, as well as other ASEAN nations, from the CEE
countries for EU FDI cannot be underestimated. Figure 7.3 also indicates
that countries with a relatively better FDI environment have made further
improvements in the time period considered. For example, the Czech
Republic, Slovenia, Singapore and Poland, which are positioned on the right
of the map, have moved further to the right, compared to say Indonesia, Lao
and Vietnam. This goes to show that once a country has tasted the benefits
of FDI, it is possible that governments of these countries create a more conducive environment to attract greater FDI. It is not surprising that a large
proportion of FDI among developing economies is concentrated in only a
few countries.

5 Conclusion

Although the regulatory regime governing FDI has had its ups and downs in
the past, the 1990s saw much liberalization as Indonesia became the third
most important destination of FDI in the ASEAN region, after Singapore and
Malaysia. This was short-lived with the advent of the 1997 crisis; the IMF
required a greater measure of openness but the results have been limited
(bbc.co.uk/1/hi/business/2238345.stm, 5 September 2002).

The EU has been a major investor in Indonesia since its colonial days.
Recent data show that EU sources account for more than a third of all FDI
that flows into Indonesia. This chapter focused on the determinants of EU
FDI in Indonesia and the position of Indonesia *vis-à-vis* these factors. Using
a panel data setting for EU FDI into ASEAN between 1992 and 1999, we find

that the domestic market and resources are the motivating reasons for FDI in the region. Indonesia, being the largest country with a massive population would naturally be attractive to foreign investors. However, we also find that cheap labour, on its own, may not be an attractive feature. This needs to be supported with productivity. Physical infrastructure and the openness to new technology are other significant factors. Indonesia, however, lacks these characteristics when compared to its neighbours, Malaysia and Singapore. These findings are further amplified when seen on a PCA map. We find that Indonesia's threat within the region comes mainly from Vietnam and the Philippines. These countries tend to have a combination of features similar to that of Indonesia in the period covered in our analysis. Outside South-East Asia, Brazil and Chile pose a similar threat. A greater threat still may come from the CEE countries, many of which are far superior in their locational advantages. Coupled with their distance from the EU and cultural similarity, the CEE countries extend serious competition to EU FDI to Indonesia. The development of the critical factors that attracted FDI from the EU between 1992 and 1999 among the CEE countries puts them at a clear advantage.

To ensure further development and economic growth, Indonesia needs FDI. The near-collapse of the domestic financial system and the increasing public debt as a result of the 1997 financial crisis makes FDI more important than ever before. Policies that enhance the factors highlighted above would make Indonesia a choice location among EU investors. FDI, being long-term in nature, also requires a government which is stable and business-friendly.

Notes

1. See Dunning (2000) for a brief and precize explanation of the OLI framework and how it is related to other existing FDI theories.
2. Divisions 1–3 refer to Agriculture, hunting, forestry and fishing; Mining and quarrying; and Manufacturing, respectively.
3. Divisions 6–9 refer to Wholesale and retail trade and restaurants and hotels; Transport, storage and communication; Financing, insurance, real estate and business services; and Community, social and personal services, respectively.
4. Earlier studies, however, produced insignificant results for the wage differential. See for example, Dunning and Buckley (1977).
5. Due to the problem of unavailability of data for other ASEAN countries, only five ASEAN countries were included in the analysis.
6. The measures of 'attribute' in consumer research are a subjective matter. Our analysis is based on objective measures of attributes. As such, the word 'perceptual' may lead to confusion.
7. The plots are divided into four panels by the x-axis and the y-axis.

References

Baltagi, B.H., *Econometric Analysis of Panel Data* (New York: John Wiley, 1995).
Bartels, F. and N. Freeman, 'Multinational Firms and FDI in Southeast Asia: Post Crisis Changes in the Manufacturing Sector', *ASEAN Economic Bulletin*, 17(3) (2000): 324–41.

Brown, J., R. Earnshaw, M. Jern and J. Vine, *Visualization Using Computer Graphics to Explore Data and Present Information* (New York: John Wiley, 1995).

Buckley, P.J. and M.C. Casson, *The Future of the Multinational Enterprise* (London: Macmillan, 1976).

Caves, R.E., M.E. Porter and A.M. Spence, *Competition in the Open Economy* (Cambridge MA: Harvard University Press, 1980).

Chandraprapalert, A. 'The Determinants of US Direct Investment in Thailand: A Survey of Managerial Perspective', *Multinational Business Review* (2000): 82–8.

Cheng, L.K. and Y.K. Kwan, 'What are the Determinants of the Location of Foreign Direct Investment? The Chinese Experience', *Journal of International Economics*, 51(2) (2000): 379–400.

Coughlin, C.C., J.V. Terza and V. Arromdee, 'State Characteristics and the Location of Foreign Direct Investment within the United States', *Review of Economics and Statistics*, 73(4) (1991): 675–83.

Coughlin, C.C. and E. Sergev, 'Foreign Direct Investment in China: A Spatial Econometric Study', *World Economy*, 23(1) (2000): 1–23.

Day, G.S., A.D. Shocker and R.K. Srivastava 'Customer-Oriented Approaches to Identifying Product-Markets', *Journal of Marketing*, 43 (1979): 8–19.

Dunning, J.H. 'Trade, Location of Economic Activity and the MNE: In Search for an Eclectic Approach', in B. Ohlin, P.O. Hesselborn and P.M. Wijkman, *The International Allocation of Economic Activity* (London: Macmillan, 1977): 395–418.

Dunning, J.H. 'Explaining the International Direct Investment Position of Countries: Towards a Dynamic or Developmental Approach', *Weltwirtschaftliches Archiv*, 117 (1981): 30–64.

Dunning, J.H. *Japanese Participation in British Industry* (London: Croom Helm, 1986).

Dunning, J.H. *Multinational Enterprises and the Global Economy* (London: Addison Wesley, 1993).

Dunning, J.H. 'The Eclectic Paradigm as an Envelope for Economic and Business Theories of MNE Activity', *International Business Review*, 9 (2000): 163–190.

Dunning, J.H. and P. Buckley, 'International Production and Alternative Models of Trade', *The Manchester School of Economics and Social Sciences*, 44 (1977): 392–403.

Eick, S. and E. Fyock, 'Visualizing Corporate Data', *AT&T Technical Journal*, 75(1) (1996): 74–86.

El-Haddad, A.B. 'Determinants of Foreign Direct Investment in Developing Countries: the Egyptian Situation', *Egypt Contemporaine*, 77 (1988): 65–93.

EU, *Delegation of European Commission to Indonesia, Brunei Darusalam and Singapore: The European Union and Indonesia Investment Relation*, Jakarta (1999–2001), http://www/delidn.cec.eu.int/.

Felker, G. and K.S. Jomo, 'New Approaches to Investment Policy in the ASEAN-4', *ADBI 2nd Anniversary Conference* 10 December (1999), Tokyo, www.adbi.org/para2000/papers/jomo.pdf.

Gray, M. 'Foreign Direct Investment and Recovery in Indonesia: Recent Events and their Impact', *IPA Backgrounder*, 14/2 (2002).

Hymer, S. H. *The International Operations of National Firms: A Study of Direct Foreign Investment* (Cambridge, MA: MIT Press, 1960).

ITU, 'Key Indicators of World Telecommunications' (2002), www.itu.int/ITU-D/ict/statistics/.

JETRO, 'White Paper on Foreign Direct Investment 1999' (1999), http://www.jetro.go.jp/it/e/pub/whitepaper/invest1999/.

Kimura, Y. and H.K. Lee, 'Korean Direct Investment in Manufacturing: Its Patterns and Determinants – An Empirical Analysis', *Journal of International Management*, 4(2) (1998): 109–27.

Kotabe, M. 'The Promotional Roles of the State Government and Japanese Manufacturing Direct Investment in the United States', *Journal of Business Research*, 27 (1993): 131–46.

Larrain, G., H. Reisen and J.V. Maltzan, 'Emerging Market Risk and Sovereign Credit Ratings', OECD Development Centre, Technical Papers, 124 (1997).

Lindblad, J.T. *Foreign Investment in Southeast Asia in the Twentieth Century* (London: Macmillan, 1998).

Love, J.H. and F. Lage-Hidalgo, 'Analysing the Determinants of US Direct Investment in Mexico', *Applied Economics*, 32 (2000): 1259–67.

Lucas, R.B. 'On the Determinants of Foreign Direct Investment: Evidence from East and Southeast Asia', *World Development*, 21 (1993): 391–406.

Macdougal, G.D.A. 'The Benefits and Costs of Private Investment from Abroad: A Theoretical Approach', *Economic Record*, 36 (1960): 13–35.

Mallampally, P. and K.P. Sauvant, 'Foreign Direct Investment in Developing Countries', *Finance & Development*, 36(1) (1999): 34–7.

Manaenkov, D. 'What Determines the Region of Location of an FDI Project? An Empirical Assessment', Working Paper, New Economic School (2000), Moscow.

Narula, R. and K. Wakelin, 'Technological Competitiveness, Trade and Foreign Direct Investment', *Structural Change and Economic Dynamics*, 9 (1998): 373–87.

Nicholas, C.J. and J. Meinke, 'The Emergence of Data Visualization and Prospects for its Business Applications', INSS 690 Professional Seminar Papers (Summer 1999), http://faculty.ed.umuc.edu/~meinkej/inss690/690Summer99.htm.

O'Donnell, S. and T. Blumentritt, 'The Contribution of Foreign Subsidiaries to Host National Competitiveness', *Journal of International Management*, 5 (1999): 187–206.

Petrochilas, G.A. *Foreign Direct Investment and the Development Process* (Avebury: Aldershot, 1989).

Porter, M. *The Competitive Advantage of Nations* (New York: Free Press, 1990).

Rugman, A.M. *Inside the Multinationals: The Economics of Internal Markets* (New York: Columbia University Press, 1981).

Scaperlanda, A. and R.S. Balough, 'Determinants of US Direct Investment in the EEC: Revisited', *European Economic Review*, 21 (1983): 381–90.

Spar, D. 'Trade, Investment and Labour: The Case of Indonesia', *The Columbia Journal of World Business*, 31(4) (1996): 30–9.

Tatoglu, E. and K.W. Glaizer, 'An Analysis of Motives for Western FDI in Turkey', *International Business Review*, 7 (1998): 203–30.

Thomas, D.E. and R. Grosse, 'Country-of-Origin Determinants of Foreign Direct Investment in a Emerging Market: The Case of Mexico', *Journal of International Management*, 7(1) (2001): 59–79.

UNCTAD, *World Investment Report 2001* (New York: United Nations, 2002).

UNCTC, *The Determinants of Foreign Direct Investment: A Survey of the Evidence* (New York: United Nations, 1992).

US Embassy, *Indonesia: Investment Climate Statement 2001* (2001), Jakarta, http://www.usembassyjakarta.org/econ/investment.html.

Vernon, R. 'International Investment and International Trade in the Product Cycle', *Quarterly Journal of Economics*, 80 (1966): 190–207.

Vernon, R. 'The Product Cycle Hypothesis in the New International Environment', *Oxford Bulletin of Economics and Statistics*, 41 (1979): 255–67.

Wilkinson, T.J. and L.E. Brouthers, 'Trade Shows, Trade Missions and State Governments: Increasing FDI and High Tech Exports', *Journal of International Business Studies*, 31(4) (2000): 725–35.

Yang, J.Y.Y., N. Groenewold and M. Tcha, 'The Determinants of Foreign Direct Investment in Australia', *The Economic Record*, 76(232) (2000): 45–54.

Young, F.W. and P. Valero, *Vista – The Visual Statistics System: Principal Components Analysis*, Visual Statistics Project Report, 99-1 (1999).

Paul Youngsworth, *Data Visualization and the Intranet*, Dimensional Insight (1999).

Zhao, H. and G. Zhu, 'Location Factors and Country-of-Origin Differences: An Empirical Analysis of FDI in China', *Multinational Business Review* (Spring 2000): 60–73.

8
Determinants of FDI Flows to Developing Economies: Evidence from Malaysia

Zubair Hasan

1 Introduction

Private foreign investment flows have emerged as the single largest source of external finance for developing countries in recent decades. These flows broadly take two forms. First is the foreign direct investment (FDI) that multinational corporations bring in to establish production units or undertake specific projects in the host country independently or in collaboration with the local entrepreneurs. FDI entails not only a transfer of resources but also the acquiring of control. The investor aims at securing a lasting interest and an active role in the company of the host country (IMF, 1993).

Second, we have the foreign portfolio investment (FPI), for example in stocks, bonds and notes in the credit and stock markets of a country by private foreign institutions – banks, mutual funds and corporations – or individuals. These investments, being liquid, are highly volatile, and move freely across national boundaries to enlarge profits and diversify investment packages (Lewis, 1999). Their movements are very susceptible to the 'herding behaviour' of investors. In this chapter we are concerned only with the FDI inflows, portfolio investment coming into the picture only indirectly.

FDI is intended to augment the production capacity of the host country, and take entrepreneurial risks for profits. Comparative location advantages mainly direct the investors in their choice of destination albeit other factors are now assuming importance. One advantage of direct investments is their 'dug-in' character: they are not prone to leave the host country at the first sign of adversity. Also, they tend to tolerate relatively less developed financial structures (Wilhelms, 1998). Flows of FDI to developing countries increased from about US$ 24 billion in 1990 to US$ 170.5 billion in 2001 – i.e. by more than sevenfold. But interestingly, their rate of growth slowed down considerably after the 1997–8 financial crisis. The year 1997 marks a sort of watershed.

FDI flows have since increased from one developed country to another, reducing the share of the developing economies (Hasan, 2003, Table 1).

The pros and cons of FDI as a source of financing development in the Third World have been discussed in the literature for years, although the debate still lingers (Loungani and Razin, 2001). However, in view of the ongoing process of liberalization and globalization the volume of private capital flows across national borders is only likely to increase with the passage of time (Dunning and Narula, 1997). The issue before the developing countries then is: how well can they manipulate the inevitable to their advantage? Indeed, countries are today competing to enlarge their share in the global pie that is tending to shrink at present. Malaysia, in particular, is eager to boost the confidence of international investors to regain if not surpass their pre-1997 level of FDI inflows.[1]

The urge to attract foreign capital naturally requires an examination of the factors that do or would determine the flow of foreign funds into the country. A number of recent works have discussed FDI flows to Malaysia as part of wider regional studies.[2] Such studies are enlightening but tend of necessity to generalize the analysis to the neglect of individual country peculiarities. Economic structures, social environment, political settings and international relations of countries pooled together are usually too diverse to allow meaningful comparisons (Hasan, 2003, p. 1). Again, the data used for the sample countries are those reduced to a common currency. This detracts from the comparability of data with reference to the conversion base or method. Even the ASEAN economies are too diverse for comparative studies beyond a certain limit: there is a strong case for country-specific studies. Rich natural resources and a cheap labour force are advantages many countries including Malaysia enjoy, but her economic achievements also owe much to the political stability, social cohesion and sensible planning: GDP has grown at an average rate of 7 per cent since 1970.

The main objectives of the present exercize are to see (a) what factors in general attract foreign capital to the developing economies, (b) which of these or other factors have been relevant in the Malaysian case and (c) what policy lessons the experience has for Malaysia or others. Section 2 sets up the background for the work: it examines the role and destination of foreign investment in Malaysia. Section 3 reviews the current literature on the subject in search of the FDI determinants. Section 4 deals with the data, variable identification and the creation of a simple descriptive model to assess the efficacy of the chosen determinants. Section 5 presents and discusses the results obtained. Finally, in Section 6, we make a few concluding remarks.

2   Background

Following global trends, FDI flows to Malaysia rose from US\$ 2.33 billion in 1990 to US\$ 5.1 billion in 1997 – i.e. equivalent to 5.2 per cent of her GDP.

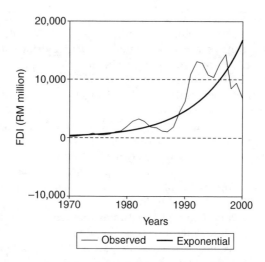

Figure 8.1   Malaysia: exponential growth of FDI, 1970–2000

However, after the financial crisis of that year, net FDI inflows dwindled to a mere US$1.5 billion – i.e. equal to no more than 1.86 per cent of GDP in 2001 (*World Development Indicators*, 2003). On the whole, net FDI has grown exponentially over the past three decades, as Figure 8.1 clearly shows.[3]

It is interesting to see that the destination of FDI flows followed quite closely the long-run changes taking place in the economic structure of the country. Possibly, Malaysia's reliance on foreign capital for development in some measure, forced such changes on the economy. Much of the foreign investment in the country is associated with the growth of modern manufacturing, including electronic goods, electrical machinery, chemicals, textiles and wood products. However, over time the services sector has tended to expand faster, inducing a corresponding shift in the destination of FDI flows. This shift picked up during the 1990s when the FDI tide was on the rise. One can easily see that the skyline of the manufacturing sector bars in Figure 8.2 is concave from below while that of the services sector is convex. In fact, by the year 2000 the share of the services sector, at 43 per cent of FDI, had already overtaken that of the manufacturing sector, at 32 per cent. Oil and gas sector was third in order of importance. The property sector has lagged far behind.

One reason for FDI playing an important role in Malaysia has been the preference of the multinational corporations to establish and finance industries geared to exports. This made the country essentially a wide-open trading economy.[4] Investment in the services sector was also linked closely to the expansion of the finance, transportation and information systems: establishment of the off-shore financial center at Labuan, port development

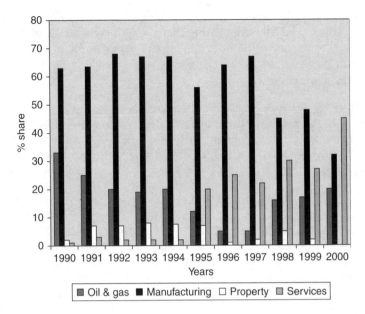

Figure 8.2 FDI (share of sectors), 1990–2000

Source: Bank Negara Malaysia, *Annual Report* (2000).

and the erection of the Multimedia Super Corridor are some examples. However, the recent decline in FDI inflows is causing concern to policymakers. Two reasons are usually advanced. The first is the wasteful inefficient use of resources claimed as epitomized in the rising capital–output ratio over the years (Star, 1999, p. 3). The second is said to be the use of capital controls the country resorted to for remedying the situation during the 1997–8 financial crisis. Both need a closer look.

Initially, we had included the incremental capital–output ratio (ICOR) in the independent variables of our model. Assuming that a rising ICOR indicates economic inefficiency, we expected it to be in an inverse relationship with FDI. We found that the relationship suffered from a high degree of serial correlation, and when combined with other regressors in the model, the coefficient was grossly insignificant, adding little to the value of R^2: in sum, it was having no impact on the FDI inflows. It was investment in the huge capital-intensive projects with long gestation periods that made the ICOR climb sharply – it rose from 3.0 in 1988 to 6.5 in 1997 – not the inefficient or wasteful use of resources.[5]

Likewise, it is difficult to accept the idea that capital controls drove FDI flows away from Malaysia (Hasan, 2002, 2003). The selective controls the country imposed were withdrawn within a year – i.e. as soon as they had served their purpose; only the currency peg remained. The cause of reduction has largely been the growing competition for the flows from other developing countries, especially China. Also, there *is* an emerging trade-off between national liberty and economic prosperity in the new world order.

3   Literature review

The literature available on FDI is quite voluminous. However, we shall focus on some of the major contributions that deal with the determinants of FDI flows to the developing economies, which will help us identify variables relevant to our work. The studies discussing the determinants raise a variety of issues but their undercurrent is the search for a theoretical basis behind the variables.

One view – in the *classical* tradition – is that the direction and magnitude of capital flows is determined by differences among countries in factor proportions that cannot be explained by international trade. A difference in factor proportions between countries stimulates an adjustment of their real exchange rates and encourages countries with abundant capital supplies and labor shortages to station their investments in developing economies where opposite conditions prevail (Krugman and Obstfeld, 1994). This, for example, brought foreign capital for the development of tin mines and plantations to Malaya. Chunlai (2002) illustrates the location theory using the Chinese experience. Opponents argue that factor proportions can rarely be the sole determinants of international capital flows, the latter being much volatile compared to the relatively stable factor endowments. Indeed, exchange rates are regarded as the major factor guiding multinational firms in their choice for FDI destinations (Nakamura and Oyama, 2001).

In Malaysia, FDI seems to integrate the national economy with those of the investors. It tends to increase exports from home country to the host country as well as imports in the reverse direction: the integrated assembly lines in the host countries require imports of intermediate goods for their production. This sort of FDI is quite sensitive to changes in exchange rates and is also linked to the volume of trade.

Again, some writers argue that the policies a country designs for increasing the FDI inflows to be effective, need the erection of an institutional infrastructure conducive to the objective. Governmental organs, markets, educational systems and social–cultural setups must be efficient and effective in transmitting the policies designed to facilitate FDI transactions. It is 'institutional fitness' that makes policies concerning FDI inflows succeed (Wilhelms, 1998). A fuller discussion of this approach is available in a working paper published in 2002 by the Bank of Japan on the determinants of FDI flows inspired by the seminal study of Goldberg and Klien (1998) on the subject. The concept implies the prior existence of appropriate policies. Of course, such policies cannot be the same for all countries.

Even so, Lewis (1999, Table 4.3) mentions among his illustrations the wide range of incentives available to FDI in Malaysia: for example, tax exemptions and reductions are available for foreign investment in promoted sectors, reduced tax rates apply for regional headquarters, companies that provide R&D services are eligible for full tax exemption of profits for five years and tariff protection can be granted based on the degree of utilization of domestic raw materials, level of local value added and level of technology in the industry. Incentives are also linked to the level of local content in the product.[6] Thus, suitable policies plus institutional fitness are the key to success. These factors are difficult to quantify, but perhaps development expenditure can, at times, be a good proxy.

Lewis contains another theory for FDI incentives in a rather negative garb: he lists the barriers to FDI inflows that may exist in a country, and provides in his Table 4.1 some of the factual examples classified as 'restrictions' on market entry, ownership, control and operations. The removal of the barriers would tend to improve the FDI flows into the developing economies.

In addition, there are works, mostly empirical, that do not care to state, at least explicitly, a theoretical basis for their position but prefer to immediately identify and explain what they consider as determinants of the FDI relevant to their immediate objective. Singh and Jun (1995), for example, analysed in their study of the determinants of FDI flows to developing economies the impact of such qualitative factors as political risk and business conditions, along with quantitative macroeconomic variables. Using a pooled model, they found that export, especially of manufactures, is the strongest variable explaining the flows to a country. They also discovered that exports (Granger) cause the FDI.

Another study that includes some qualitative factors as well is Lim (2001). He summarizes recent arguments and findings on two aspects of FDI: the FDI correlation with growth, and with its own determinants. In the first case he finds that while substantive support exists for positive spillages from FDI, there is no consensus on causality. Among the determinants he finds that market size, infrastructure quality, political and economic stability and free trade zones (FTZs) are important for FDI. However results are mixed regarding the importance of fiscal incentives, the business or investment climate, labour costs and openness.

Phang Hooi Eng, a Senior Manager in the Economics Department at Bank Negara Malaysia (1998) found that the net effect of FDI on the balance of payments had been negative, and FDI appeared to have taken more out of the economy than it had put in, even though this negative effect may have been more than offset by retained earnings which are ploughed back either for reinvestment in business or for new investment in related or new areas of business. Her argument implies a negative relationship between FDI flows and the balance of payments (BOP) in developing countries.

Nina Bandelj (1998–9) considers FDI a powerful catalyst in transition to a market economy. Being a sociologist, she examines the effects of institutional, cultural and social structure embeddedness of investor and host countries as determinants of FDI in transition economies. The results of her regression analysis indicate that net of host country characteristics the inflows depend significantly on the institutional arrangements, shared cultural understandings, presence of migration net works and trade ties between a pair of countries. These findings highlight the importance of a relational perspective in understanding macroeconomic processes and are found to be relevant to the Malaysian case as well.

With the increasing net FDI inflows, developing countries have also experienced large-scale capital flights in recent decades. Is there any linkage between the two? Chander Kant (1996) seeks to answer this important question. He postulates that if the investment climate improves, FDI must increase and capital flights should decrease; the relationship between the two must, therefore, be negative. He constructs three versions of capital flight. Employing correlation and PCA techniques, he finds ample support for his proposition.

Finally, we must mention two important publications that provided inspiration and material for many of the works dealing with issues concerning foreign capital flows across national borders: World Bank (1997) and UNCTAD (1998).[7]

4   Variables, data and model

The above literature review shows that there are a variety of factors – economic and non-economic, qualitative and quantitative – that can be viewed as determinants of FDI in a country. We have chosen six variables as determinants of the net private FDI flows to Malaysia. We would have preferred to work with quarterly data that could have allowed the study restricted to more recent years, the data would have also been more compact with an adequate number of observations for analysis. However, quarterly data for *all* the variables in the scheme were not available. Also, being a country-specific study, it could not use a panel model, as do most of the empirical studies on the subject. We perforce decided to use annual data over a thirty-one-year time span (from 1970 to 2000). As qualitative factors tend to change rather fast over time and are difficult to keep track of, we restricted the choice to quantitative variables. Even in their case, the available data was not always very satisfactory, and approximations and proxies had to be used. The variables for the study are:

FDI   Foreign Direct Investment
CF   Capital flight
EXR   Exchange rate

RG Rate of growth
CAB Current account balance
DEX Development expenditure
ER Export to GDP ratio

FDI comprises net private FDI. The entry has different titles over different time spans in the BOP statistics Bank Negara has published – corporate investment, corporate investment (net) and private FDI. FDI in Malaysia comes in public sector projects as well, but it is omitted for this work, as market forces do not guide the flow. Likewize, the Ringgit loans raised by MNCs in the local market to finance the assets they import, as also the earnings they retain (e.g. for reinvestment), are not included owing to the lack of necessary details.

Institutions and individuals have both evolved methods for estimating the magnitude of capital flight (**CF**) from a country. Chander Kant (1996) compares methods designed by the World Bank, Dooley and Cuddington. He modifies the Cuddington's study to produce his own version (pp. 6–10). Israel Pinheiro (1997) provides alternative estimates for Brazil from 1971 to 1987 using the World Bank, Morgan and Cuddington methods (pp. 8–11). We have more or less followed the Cuddington method for the present work in view of the information, as it is available in the Malaysian balance of payments statistics.[8] We have taken the sum of rows shown in Section V of the Bank Negara reports up to 1986 under the title 'Private Financial Capital'. These included sub-heads 'Commercial Banks', 'Others' and 'Errors and Omissions including other Short-Term capital'. The items were lumped together from 1987 in a BOP sub-division containing 'Private Short-Term capital', and 'Errors and Omissions.' The sum of the items is multiplied by (−1) for each year to make the series compatible with its heading, 'Capital Flight', (+) values showing the *outward* flows, and (−) values the *inward*.

Rate of exchange or **EXR** has long been regarded as an important determinant of FDI flows. We have taken the nominal end-year Ringgit price of the US dollar as our variable. An increase in **EXR** so defined would mean a depreciation of the local currency *vis-à-vis* the US dollar in the foreign exchange market. As all trade in Malaysia is in terms of dollars, FDI flow is expected to increase in response to a fall in the value of the Malaysian currency. As such, we expect a positive relationship between **EXR** and FDI.

RG is the rate of growth of real GDP, and is expected to have a positive linkage with foreign investment flows. An economy that grows at an adequate and rising rate offers the chance to the foreign investor to earn attractive and regular profits at lower risks. Malaysia has maintained high rates of growth over fairly long periods of time, and FDI flows have also been substantial. Evidently, the two must be directly related.

BOP surpluses are one indicator of the financial and economic health of a developing country and may contribute to attract foreign investment, their relationship with FDI flows usually is expected to be positive. We have taken only the current account balance **CAB** for the present exercise, to keep the variable independent of the FDI which influences, sometimes considerably, the overall BOP.

One prerequisite for an economy to stimulate FDI inflows is the expansion of various sorts of infrastructural facilities, including means of transportation and communication, power supply, educated skilled workers, accommodation and the like. We have taken the annual net developmental expenditure or **DEX** of the public sector as a proxy for the provision of such facilities. We have not related it to GDP as some writers have done, for any net expenditure incurred on infrastructural facilities would add to their availability irrespective of a rise or fall in their ratio to the country's GDP. Increase in **DEX** is expected to have a direct impact on the FDI.

Growth of exports and its pace measure the extent of a country's integration with the global economic network. Exports, especially of manufactures, rising fast over the years, as in Malaysia, improve investors' confidence in the economy and spur the flow of foreign capital to the country. We have taken **ER** as the ratio of exports to the GDP expressed as percentages, measuring the change in both the level and pace of the variable. The data is presented in Table 8.1.

We set up the following multivariate regression model:

$$\text{FDI} = \beta_0 + \beta_1\,\text{CF} + \beta_2\,\text{EXR} + \beta_3\,\text{RG} + \beta_4\,\text{CAB}$$
$$+ \beta_5\,\text{DEX} + \beta_6\,\text{ER} + u \tag{1}$$

In this equation, u is a catch-all variable allowing for the influence on FDI of all other variables that are not included in the independent variables' list. It follows from Table 8.2 that the net flow of private FDI to Malaysia over the thirty-one years of our study aggregated to around 146 billion US dollars, giving a handsome average of \$ 4.728 billion a year. The outflow of the volatile portfolio investment has averaged a little more than half of that amount. The exchange rate has been quite stable over the years with a standard deviation of 0.4870 for an average of RM 2.6946 to the US dollar for the period. The economy grew on an average by almost 7 per cent a year, real per capita income more than doubled after 1987 and the current account showed an overall surplus.

A comparison of the averages over the decades, as given in Table 8.2, is even more interesting. We find that most of the foreign investment came into the country during the 1980s and 1990s, and at an increasing rate, as depicted in Figure 8.1. The exchange rate went up only in the 1990s mainly because of the 1997–8 turmoil that resulted in the devaluation of the Ringgit by 34 per cent. In fact, the currency strengthened during the 1980s, the average Ringgit price of dollar even falling slightly. The openness of the economy grew, especially during the 1990s, when the ratio of exports to GDP shot up, averaging 90 per cent. Average development expenditure rose by almost six times over the twenty years. The average rate of growth dipped but looked up again in the 1990s.

Table 8.1 Determinants of FDI in Malaysia, 1970–2000 (RM million)

Years	Foreign direct invest	Capital flight	Exchange rate	Growth rate	Current account balance	Develop. exp.	Export GDP ratio
Y	FDI	CF	EXR	RG	CAB	DEX	ER
1970	290	282	3.0775	5.1	25	725	44.40
1971	305	182	2.8863	10.0	−329	1,085	41.25
1972	477	82	2.8170	9.6	−698	1,242	37.61
1973	480	270	2.4545	11.8	246	1,128	51.38
1974	833	−225	2.3095	8.2	−781	1,876	56.10
1975	532	895	2.5857	2.5	−421	2,151	49.00
1976	498	1,059	2.5352	11.7	1,686	2,378	56.23
1977	648	2,907	2.3641	7.9	1,198	3,217	46.37
1978	1,158	1,213	2.2077	6.9	249	3,782	46.91
1979	1,255	2,299	2.1887	9.1	2,033	4,281	54.53
1980	2,033	791	2.2175	7.5	−620	7,470	54.29
1981	2,914	1,423	2.2433	6.9	−5,633	11,358	48.41
1982	3,263	617	2.3185	5.2	−8,409	11,485	45.93
1983	2,926	1,148	2.3387	5.9	−8,117	9,670	46.88
1984	1,859	2,331	2.4263	7.6	−3,917	8,407	48.55
1985	1,725	−502	2.4135	−1.0	−1,522	7,142	49.05
1986	1,262	−1,275	2.6015	1.2	−316	7,559	49.68
1987	1,065	2,344	2.4915	5.2	6,642	4,741	55.77
1988	1,884	2,627	2.7125	8.7	4,739	5,231	59.82
1989	4,518	−574	2.6991	8.8	698	7,696	64.45
1990	6,309	−4,375	2.6981	9.8	−2,483	10,689	66.88
1991	10,996	−4,740	2.7235	8.7	−11,644	9,565	69.93
1992	13,204	−12,038	2.6065	7.8	−5,622	9,688	68.79
1993	12,885	−23,301	2.7011	8.3	−7,926	10,124	70.41
1994	10,798	5,151	2.5578	9.2	−14,770	11,277	91.33
1995	10,454	−633	2.5405	9.5	−21,647	14,051	94.09
1996	12,777	−3,946	2.5279	8.6	−11,226	14,628	91.58
1997	14,450	13,290	3.8883	7.8	−15,820	15,750	93.20
1998	8,490	7,720	3.8000	−7.5	36,794	18,103	105.24
1999	9,397	42,681	3.8000	5.8	47,895	22,615	107.45
2000	6,894	46,681	3.8000	8.3	31,958	23,512	109.76
Mean	4,728	2,722	2.6946	7.0	396	8,472	63.72

Source: Estimates are based on data published in Bank Negara Malaysia, *Annual Reports*.

Table 8.2 Mean values of the variables (RM million)

Periods	FDI	CF	EXR	RG	CAB	DEX	ER	N
1970–80	773	887	2.5131	8.2	235	2,667	48.92	11
1981–90	2,773	376	2.4942	6.0	−1,832	8,398	53.54	10
1991–2000	11,034	7,087	3.0954	6.6	2,799	14,931	90.18	10

Source: Data as given in Table 8.1.

A major policy shift took place towards improving, and expanding local infrastructural facilities, that involved much longer gestation periods. Development of the Labuan off-shore financial centre, the Kuala Lumpur International Airport (KLIA), the Langkawi tourist complex, the KL city centre, the construction of North–South expressway, the erection of rapid-transit railway systems, the building of a new administrative district and a Multimedia Super Corridor are some of the examples of works that needed exceptional investment, and with the returns that could grow only at a slower pace. This capital deepening will attract even more FDI to the country in the course of time, and the expenditure extends the benefits of development to future generations.

5   Results and their analysis

The data were subjected to unit root and cointegration tests; both were negative. Table 8.3 presents the results for the regression model of (1). The results are quite robust. Adjusted R^2 explains almost 90 per cent of the variation in the FDI, and is free of serial correlation. All coefficients are significant at 5 per cent level. Collinearity, as is common for time series models, does exist but is not of a serious dimension.[9] The direction of the relationship of various explanatory variables with the dependent variable FDI is along the expected lines. Figure 8.3 (p. 165) shows the extent of the regression fitness and Figure 8.4 (p. 166) shows that the residuals are trend-free. The coefficient for capital flight (**CF**) is negative. But an increase of 1 million Ringgit in **CF** is likely to go with a reduction in FDI inflows by a much lesser amount – RM 213,000 only. This conforms well to the difference in the nature and causes of the two factors explained in the introduction.

The negative relationship of **CAB** with FDI is unexpected and rather intriguing, as it is in line with Eng's finding reported earlier (p. 159). One plausible explanation may be that the increasing surplus on current account indicates the inability of a country to make gainful use of available foreign exchange resources, and FDI flows, therefore, tend to taper off. Alternatively, the surpluses may increase because the necessary complementary foreign investment is not coming in. The latter is probably truer for Malaysia as the local savings for 2000–2 have, for instance, been larger than what the economy could

Table 8.3A   Model summary

R	R^2	Adjusted R^2	Standard error of the estimate	F	Durbin–Watson
0.957	0917	0.896	1541.72	541.75*	2.190

Note: * *p*-value for *F* is (0.000). Upper limit for Durbin–Watson at 5 per cent for $k=7$ and $n=31$ is 2.018.

Table 8.3B   Coefficients (dependent variable FDI)

	Constant	CF	EXR	RG	CAB	DEX	ER
			Explanatory variables				
Coefficients:	−14,828.705	−0.213	2,894.459	194.658	−0.0717	0.411	118.216
t-values	−6.355	−5.302	3.007	2.135	−2.193	4.112	4.023
Significance	(0.000)	(0.000)	(0.006)	(0.043)	(0.038)	(0.000)	(0.000)
Elasticity*		0.1232	1.650	0.287	0.006	0.736	1.593
Collinearity statistics:							
Tolerance	0.304	0.361	0.652	0.357	0.214	0.203	
Variance Inflation Factor	3.288	2.773	1.534	2.803	4.677	4.926	

Notes
* We have used the mean in calculating elasticity instead of the usual geometric mean.
Some of the values in the data were negative.

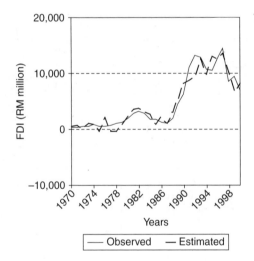

Figure 8.3   Observed and estimated values of FDI, 1970–98

invest. The positive sign for the RM–dollar exchange rate is in line with the empirical evidence that a weak currency is likely to increase the foreign investment flows to a country over time (Toro, 1999). Indeed, the rate has been the most dominant determinant of the FDI flows into Malaysia: over the period under review a 0.01 rize in the rate has, *ceteris paribus*, induced a net flow of about US$ 27 million to the country. Still, notice that **EXR** Granger caused the FDI and the reverse was not true – i.e. in Malaysia the relationship between the two variables has been unidirectional (see Table 8.4).

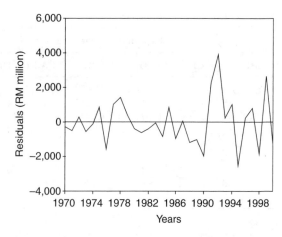

Figure 8.4   Residuals of the model, 1970–98

Table 8.4   Granger bi-variate *F*-test for causality

Null hypothesis (H_0)**	*F*-statistics	Critical value*	Result	N
FDI dnc[†] **EXR** (1)**	0.1312	4.24	Accept H_0	31
EXR dnc **FDI** (2)	4.1513	3.42	Reject H_0	31
FDI dnc **ER** (3)	0.4171	2.93	Accept H_0	31
ER dnc **FDI** (2)	3.5318	3.42	Reject H_0	31
FDI dnc **EXR** (3)	0.4171	2.91	Accept H_0	31
EXR dnc **FDI** (2)	3.5318	3.42	Reject H_0	31
FDI dnc **RG** (2)	0.9775	3.44	Accept H_0	29***
RG dnc **FDI** (1)	7.9506	4.24	Reject H_0	29***

Notes
* Critical values are at 5 per cent level of significance.
** The numbers in parenthesis are the optional lag lengths of the causal variable as chosen according to the FPE criterion.
*** Negative **RG** is excluded.
[†] dnc=does not cause.

Rate of growth (**RG**) has the usual positive relationship with FDI. A 1 per cent rise in **RG** tends to induce a capital flow of about RM 204 million for the economy. This presumably explains in part why the economic managers in Malaysia, as elsewhere, place emphasis on promoting growth rather than distributive justice. Based on a 1997 survey the Gini coefficient for Malaysia climbed to over 49 per cent (*World Development Indicators*, 2003, Table 2.3), and remains among the highest in the world. It is also interesting to note that, like the rate of exchange, it is growth that Granger causes the FDI, and not vice versa.

As expected, development expenditure **DEX** has a positive relationship with FDI inflows and the coefficient too is not small: a 1 million Ringgit increase in **DEX** is likely to bring in no less than RM 411,000 in foreign investment. This justifies the huge infrastructural investment the country has undertaken in recent decades.

Exports play a crucial role in attracting foreign capital to Malaysia. A 1 per cent rise in **ER** is likely to increase FDI inflow by around RM 120 million! This endorses the fact that Malaysia is essentially a trading country and exports remain her engine of growth. Finally, notice that the row recording the elasticity of regression coefficients in Table 8.3A shows the exchange rate as the leading determinant of FDI inflows, followed by exports and infrastructural development.

6 Concluding remarks

The economic achievements of Malaysia since independence, especially during the 1980s and 1990s, make the country one of the brightest stars in the firmament of the developing world. Every country today has to move forward with the traffic on the globalization road even if the rules of the game do not always look equitable. Malaysia chose that path much earlier, as though the country could see the shape things were going to take. The country opened her gates to the world much earlier for the free flow of capital and goods across the national borders and erected production facilities to take advantage of her rich natural resources and cheap labor force. This encouraged the private sector not only to flourish but to become partners with the public sector in the process of national advancement. It advocated a 'prosper-thy-neighbour policy' in trade for mutual benefit. The business-friendly environment in Malaysia resulted in making the country one of the largest recipients of FDI among the developing countries.[10]

Malaysia had location advantage, and created fast a physical and social infrastructure matching with foreign investors' expectations. The results of our model, as described above, bear ample testimony to this. The leadership ensured peace and stability in the country that encouraged the growth of the non-quantifiable factors that are stressed in the literature for attracting FDI. It put in place an educational system including twinning programs with foreign universities to create a growing pool of skilled manpower. Proper linkages between different sectors of the economy were forged and maintained to avoid bottlenecks. Everything was geared to fit into a long-run national aspiration epitomized in the realistic targets of 'Vision 2020'. The country is well on road to that destination.

Foreign capital flowed in abundance to take advantage of the profit-earning opportunities the country offered and these tended to expand because of well-coordinated monetary and fiscal policies. It is a measure of the efficacy of these policies that over the range of regression FDI in Malaysia followed growth, did not lead it, as was the case with the exchange rate. Even exports, the crucial variable for Malaysia, are not found to lead growth, in contrast to what Singh and Jun (1995) found for developing economies in general. In other words, the country has been an equal partner in the progress and reward-sharing of a flourishing economy, not a taker of dictation from foreign investors.

Since the competition for attracting FDI is on the rise, and political equations rather than economics are becoming more important, the country must add newer global links and promote self-reliance. The infrastructure, socio-political stability and a savings rate running at over 40 per cent of GDP can help Malaysia sail with confidence through any rough waters.

Notes

1. On the Malaysian approach to foreign capital flows, see the Bank Negara *Annual Report* (2000), pp. 199–200.
2. See for example, Chadee and Schlichting (1997), Mehmet and Tavaloki (2003) and Zhang (2001).
3. The data used to draw the curve is from Table 8.1. Of the several curves tried the exponential growth of the form Ab^x gave the best fit. The equation is $\text{FDI} = (329.28)(1.1138)^x$, where 1970 is the origin, and x is the year unit.
4. The ratio of trade volume – exports + imports – of a country to GDP has a positive relationship with the country's degree of openness. In the case of Malaysia, this ratio went up from 133 per cent in 1990 to 184 per cent in 2001, lower only than Singapore in the region (see *World Development Indicators*, 2003, Table 6.1).
5. The Crisis and Policy Response (*Star*, 1999) argued that the steeply rising ICOR indicated that the use of capital had become increasingly less efficient. Interestingly, in the next sentence the report agreed that the rise could also be attributed to increasing investment in capital-intensive projects with long gestation periods (p. 3). See also the comment in Hasan (2002, n. 7)
6. See Bank Negara Malaysia policy statements on foreign capital, in their various *Annual Reports*.
7. The UNCTAD Report noting that the developing countries were strongly interested in attracting FDI for accelerating growth and economic transformation listed the principal determinants influencing the location choices of the foreign investors (Table 2), reproduced in Mallampally and Sauvant (1999).
8. To explain these methods, we list the relevant BOP items as in IMF (1993): A Current Account Surplus; B Net Foreign Direct Investment; C Short Term Capital; D Portfolio Investment; E Banking System Foreign Assets; F Changes in Reserves; G Errors and Omissions; H Changes in Debt or Current Account:

   Capital flight estimates

World Bank	A+B +F +H
Morgan	A+B +F + H−E
Cuddington	−C−G
Hasan	−C −G −E

9. The issue concerning collinearity is not its existence or absence in multivariate regression results. It is the *degree* of collinearity that matters. Even here, it essentially is a heuristic concept. Furthermore the presence of collinearity, unless it really is very serious, does not destroy the validity of results. For an elementary discussion of the issue see Gujarati (1992, Chapter 10).

10. Weigel (1997) reports that among the top 12 countries ranked with reference to FDI flows, Malaysia ranked fourth during the 1970–89 period. Its rank improved to third position for 1990–6 period after only China and Mexico.

References

Bandelj, N., 'Embedded Economies: Determinants of Direct Foreign Investment in the Central and Eastern Europe', Department of Sociology, Princeton University, Princeton (1998–1999).

Bank Negara Malaysia, *Annual Report*, Kuala Lumpur (2000).

Bevan, A.A. and S. Estri, 'The Determinants of Foreign Direct Investment in Transition Economies', Working Paper 342, Centre for New and Emerging Markets, London Business School (2000).

Chadee, D.D. and D.A. Schlichting, 'Foreign Direct Investments in the Asia-Pacific Region: Overview of Recent Trends and Patterns', *Asia Pacific Journal of Marketing and Logistics*, 3(9) 1997): 3–15.

Chakrabarti, R. and B. Scholnick Barry, 'Exchange Rate Expectations and FDI Flows', Financial Working Paper Series, 00-15, Dupree College of Management, Georgia Institute of Technology (2000).

Chunlai, C., 'The Location Determinants of Direct Foreign Investment in Developing Countries', Working Paper, **CFIS**-China Program, Adelaide University Australia, (2002).

Dunning, J.H. and R. Narula, 'Developing Countries versus Multinationals in a Globalizing World: The Dangers of Falling Behind', in P. Buckley and P. Gauri (eds.), *Multinational Enterprises and Emerging Markets* (London: Dryden Press, 1997).

Eng, Phang Hooi, 'Malaysia: FDI has Negative Effects on BOP Savings Says New study', Report (Geneva). Goldberg, L. and M. Klien 'Foreign Direct Investment, Trade and Real Exchange Rate Linkages in Developing Countries', in R. Glick (ed), *Managing Capital Flows and Exchange Rates* (Cambridge: Cambridge University Press, 1998).

Gujrati, D., *Essentials of Econometrics* (New York: McGraw-Hill, 1992).

Hasan, Z., 'The 1997–1998 Financial Crisis in Malaysia: Causes, Response, and Results', *Islamic Economic Studies*, 9(2) (2002): 1–16.

Hasan, Z., 'Determinants of Foreign Direct Investment in Developing Economies: Evidence from Malaysia': Eleventh Inaugural Lecture, Research Centre, International Islamic University of Malaysia (2003): 1–28.

International Monetary Fund (IMF) Balance of Payments Manual, 5th edn, (Washington, DC: IMF, 1993).

Kant, C., 'Foreign Direct Investment and Capital Flight', Princeton Studies in International Finance, 80, Department of Economics, Princeton University (1996).

Krugman, P. and M. Obstfeld, *'International Economics*, 3rd edn (New York: HarperCollins, 1994).

Lewis, J., *Factors Influencing Foreign Direct Investment in Lesser Developed Countries* (Park Place Economist, 1999).

Lim, Ewe-Ghee, 'Determinants of, and the Relation Between, Foreign Direct Investment and Growth: A Summary of Recent Literature', IMF Working Paper, WP/01 (2001): 175.

Loungani, P. and A. Razin (2001), 'How Beneficial is Foreign Direct Investment for Developing Countries, *Finance & Development*, 38(2).

Mallapally, P. and K. Sauvant, 'Foreign Direct Investment in Developing Countries', *Finance & Development*, 36(1) (1999).

Mehmet, O. and A. Tavaloki, 'Does Direct Foreign Investment Cause a Race to the Bottom? Evidence from Four Asian Countries', *Journal of Asia Pacific Economy*, 2(8) (2003): 133–56.

Misra, D., A. Mody and A.P. Murshid, 'Private Capital Flows and Growth', *Finance & Development*, 38(2) (2001).

Nakamura, S. and T. Oyama, 'The Determinants of Foreign Direct Investment from Japan and United States to East Asian Countries, and the Linkage between FDI and Trade', Working Paper, 98-11 Research and Statistics Department, Bank of Japan (2001).

Pinheiro, I., 'Considerations for Exchange Controls, Capital Flight, and Country Risk', Institute of Brazilian Issues-IBI, George Washington University, Washington, DC (1997).

Singh, H. and K.W. Jun, 'Some New Evidence on the Determinants of Foreign Direct Investment in Developing Countries', WPS, 1531 (Washington, DC: World Bank, 1995).

Star, 'The Crisis and Policy Response', NEAC'S Agenda for Action, Star Publications (Malaysia), Bhd (1999).

Toro, E., 'Exchange Rates and Foreign Direct Investment: The Role of Mobility', Working Paper Series in Economics and Finance, 59, Department of Economics, Stockholm School of Economics (1999).

UNCTAD, *World Investment Report* (1998).

Weigel, D.R., 'Foreign Direct Investment', International Finance Corporation & Foreign Investment Advisory Service USA (1997).

Wilhems, S.K.S., 'Foreign Direct Investment and its Determinants in Emerging Economies', African Economic Policy Paper, Discussion Paper 9 (1998), (Washington, DC: Word Bank).

World Bank, *Private Capital Flows to Developing Countries* (Washington, DC: World Bank, 1997).

World Bank, *World Development Indictors* (Washington, DC: Workd Bank, 2003).

Zhang, K.H., 'Does Foreign Direct Investment Promote Economic Growth? Evidence from East Asia and Latin America', *Contemporary Economic Policy*, 19(2) (2001): 175–85.

9
What Does the Economic Rise of China Imply for ASEAN and India?: Focus on Trade and Investment Flows

Sadhana Srivastava and Ramkishen S. Rajan[1]

1 Introduction

The People's Republic of China (PRC)[2] has been opening up its economy to the outside world in a carefully managed and phased manner since 1979. The PRC's economy grew at an annual average rate of 9.2 per cent between 1980 and 2000, and its merchandize exports expanded by more than 15 per cent annually over the same period. With the PRC's phenomenal growth since the 1980s, it has emerged as a major economic power in Asia. The PRC is the most populous country in the world, the second largest economy in terms of GDP at purchasing power parity (PPP), the world's sixth biggest merchandize trading nation, the twelfth largest global exporter of commercial services and the largest recipient of foreign direct investment (FDI) among developing countries. The PRC's accession to the World Trade Organization (WTO) in December 2001 is widely expected to give a further fillip to the country's FDI, export and overall growth prospects over the medium and longer term.

Against this background, an important and vigorous ongoing policy debate in Asia concerns the impact of the economic rise of the PRC on the rest of the region. The general perception is that there is a likelihood of substantial diversion of FDI from other developing countries in Asia towards the PRC in order to service the large domestic market and in search of more cost-efficient production locations (Rajan, 2003a, 2003b).

Members of the Association of Southeast Asian Nations (ASEAN) are expected to face particularly intense competitive pressures from the PRC in view of the overlap in relative factor endowments, export markets (the USA) and heavy reliance on FDI inflows from similar sources. The economic emergence of the PRC may also significantly impact another large emerging economy in Asia, India. India has been positioning itself relatively favourably

171

to attract and benefit from FDI since 1991, the year when wide-ranging measures were introduced to liberalize the economy. These reform measures
have continued over the 1990s, though the pace has been uneven at times.
The Indian economy is the second most populous in the world, is ranked
fourth largest in terms of GDP at PPP and has been one of the world's fastest-
growing economies over the 1990s (World Bank, 2002a).

Some studies warn that the 'China threat' to ASEAN and India may be
immediate and severe in labour-intensive products in which the PRC has a
strong comparative advantage, but could move on to impact the broader
technological spectrum (Lall and Albaladejo, 2001; Lall, 2003). However,
such negatives from stiffened competition could be outweighed by the
potential for mutually beneficial and complementary relationships that may
accrue to its trading partners from the PRC's growth and trade expansion. It
is thus important to study the relative performances of the PRC, ASEAN
countries and India over time, as well as the intensity and changing dynamics of their intra-regional economic interactions.

The remainder of this chapter is structured as follows. Section 2 briefly
examines the dynamics of economic interactions among these economies
since the mid-1980s and concerns itself with the impact of the PRC's rise on
ASEAN's and India's FDI prospects. Section 3 attempts to analyse the impact
of the PRC's emergence on the more advanced ASEAN members (Indonesia,
Malaysia, the Philippines, Singapore and Thailand) – henceforth referred to
as ASEAN-5 – with regard to export competitiveness in manufacturing and
the services sector at a disaggregated product level. Section 4 offers few
concluding remarks regarding bilateralism and regionalism in Asia.

2   Economic interactions between the PRC, ASEAN-5 and India, 1984–2001

This section briefly examines economic interactions between these economies
since the mid-1980s.

The PRC and ASEAN-5

Merchandise trade

Figure 9.1 reveals trends in bilateral trade between ASEAN-5 and the PRC
between 1985 and 2001. A few noteworthy points warrant highlighting.
Between 1985 and 1992, while bilateral trade did rise, the rate of increase
was rather gradual. Bilateral trade rose sharply between 1992 and 1996. This
period corresponds to a time when FDI began to surge into the PRC. Trade
between the two stagnated between 1996 and 1998 during the economic
crisis in South East Asia,[3] though it has rebounded since then. Bilateral trade
between ASEAN-5 and the PRC totalled US$ 39.5 billion in 2002, growing at
an annual average of slightly over 20 per cent since 1991 when overall trade
amounted to only US$ 7.9 billion (ASEAN–China Expert Group on Economic

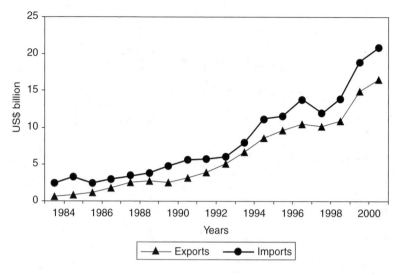

Figure 9.1 Trends in bilateral merchandise trade of ASEAN with China, 1984–2001
Source: ADB (2002).

Cooperation, 2002). While both ASEAN's exports to and imports from the PRC have increased in tandem, the latter has consistently exceeded the former, ensuring that the PRC has enjoyed a persistent trade surplus with ASEAN. The PRC's share of ASEAN's trade remained rather stagnant between 1985 and 1994, but has shot up since then, particularly with regard to the PRC as a source of ASEAN's imports.

In order to analyse changes in export composition of ASEAN's trade with the PRC, Tables 9.1 and 9.2 present the top ten exports and imports in ASEAN's trade with the PRC between 1993 and 2000. In comparison to 1993, when ASEAN's exports to the PRC were dominated more by primary products like Wood & Wood articles and Mineral Fuels, by 2000 the product composition had shifted markedly to manufactured products, particularly Electrical and Electronic and Nuclear Boiler products. This is evident in the increasing share of these products in ASEAN's exports to the PRC over the 1993–2000 period. These products, along with that of Nuclear Boilers and Parts, accounted for about half of ASEAN's imports from the PRC by 2000. There is, therefore, increasing evidence of intra-industry trade in these products between ASEAN-5 and the PRC. The PRC is rapidly improving its production and export capacity in light manufactured products as well as in the assembly of parts and components of a limited number of capital goods. Its exports of light manufactured goods compete mainly with South Asian countries and a few Latin American and African countries in third markets, while it competes head-on with some lower- and middle-income ASEAN countries

Table 9.1 Share of ten major products in ASEAN's* exports to PRC China, 1993–2000

1993			1996			1999			2000		
HS	Products	Share (%)	HS	Products	Share (%)	HS	Products	Share (%)	HS	Products	Share (%)
27	Mineral Fuel Oils, Waxes and Products, etc.	32.3	27	Mineral Fuel Oils, Waxes and Products, etc.	23.3	84	Nuclear Reactors, Boilers, etc. and Parts	20.3	85	Electrical Machinery, Sound Recorders, etc.	21.0
44	Wood and Articles Thereof	22.6	84	Nuclear Reactors, Boilers, etc. and Parts	13.2	85	Electrical Machinery, Sound Recorders, etc.	17.9	84	Nuclear Reactors, Boilers, etc. and Parts	17.5
15	Animal Vegetable Oils Fats, Waxes, etc.	8.4	85	Electrical Machinery, Sound Recorders, etc.	9.0	27	Mineral Fuel Oils, Waxes and Products, etc.	11.4	27	Mineral Fuel Oils, Waxes and Products, etc.	17.0
84	Nuclear Reactors, Boilers, etc. and Parts	6.4	44	Wood and Articles Thereof	8.8	15	Animal Vegetable Oils, Fats, Waxes, etc.	5.4	39	Plastics and Articles Thereof	6.1
85	Electrical Machinery, Sound Recorders, etc.	6.0	15	Animal Vegetable Oils, Fats, Waxes, etc.	6.7	44	Wood and Articles Thereof	5.3	44	Wood and Articles Thereof	4.9
39	Plastics and Articles Thereof	3.2	40	Rubber and Articles Thereof	4.2	39	Plastics and Articles Thereof	5.1	29	Organic Chemicals	4.3
72	Iron and Steel	2.3	24	Tobacco and Manufacture of Tobacco Substitutes	3.9	29	Organic Chemicals	3.7	15	Animal Vegetable Oils, Fats, Waxes, etc.	3.9
98	Postal Packages and Special Transactions	2.1	10	Cereals	3.7	38	Miscellaneous Chemical Products	3.5	47	Wood Pulp and Waste of Paper or Paperboard	3.0
74	Copper and Articles Thereof	1.8	74	Copper and Articles Thereof	3.1	48	Paper and Paperboard Articles of Paper Pulp	3.4	48	Paper and Paperboard Articles of Paper Pulp	2.2
29	Organic Chemicals	1.5	39	Plastics and Articles Thereof	3.0	40	Rubber and Articles Thereof	2.9	90	Optical Photographic Measuring Instruments, etc.	1.8
	10 Major	86.8		10 Major	78.8		10 Major	78.9		10 Major	81.8
	Others	13.2		Others	21.2		Others	21.1		Others	18.2
	Total	100.0		Total	100.0		Total	100.0		Total	100.0

Notes

* Covers only ASEAN-5 plus Brunei.

Source: ASEAN Trade Statistics Database (2002).

Table 9.2 Share of ten major products in ASEAN's* imports from PRC China, 1993–2000

	1993			1996			1999			2000	
HS	Products	Share (%)	HS	Products	Share (%)	HS	Products	Share (%)	HS	Products	Share (%)
85	Electrical Machinery, Sound Recorders, etc.	11.1	85	Electrical Machinery, Sound Recorders, etc.	21.5	85	Electrical Machinery, Sound Recorders, etc.	26.6	85	Electrical Machinery, Sound Recorders, etc.	34.8
84	Nuclear Reactors, Boilers, etc. and Parts	9.7	84	Nuclear Reactors, Boilers, etc. and Parts	14.7	84	Nuclear Reactors, Boilers, etc. and Parts	20.0	84	Nuclear Reactors, Boilers, etc. and Parts	16.2
27	Mineral Fuel Oils, Waxes and Products, etc.	9.0	72	Iron and Steel	5.6	10	Cereals	4.3	27	Mineral Fuel Oils, Waxes and Products, etc.	6.9
52	Cotton	5.6	27	Mineral Fuel Oils Waxes and Products, etc.	5.2	27	Mineral Fuel Oils Waxes and Products, etc.	3.6	10	Cereals	3.1
24	Tobacco and Manufacture of Tobacco Substitutes	4.2	25	Salt, Sulphur, Earths, Stones, Lime, Cement, etc.	3.2	89	Ships, Boats and Floating Structures	2.5	52	Cotton	2.3
10	Cereals	3.7	73	Articles of Iron or Steel	2.7	28	Inorganic Chemical, Rare-Earth Metals, etc.	2.1	90	Optical Photographic Measuring Instruments, etc.	2.1
73	Articles of Iron or Steel	3.3	07	Edible Vegetable Roots and Tubers	2.5	29	Organic Chemicals	2.0	72	Iron and Steel	2.0
28	Inorganic Chemical, Rare-Earth Metals, etc.	3.0	28	Inorganic Chemical, Rare-Earth Metals, etc.	2.4	73	Articles of Iron or Steel	1.8	28	Inorganic Chemical, Rare-Earth Metals, etc.	1.7
55	Man-Made Staple Fabrics Oil Seeds, Fruits, Medicinal	3.0	29	Organic Chemicals	2.4	52	Cotton	1.7	29	Organic Chemicals	1.5
12	Plants, Fodder, etc.	3.0	89	Ships, Boats and Floating Structures	1.7	07	Edible Vegetable Roots and Tubers	1.4	73	Articles of Iron or Steel	1.4
	10 Major	55.5		10 Major	61.9		10 Major	66.0		10 Major	72.0
	Others	44.5		Others	38.1		Others	34.0		Others	28.0
	Total	100.0		Total	100.0		Total	100.0		Total	100.0

Notes
* Covers only ASEAN-5 plus Brunei.

Source: ASEAN Trade Statistics Database (2002).

in the production and assembly of some capital goods. However, insofar as the intermediate goods used in the manufacture of the PRC's exports of capital goods are largely imported from ASEAN and other East Asia countries, trade is as much complementary as it is 'competitive' (Shafaeddin, 2002).

FDI

In order to analyse the patterns of FDI inflows in ASEAN member countries, and the role of PRC (as well as 'Greater China', i.e. Hong Kong and Taiwan), Table 9.3 presents trends in net FDI inflows into ASEAN-5 countries between 1995 and 2000, while Table 9.4 presents the data as a share of total FDI inflows into individual ASEAN countries.

While intra-regional FDI within ASEAN has declined significantly with the advent of the crisis in 1997–8, especially due to large FDI outflows from Indonesia, extra-regional FDI flows to ASEAN-5 also registered a significant decline since 1996. The share of ASEAN-5 in total Asia-bound FDI also fell dramatically (from 51 per cent in 1990 to only 11 per cent in 2001).

The PRC's direct investment in ASEAN-5 is non-negligible. It tends primarily to be market- and resource-seeking. However, consistent with the merchandize trade data, Chinese companies have invested in particular in electronics and electrical industries in Malaysia and Thailand (MTI, 2001). The data reveal that the PRC accounted for less than 1 per cent of ASEAN's total FDI inflows on average, except for 1998 (when it was 1.7 per cent). On the other hand, Hong Kong and Taiwan each accounted for about 4 per cent–5 per cent of ASEAN-5 total net FDI inflows during this period (Table 9.4). As of 2000, Greater China accounted for nearly 14 per cent of net FDI inflows into ASEAN, having averaged 9 per cent over the five-year period. However, there exists a great deal of intra-ASEAN variation. Greater China accounted for about 13 per cent of total inflows into the Philippines and Thailand. For the remainder of the ASEAN countries, FDI from Greater China hovered at between 5 per cent and 10 per cent.

Available data on ASEAN's cumulative FDI into the PRC suggests a marked rise from about US$ 290 million in 1990 to over US$ 20 billion by 2000 (Figure 9.2). This indicates increasing interest of ASEAN investors – particularly those from Singapore – in the PRC, especially since the post-crisis period. However, even at a superficial level one must doubt the importance of direct competition from the PRC as it too suffered a marginal decline in net FDI inflows, albeit less than ASEAN (see Wu *et al.*, 2002b). As discussed, the relatively sharp decline in ASEAN's FDI flows was primarily due to Indonesia which was the only ASEAN country to experience an outright erosion in the cumulative stock of FDI after 1997, as there was a sharp outflow of FDI between 1998 and 2000 (Rajan and Siregar, 2002). Indonesia in turn has been hurt by domestic socio-political convulsions and investor uncertainty as opposed to competition from the PRC *per se*. Similarly, stagnation in FDI flows to Malaysia in the late 1990s and early 2000 were probably more due

Table 9.3 Trends in net FDI inflows to ASEAN, 1995–2000

Net FDI inflows from the PRC

	Amount (US$ million)						Share in total (%)					
	1995	1996	1997	1998	1999	2000	1995	1996	1997	1998	1999	2000
Indonesia	5.7	0.0	8.0	−44.0	−1.2	−2.8	5.1	0.0	−55.8	−16.3	−1.4	−9.9
Malaysia	22.5	13.3	43.6	5.5	3.2	1.3	20.3	13.1	−304.5	2.1	3.8	4.7
Philippines	7.4	3.8	2.4	143.0	65.0	0.0	6.7	3.7	−16.5	52.9	78.0	0.0
Singapore	73.5	80.7	−60.5	160.8	18.6	22.5	66.2	79.4	422.4	59.5	22.3	79.7
Thailand	1.9	3.9	−7.8	5.1	−2.2	7.2	1.7	3.8	54.4	1.9	−2.6	25.6
Total (ASEAN-5)	110.9	101.7	−14.3	270.4	83.4	28.3	100.0	100.0	100.0	100.0	100.0	100.0

Net FDI inflows from ASEAN (intra-ASEAN FDI)

	Amount (US$ million)						Share in total (%)					
	1995	1996	1997	1998	1999	2000	1995	1996	1997	1998	1999	2000
Indonesia	608.9	193.3	272.2	−37.1	−427.8	−232.6	19.3	8.1	5.3	−3.0	−39.8	−30.3
Malaysia	1,676.5	1,475.8	2,261.5	469.9	536.0	365.6	53.2	61.9	44.3	37.6	49.8	47.6
Philippines	204.8	73.9	139.4	109.9	114.2	88.5	6.5	3.1	2.7	8.8	10.6	11.5
Singapore	503.2	332.9	2,131.3	136.5	283.7	157.8	16.0	14.0	41.8	10.9	26.4	20.5
Thailand	160.6	308.1	297.5	569.6	569.5	389.0	5.1	12.9	5.8	45.6	52.9	50.6
Total (ASEAN-5)	3,154.1	2,384.0	5,101.9	1,248.8	1,075.5	768.5	100.0	100.0	100.0	100.0	100.0	100.0

Table 9.3 Continued

Net FDI inflows from Hong Kong

	Amount (US$ million)						Share in total (%)					
	1995	1996	1997	1998	1999	2000	1995	1996	1997	1998	1999	2000
Indonesia	106.8	94.5	232.3	13.3	-143.9	-122.2	10.8	8.6	18.5	1.8	-29.8	-18.2
Malaysia	198.0	337.1	315.8	126.3	234.0	269.2	20.0	30.7	25.2	17.4	48.4	40.1
Philippines	440.8	90.4	70.9	42.1	64.6	45.9	44.6	8.2	5.7	5.8	13.4	6.8
Singapore	-35.4*	361.9	191.2	150.6	94.8	147.0	-3.6	32.9	15.3	20.7	19.6	21.9
Thailand	279.1	215.1	442.4	393.9	233.7	331.3	28.2	19.6	35.3	54.2	48.4	49.4
Total (ASEAN-5)	989.3	1,099.1	1,252.7	726.2	483.1	671.2	100.0	100.0	100.0	100.0	100.0	100.0

Net FDI inflows from Taiwan, ROC

	Amount (US$ million)						Share in total (%)					
	1995	1996	1997	1998	1999	2000	1995	1996	1997	1998	1999	2000
Indonesia	-14.1	19.5	7.7	-6.9	-20.5	-4.9	-2.4	4.6	1.1	-1.2	-6.5	-0.8
Malaysia	322.9	21.0	119.5	73.5	56.8	78.0	54.3	5.0	17.3	12.6	18.1	12.3
Philippines	13.3	56.1	23.4	100.7	9.0	8.3	2.2	13.3	3.4	17.3	2.9	1.3

		Amount (US$ million)						Share in total (%)				
Singapore	175.9	187.6	404.8	310.2	146.5	393.5	29.6	44.4	58.7	53.1	46.7	62.1
Thailand	96.6	138.0	133.8	106.3	121.6	159.0	16.2	32.7	19.4	18.2	38.8	25.1
Total (ASEAN-5)	594.6	422.2	689.2	583.9	313.4	633.9	100.0	100.0	100.0	100.0	100.0	100.0

Net FDI inflows from rest of the world

	Amount (US$ million)						Share in total (%)					
	1995	1996	1997	1998	1999	2000	1995	1996	1997	1998	1999	2000
Indonesia	3,737.1	6,000.7	4,405.5	−318.1	−2,317.2	−4,317.4	21.0	25.0	20.8	−2.0	−15.6	−43.8
Malaysia	4,138.5	5,821.2	4,061.5	2,244.1	3,359.1	3,421.5	23.3	24.3	19.2	13.9	22.6	34.7
Philippines	1,373.2	1,558.1	1,145.6	1,680.2	1,586.8	1,637.5	7.7	6.5	5.4	10.4	10.7	16.6
Singapore	6,705.1	8,651.2	8,202.7	5,654.7	6,684.7	6,232.4	37.7	36.1	38.8	35.1	44.9	63.2
Thailand	1,843.4	1,962.5	3,329.3	6,864.0	5,580.3	2,891.2	10.4	8.2	15.7	42.6	37.5	29.3
Total (ASEAN-5)	17,797.3	23,993.7	21,144.6	16,124.8	14,893.6	9,865.1	100.0	100.0	100.0	100.0	100.0	100.0

Note: * Minus sign means disinvestment.

Source: Computed from ASEAN Secretariat: ASEAN FDI Database (2002).

Table 9.4 Shares in net FDI inflows to ASEAN, 1995–2000 (per cent)

Share of PRC China in net FDI inflows in ASEAN member countries

	1995	1996	1997	1998	1999	2000	Average
Indonesia	0.03	0.0	0.0	−0.3	0.0	0.0	0.0
Malaysia	0.1	0.1	0.2	0.0	0.0	0.0	0.1
Philippines	0.0	0.0	0.0	0.9	0.5	0.0	0.2
Singapore	0.4	0.4	−0.3	1.0	0.1	0.3	0.3
Thailand	0.0	0.0	0.0	0.0	0.0	0.1	0.0
Total (ASEAN-5)	0.7	0.5	0.1	1.7	0.7	0.7	0.7

Share of intra-ASEAN net FDI inflows in ASEAN member countries

	1995	1996	1997	1998	1999	2000	Average
Indonesia	14.0	3.1	5.8	10.4	15.6	5.1	9.0
Malaysia	28.8	20.2	35.8	17.3	13.8	9.7	20.9
Philippines	13.0	4.5	10.8	6.1	6.7	5.1	7.7
Singapore	7.0	3.7	20.6	2.4	4.1	2.5	6.7
Thailand	8.0	13.6	8.2	7.7	9.3	11.9	9.8
Total (ASEAN-5)	15.2	10.2	19.8	9.6	8.5	9.4	12.1

Share of Hong Kong's net FDI inflows in ASEAN member countries

	Share in total (%)						
	1995	1996	1997	1998	1999	2000	Average
Indonesia	2.5	1.5	5.0	−3.7	5.2	2.7	2.2
Malaysia	3.4	4.6	5.0	4.7	6.0	7.1	5.1
Philippines	27.9	5.5	5.5	2.3	3.8	2.7	8.0
Singapore	−0.5	4.0	1.9	2.6	1.4	2.3	1.9
Thailand	13.9	9.5	12.2	5.3	3.8	10.1	9.1
Total (ASEAN-5)	5.0	4.4	5.2	4.8	3.0	5.9	4.7

Share of Taiwan's net FDI inflows in ASEAN member countries

	Share in total (%)						
	1995	1996	1997	1998	1999	2000	Average
Indonesia	−0.3	0.3	0.2	1.9	0.7	0.1	0.5
Malaysia	5.6	0.3	1.9	2.7	1.5	2.1	2.3
Philippines	0.8	3.4	1.8	5.6	0.5	0.5	2.1
Singapore	2.4	2.1	3.9	5.4	2.1	6.2	3.7
Thailand	4.8	6.1	3.7	1.4	2.0	4.8	3.8
Total (ASEAN-5)	3.4	2.6	3.7	4.4	2.5	7.8	4.1

Table 9.4   Continued

Share of PRC and Greater China's net FDI inflows in ASEAN member countries

	Share in total (%)						
	1995	1996	1997	1998	1999	2000	Average
Indonesia	7.1	1.8	−210.5	14.2	7.3	7.7	−28.7
Malaysia	20.8	11.4	−614.0	8.6	8.8	9.3	−92.5
Philippines	35.3	12.8	−56.5	59.9	76.9	3.1	21.9
Singapore	66.5	86.3	−1,625.7	66.4	24.2	47.9	−222.4
Thailand	20.4	19.4	−194.4	8.6	8.2	27.6	−18.3
Total (ASEAN-5)	9.1	7.5	9.0	10.8	6.1	14.5	9.5

Note:
Negative sign means disinvestment.

Source: Computed from ASEAN Secretariat: ASEAN FDI Database (2002).

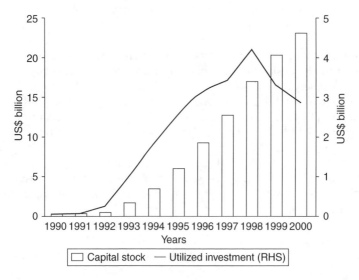

Figure 9.2   ASEAN-5 investments in China, 1990–2000
Source: MTI (2001).

to policy uncertainty following the imposition of currency and capital controls in September 1998 (Bhaskaran, 2003).

This said, in the current environment where there is a global race for FDI on the one hand, and the emergence of the PRC as a viable and promising investment alternative on the other, investors are obviously far less tolerant of actual or perceived economic weaknesses in any potential host country or region (Rajan, 1994). Insofar as the accession of the PRC to the rules-based

WTO system makes it an even more attractive host for FDI, there may well be (further) diversion of FDI from 'unstable ASEAN'.[4]

To the extent that domestic growth rates have often showed up as a significant factor in attracting FDI, continued outpacing of PRC growth relative to ASEAN may well personify the diversion of FDI from the PRC to ASEAN. This is particularly so as the PRC remains an underperformer in attracting FDI inflows when one considers FDI as a proportion of GDP.[5] This is apparent from UNCTAD (2002, p. 25) which reveals that in a ranking of FDI performance of 140 countries based on the FDI–GDP ratio between 1998 and 2000, the PRC comes in at 47. While this is an improvement from its 1988–90 ranking (61), it is by no means suggestive that the PRC is attracting more than its 'fair share' of FDI.[6] Indeed, the PRC's rise in the rankings has not even been the most impressive in Asia. For instance, Vietnam's ranking rose from 53 to 20. However, what is revealing is the sharp drop in rankings of the other ASEAN countries between 1998–90 and 1998–2000. Among the most dramatic declines was Indonesia (from 63 to 138). Malaysia's ranking declined from 8 to 44, Thailand's from 25 to 41, Singapore from 1 to 18 and the Philippines from 39 to 89. This adds further weight to the foregoing argument that the recent 'shift' of FDI flows from ASEAN to the PRC in relative tests is far more due to the severe crisis in 1997–8 and resulting loss of confidence and structural weaknesses in the ASEAN economies made apparent by the crisis than to competition from the PRC *per se*.

More detailed analysis of the sources of FDI into ASEAN and the PRC is also suggestive of limited direct 'competition' between the two. For instance, the bulk of FDI to the former has been from Japan and the USA in particular. Japan has hitherto been a rather reluctant investor in the PRC. The recent declines in FDI flows to ASEAN have in large part been due to lower investment levels from Japan (Figure 9.3). The extent of fall in Japanese FDI can be seen from the fact that while it has consistently been the single largest investor in ASEAN since the late 1980s, it did not even figure as one of the region's top ten investors in 2000 (Table 9.5).

As already noted, the bulk of investments to the PRC has been from overseas Chinese in Hong Kong and Taiwan. Analysis of FDI data from the USA and the EU reveals a fairly sharp turnaround (i.e. boom–bust–partial recovery) in investments from the EU and the USA to Malaysia, Thailand and the Philippines between 1996 and 2000 (Wu *et al.*, 2002b). These dynamics of FDI flows were out of sync with those to the PRC which remained stable though the period. As noted by Wu *et al.* (2002b):

[S]ource-country data show that, despite a booming FDI market in China, developed countries have so far not diverted investments away from ASEAN-5 to China. Arguably, if investors did not have an alternative investment location in China, the reduction in FDI to ASEAN-5 might not have been so drastic...However, because the decline in FDI to

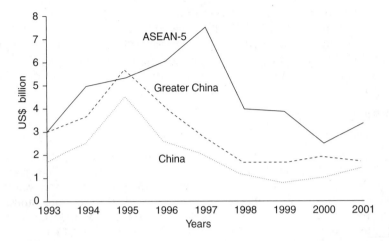

Figure 9.3   FDI flows from Japan to Greater China and ASEAN-5, 1993–2001
Source: Wu *et al.* (2002b).

Table 9.5   Top ten investors in ASEAN, 1995–2000 (balance of payments flow data, US$ million)

No	1998		1999		2000		1995–2000	
	Country	Value	Country	Value	Country	Value	Country	Value
1.	Japan	2,826	USA	2,960	USA	2,320	Japan	19,194
2.	USA	2,759	Netherlands	2,833	UK	1,493	USA	17,975
3.	Netherlands	1,790	Bermuda	1,355	Bermuda	889	UK	9,654
4.	Singapore	1,443	Japan	762	Taiwan (ROC)	802	Singapore	9,241
5.	UK	1,166	UK	742	France	772	Netherlands	8,141
6.	Hong Kong	918	France	655	Germany	696	Hong Kong	5,602
	Taiwan						Taiwan	
7.	(ROC)	842	Singapore	629	Singapore	684	(ROC)	4,454
	South Korea							
8.	(ROK)	643	Canada	489	Hong Kong	611	Germany	3,685
9.	Germany	547	Hong Kong	483	Malaysia	273	France	3,456
					South Korea		South Korea	
10.	France	465	Germany	482	(ROK)	180	(ROK)	2,996
Total		**13,400**		**11,391**		**8,720**		**84,398**

Source: Mirza (2001).

ASEAN-5 has been an abrupt turnaround, it does not appear to be very closely related to China's increasing attractiveness as FDI destination, which has been more of a gradual process ... [U]nless ASEAN gets its own house in order, there can be no guarantee that investments would flow back to ASEAN as before. (2002b, p. 107)

The lowering of import barriers (both actual trade barriers as well as 'behind the border' ones) in the PRC may reduce the incentive to establish tariff-jumping FDI in the PRC, as the market may, in some instances, be served via exports. This appears to be the case in some areas such as automobiles and petrochemicals which have hitherto been heavily protected in the PRC.[7]

The PRC and India

Merchandise trade

Figure 9.4 illustrates the trends in India–PRC bilateral trade over the period 1985–2001. There has been a discernible upward trend in bilateral merchandize trade between the two countries since the economic reforms undertaken in India in 1991–2. In particular, trade between India and the PRC more than doubled over the period 1992–2001, with the share of the PRC in India's exports increasing to about 3.3 per cent in 2001 compared to less than 1 per cent in 1991. The share of the PRC in India's imports was even higher than that of exports during this period. The pace of expansion of bilateral trade has been particularly strong since 1999, with imports expanding at a much more rapid rate than that of exports.

The bilateral merchandise trade between India and the PRC jumped from US$ 265 million in 1991 to US$ 4,950 million in 2002, with the annual average growth rate exceeding 30 per cent between 1998 and 2002 (*Business Times*, Singapore, 30 April 2003). However, large data discrepancies exist in the reported data published from both the PRC and India.[8]

FDI

As bilateral relations between India and the PRC continue to improve, it is anticipated that trade and investment relations will deepen. The sectors that

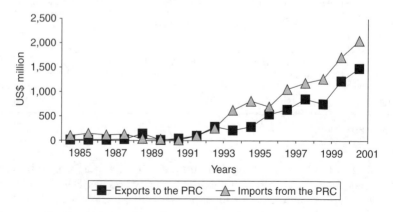

Figure 9.4   India's bilateral trade with PRC China, 1985–2001
Source: ADB (2002).

have attracted investment from Chinese companies in India are particularly in information technology (IT), natural resources, light engineering and white goods.[9] To some extent, an intra-industry division of labour is also observed between the two countries in pharmaceuticals, and engineering industries (Asher, Sen and Srivastava, 2003).

ASEAN and India

Merchandise trade

Figure 9.5 illustrates the trends in ASEAN–India bilateral trade over the period 1991–2 to 1999–2000. There has been a discernible upward trend in bilateral merchandise trade between the two countries, except the year 1998–9 as a result of the regional crisis. In particular, trade between ASEAN and India more than tripled over the period 1991–2 to 2000–1, with India's share in ASEAN's exports increasing to about 3.3 per cent in 2001 compared to less than 1 per cent in 1991. As India's imports from ASEAN outpaced its exports to ASEAN, the balance of trade has shifted sharply in ASEAN's favour.

It is important to note that India's current average tariff remains still high, at about 29 per cent compared to ASEAN's average of about 10–12 per cent. Thus, a speedy alignment in tariff levels with the ASEAN countries would be the foremost requirement for an increase in market access between these countries. Sarma and Mehta (2003) observe that some of the products that hold potential for expansion in ASEAN–India merchandise trade include pharmaceuticals, metal scrap, leather goods, textile machinery components and gems and jewellery. India has a vast potential in business services, such as medical, accountancy and legal services and software, while the ASEAN-5

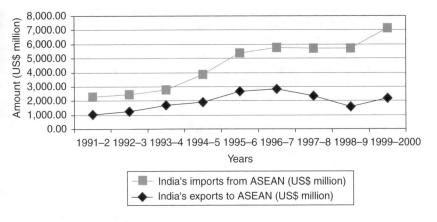

Figure 9.5   India–ASEAN bilateral trade, 1991–2000

Source: ASEAN Trade Statistics Database (2002).

countries, particularly Singapore and Malaysia, have significant expertise in infrastructure development which would be beneficial for India.

FDI

The existing investment relations between ASEAN and India have started growing since 2001. Malaysia and Singapore in particular have been invest-ing fairly aggressively in India. Investments in India by Malaysia have been primarily in infrastructural projects such as roads. The establishment of a representative office of the Confederation of Indian Industry (CII) in Kuala Lumpur laid the foundation for greater investment collaboration by com-panies, including small and medium enterprises (SMEs), between the two countries. There has also been steady investment by Singapore-based com-panies in India, primarily in the telecommunications, IT, ports, logistics and health care sectors (Asher, Sen and Srivastava, 2003).

The substantially liberalized policy framework in India has facilitated Indian companies and financial institutions in investing abroad as well. Specifically, Indian companies are investing in significant magnitudes in the PRC and selected ASEAN countries – Singapore, Malaysia and Thailand (Kumar, 2002, Table 10), although currently Indian companies contribute only about 0.2 per cent of FDI in the region. This suggests that India is grad-ually but definitely integrating with its neighbours in East Asia.

There are a number of reasons to remain positive about ASEAN's and India's FDI potential. First, some multinationals that are concerned about what might be 'excessive' exposure to the PRC are considering setting up factories in India or some other ASEAN countries such as Vietnam as a form of 'risk hedging' strategy. Second, the PRC's continued opening up and growth may lead some Chinese businesses to make investments in ASEAN countries and India. Third, since the majority of FDI in India is directed towards the services sector, it is not a direct competitor of ASEAN with respect to seeking FDI in labour-intensive manufacturing industries. In this aspect, Malaysia's and Singapore's experience and competencies in infra-structural development complements India's need for physical infrastruc-ture. At the same time, India is in a position to cooperate with ASEAN in substantially lowering costs of essential drugs, including those for HIV-AIDS, as well as cooperating in food and energy security.

3   Is the PRC a threat to ASEAN and India's export competitiveness?

In order to obtain a better understanding of the implications of the PRC's ongoing integration with the world economy – including its WTO accession – on both ASEAN and India, it would be useful to chart the comparative advantage positions of both countries in the manufacturing as well as the services sector.

Complementarities or competition in manufacturing trade?

The PRC and ASEAN-5

The persistently sharp increase in the PRC's share of global exports, on the one hand, and the inconsistent growth of ASEAN's exports over the last few years, on the other, is often portrayed as 'evidence' of the adverse impact of the rise of the PRC on ASEAN. Analysis of the extent of export competition between ASEAN and the PRC between 1990 and 2000 in the US market offers some useful insights (Kwan, 2002).

Singapore, Malaysia and Thailand have been increasing their respective export shares to the USA in certain products that coincide with the PRC's exports to the USA. The largest increase is observed for Singapore; the per centage of its exports to the USA in products that were similar to the PRC's exports to the USA increased from 19.2 per cent in 1995 to 35.8 per cent in 2000. However, the actual share of Singapore's export similarity with the PRC was the lowest among all the ASEAN-5 economies in 2000, with Indonesia having the highest share of about 82.8 per cent, followed by Thailand with 65.4 per cent. All in all, there seems a rather high and growing degree of product overlap in the exports of the PRC and ASEAN-5 to the USA, suggesting increased export competition between ASEAN-5 and the PRC.

Analysis of revealed comparative advantage (RCA) indices at the three-digit level leads to a slightly different conclusion. Between 1992 and 1998, the PRC's export structure appears to have been most similar to Malaysia's in the final market for a number of 'finished' capital goods, particularly data processing equipment, telecoms equipment and some electric machinery, but not so much for light manufactured goods. Thailand's export structure is similar to that of the PRC with respect to clothing, miscellaneous household equipment and electric machinery. Indonesia appears to share few export similarities with the PRC except for furniture (Shafeddin, 2002, Table 9).

The inconsistency in conclusions offered by the analysis of export similarity indices and RCA indices as noted above (particularly with regard to Indonesia), may be at least partly due to the fact that the former focused on East Asia's exports to the US market only, while the latter involved East Asia's global exports. This said, there is a more general problem with such trade data analyses. While somewhat informative, they tend to offer limited insights as they are based on fairly aggregated data. However, within each product category, goods could be differentiated according to quality and brand (horizontal differentiation) or they could be further differentiated into sub-parts and components with differing factor intensities (vertical specialization). Thus, just because a study finds that the PRC and ASEAN share similar degrees of export similarity at the 2-, 3- or even 4- digit or even finer product categories, that in and of itself need not suggest that countries are direct competitors.

In addition to vertical specialization, openness to international trade allows countries also to specialize horizontally based on price/quality. Thus, even if a country's comparative advantage happens to coincide exactly with the that of PRC (which may be likely given the vastness and differing levels of development of various regions in the PRC), it can still develop its own export market niche by specializing in differentiated products. This said, a concern about the PRC's ascendancy and price competitiveness is that 'cheap Chinese imports' will keep the price pressures on imperfect substitutes down – i.e. other countries will import price deflation from the PRC with consequent depressing effects on business margins and factor returns, including wages. It is in this sense that ASEAN countries may have complementarities with the PRC in production and export structures (i.e. vertical specialization), while other parts are simultaneously competitive (horizontal specialization).

These global competitive pressures emanating from the PRC and the potential deflationary effects are of particular concern in the areas of textiles and clothing where the PRC's WTO accession is expected to be a significant boon to Chinese exporters who are no longer limited by the quantitative restrictions (QRs) under the Multifibre Arrangement (MFA). Quantitative analyses suggest that the removal of these quotas (in 2005) will lead to a significant increase in the PRC's exports in these areas at the expense of many ASEAN countries as well as other Asian countries more generally (Martin and Ianchoviachina, 2001; Adhikari and Yang, 2002). A study by Francois and Spinanger (2001) summarizes the welfare impacts on selected Asian countries. It observes that while the possibility of horizontal specialization suggests that the above costs are overestimates, there are bound to be non-negligible price pressures and adjustment cost effects on other textile and clothing exporting countries.

With the PRC's continued opening up and growth effects spreading to the inland regions, there are real concerns that small variations in costs could lead to large shifts in comparative advantage, thus necessitating large and sudden domestic adjustments. Bhagwati (1997) refers to this phenomenon as 'kaleidoscope' or 'knife-edge' comparative advantage. Countries need to be ever aware of these potential cost shifts and ensure constant industrial upgrading so as to remain important cogs in the larger regional production network. In other words, the continued opening of the PRC may well contribute to a far more uncertain and competitive environment for ASEAN countries (especially as PRC's western regions develop and labour-intensive industries migrate to the inland regions). Opportunities for lower-income ASEAN countries to upgrade to higher-value added stages of production might then be harder to come by compared to the transition made by their higher-income neighbours in earlier periods.

Nonetheless, accession to the WTO ought to offer even more benefits to regional countries as it will involve increased access to the Mainland's domestic market, allowing ASEAN countries the possibility of enhancing exports. Thus, while the PRC has remained an important import source for ASEAN, as discussed previously, it has also become an increasingly important export market. If current trends persist, the growing importance of the

PRC – and Greater China more generally – may well provide a much-needed cushion to smaller ASEAN countries against gyrations in the industrial country economic environment.

The PRC and India

Much of the preceding arguments also hold in the case of India's interaction with the PRC.

Table 9.6 estimates the Export Revealed Comparative Advantage (XRCA) indices as in Balassa and Noland (1989) for manufacturing sector exports of India and the PRC over the period 1987–98. We use the Garnaut and Anderson (1980) classification of products according to relative factor intensities (see the Appendix 9A.1, p. 200). An individual XRCA index value of greater than one indicates RCA, while a value less than one, indicates comparative disadvantage in the exports of a particular commodity category. Table 9.7 analyses the export pattern of these commodities in the two countries.[10]

Compared to the PRC, the only category in which India continues to have a comparative advantage in exports is in unskilled labour-intensive (ULI) manufacturing goods, especially textiles and textile yarns and in clothing and accessories. However, even within this category, while the PRC has increased its specialization and expanded its share in world exports, India has not been able to do so despite a decade of economic reforms. The PRC has also gained a comparative advantage in technology-intensive (TI) goods and has improved its capability in production and exports of components. Thus, in 1985, out of sixty components, the PRC had a comparative advantage in 6.7 per cent of them, which increased to 8.3 per cent in 1996 (Ng and Yeats, 2001, Table 1). Although India could benefit from exporting those necessary inputs for production of many labour-intensive products in this sector, competition is unlikely in the area of office machines and data processing machines, as India is not a major producer or exporter of these products.

From the estimates in Table 9.7, it is evident that in the manufacturing sector, the only sector in which some competition could emerge between India and the PRC would be in ULI goods, especially in textiles and clothing. However, using further disaggregated data within the textiles and clothing sector, Shafaeddin (2002) finds that the PRC's competitive strengths are in outer garments, whereas India's exports are concentrated in textiles and non-knitted undergarments. This indicates that the possibilities of competition in the manufacturing sector appear limited, suggesting greater complementarities. Nevertheless, India is unlikely to gain from complementary effects from the PRC's accession in an important area of exports of parts and components of electronic products, since it has not been a part of the regional division of labour in this area which has been largely concentrated in East Asia (Rajan and Sen, 2002, 2003a).

Recent estimates of the welfare effects of the PRC's accession to the WTO reveal that while the more advanced developing countries in Asia gain, the

190

Table 9.6 Export revealed comparative advantage (XRCA) estimates of India and China, manufacturing sector, 1987–98 (according to Garnaut and Anderson classification of products by factor intensities)

		Unskilled labour-intensive goods				
Countries	XRSCA	1987	1992	1996	1997	1998
India	XRCA > 1	2.62	2.29	3.57	2.5	2.16
	XRCA < 1					
China	XRCA > 1	2.5	3.69	3.54	4.06	4.29
	XRCA < 1					

		Technology-intensive goods				
Countries		1987	1992	1996	1997	1998
India	XRCA > 1					
	XRCA < 1	0.27	0.27	0.22	0.29	0.25
China	XRCA > 1					
	XRCA < 1	0.26	0.6	0.82	0.93	1

		Physical capital-intensive goods				
Countries	XRSCA	1987	1992	1996	1997	1998
India	XRCA < 1					
	XRCA < 1	0.26	0.51	0.49	0.61	0.53
China	XRCA > 1					
	XRCA < 1	0.28	0.46	0.61	0.71	0.74

		Human capital-intensive goods				
Countries	XRSCA	1987	1992	1996	1997	1998
India	XRCA > 1					
	XRCA < 1	0.29	0.49	0.31	0.46	0.36
China	XRCA > 1					
	XRCA < 1	0.41	0.51	0.59	0.66	0.73

Notes: Refer to the Appendix (p. 200) for a list of commodities under this classification.

Source: Computed from United Nations, *UN International Trade Statistics Yearbook* (2000).

$$XRCA = \frac{X_i^k/X_w^k}{X_i/X_w} = \frac{X_i^k/X_i}{X_w^k/X_w}$$

Where X_i^k = Exports by country i of commodity k
X_w^k = World exports of commodity k
X_i = Total exports oof country i
X_w = Total world exports

Table 9.7 Export pattern of commodities among India and China, manufacturing sector, 1987–98 (according to Garnaut and Anderson classification of products by factor intensities)

Unskilled labour-intensive goods						
Countries	RCA	1987	1992	1996	1997	1998
India	S_w	1.15	1.12	1.4	1.5	1.45
	S_{ct}	32.5	31.4	31.39	32.82	28.34
China	S_w	4.98	8.42	10.13	11.95	11.96
	S_{ct}	31.2	51	45.26	52.76	56.12

Technology-intensive goods						
Countries		1987	1992	1996	1997	1998
India	S_w	0.12	0.13	0.17	0.18	0.17
	S_{ct}	4.79	5.09	6.76	6.88	5.9
China	S_w	0.51	1.37	2.34	2.73	3.11
	S_{ct}	4.7	11.6	17.96	21.37	26.48

Physical capital-intensive goods						
Countries	RCA	1987	1992	1996	1997	1998
India	S_w	0.12	0.25	0.31	0.37	0.35
	S_{ct}	5.07	9	9.19	10.27	8.9
China	S_w	0.56	1.05	1.75	2.08	2.05
	S_{ct}	5.5	8.2	10.51	11.67	12.43

Human capital-intensive goods						
Countries	RCA	1987	1992	1996	1997	1998
India	S_w	0.13	0.24	0.28	0.28	0.24
	S_{ct}	5.48	9.62	8.24	8.24	6.92
China	S_w	0.81	1.16	1.7	1.93	2.02
	S_{ct}	7.9	9.9	10.18	11.56	13.83

Notes
S_w indicates country share in world exports of a particular commodity group.
S_{ct} indicates country share in its total exports to the world.

Source: Computed from WTO, *International Trade Statistics Yearbook* (2000).

less advanced ones tend to lose over the shot and medium run (Martin and Ianchovichina, 2001). However, over time, the PRC could well be a growth locomotive for the region (Fernald, Edison and Lougani, 1999) or at least act as a buffer against possible downturn in other major export markets in the USA, the EU and Japan. In addition, as the PRC expands, its demand for agricultural and mineral products and raw materials – including energy products, forestry, agriculture and fishery and aquaculture products – will continue to rise, benefiting a number of resource-rich countries in ASEAN and elsewhere, particularly Indonesia (Adhikari and Yang, 2002).

Complementarities or competition in services trade?

With services trade gaining importance in world trade, it is essential also to analyse the complementarities and competition in the services sector between the PRC, ASEAN and India. Indeed, services trade liberalization is an important dimension of the PRC's WTO accession. As Mattoo (2002) notes:

> [The PRC's] GATS commitments represent the most radical services reform program negotiated in the WTO...The PRC...has promised to eliminate over the next few years most restrictions on foreign entry and ownership, as well as most forms of discrimination against foreign firms. (2002, p. 22)

The PRC and ASEAN

With WTO accession there will be greater scope and demand for services by the PRC, particularly with regard to distribution, professional and infra-structural services (telecoms and financial). As the PRC continues to rapidly urbanize and industrialize, there will invariably be vast opportunities for ASEAN businesses to be involved in major infrastructural development projects. Thus, richer and more developed ASEAN countries such as Singapore and Malaysia, which have growing strengths in these areas, should benefit significantly from the PRC's continued economic transformation.

With respect to the PRC and ASEAN-5, there appears to be greater potential in cooperating in travel and tourism services, given the strong comparative advantage that most ASEAN-5 economies enjoy in this area. Indeed, there is significant tourism potential from the PRC as average Chinese household incomes rise. The PRC is the world's fastest-growing tourist market in both inbound and outbound travel. Two-way flows between ASEAN and the PRC have been on an increase. ASEAN tourists visiting the PRC reached an estimated 1.8 million in 2000; while ASEAN-5 received about 0.8 million tourists from the PRC in 1995, this number almost tripled to 2.3 million persons in 2000. Conversely, ASEAN tourists were fewer than 8 per cent of the total tourist arrivals to the PRC during 1999, while Chinese tourists in ASEAN made up just 10 per cent of the persons visiting ASEAN in 2000 (Wattanapruttipaisan, 2002). The growth in tourists from the PRC was particularly significant in Malaysia and Singapore, where Chinese visitors increased from the tenth largest visitor group in 1995 to fourth and fifth positions, respectively in 2001 (Wu *et al.*, 2002a). Between 1995 and 2001, the number of Mainland Chinese visitor arrivals to Malaysia quadrupled, while they doubled to Thailand and Singapore.

A number of ASEAN countries such as Malaysia, Thailand and Singapore are taking specific steps to enhance their attractiveness as tourist destinations to PRC residents. More can be done in this regard, particularly with ASEAN countries working in tandem or as clusters to promote the region as a whole (also see Wu *et al.*, 2002a). There have been important initiatives in this direction, with an announcement by the ASEAN Secretariat that ASEAN planned to forge closer tourist relations with the PRC, Korea and Japan. The areas of ASEAN-wide collaboration are expected to span tourism promotion, human resource development (HRD), use of IT and public–private sector cooperation.

The PRC and India

The services sector in India has outperformed merchandise trade, especially over the post-reform period. The average annual growth of services trade over the 1990–8 period was about 15 per cent. India's growth in services trade was nearly double that of merchandize trade during the 1992–8 sub-period.

Within the service sector, while information and communications technologies (ICTs) and related services were viewed as being non-tradable only a few years ago, they have in fact been the main thrust of rapid expansion of services trade in India, accounting for about 70 per cent of service exports in the year 2000 (World Bank, 2002b). The ICTs share in India's services exports in 2000 was almost double that in 1995. The development of the ICT industry in India has primarily been attributable to the software and product services segments, that registered an average revenue growth of about 50–60 per cent annually during the 1990s. The development of this sector has been largely market-driven and propelled by the nurturing of a pool of skilled IT professionals, coupled with an increasing international demand for such workers. However, despite rapid growth, India's share in the total global software market remains very low, suggesting significant scope for further expansion. The Indian government has identified the software industry as a major export and growth thrust area.

How competitive are the PRC's service exports, including ICT services exports, *vis-à-vis* ASEAN-5 and India? Since the concept of comparative advantage can be extended to services trade, a similar set of XRCA indices is estimated Table 9.8 for the four major categories of service exports within India, ASEAN-5 and the PRC over the period 1990–2000. It is observed that India clearly enjoys a comparative advantage in exports of ICT services (communications, computer-related services) *vis-à-vis* the PRC and most of the ASEAN-5 economies (except for Malaysia and Singapore) during this period, while the PRC appears well on the way to attaining comparative advantage in this area. Apart from this sector, India has not gained or improved its comparative advantage position in exports of other services.

With the PRC's entry into the WTO and resultant liberalization of its services sectors (telecommunications and finance), the demand for software services is projected to increase. With the PRC strengthening its competitive position in hardware and focusing on software development through setting

Table 9.8 Export revealed comparative advantage (XRCA) estimates of India, China and ASEAN, services trade, 1990–2000

Communications, computer, etc. – related services				
Countries	XRCAs	1990	1995	2000
India	XRCAs > 1	1.15		1.84
	XRCAs < 1		0.82	
China	XRCAs > 1			
	XRCAs < 1	0.54	0.71	0.88
Indonesia	XRCAs > 1			
	XRCAs < 1	0.29	0.11	0.12
Malaysia	XRCAs > 1		1.16	1.25
	XRCAs < 1	0.69		
Singapore	XRCAs > 1	1.25	1.46	1.45
	XRCAs < 1			
Thailand	XRCAs > 1			
	XRCAs < 1	0.32	0.75	0.57
Philippines	XRCAs > 1	2.12	2.19	
	XRCAs < 1			0.50

Insurance and financial services				
Countries	XRCAs	1990	1995	2000
India	XRCAs > 1			
	XRCAs < 1	0.51	0.44	0.17
China	XRCAs > 1		1.68	
	XRCAs < 1	0.73		0.08
Indonesia	XRCAs > 1			
	XRCAs < 1			
Malaysia	XRCAs > 1			
	XRCAs < 1	0.01	N.A	N.A
Singapore	XRCAs > 1			
	XRCAs < 1	0.11	0.21	0.37
Thailand	XRCAs > 1			
	XRCAs < 1	0.03	0.11	0.07
Philippines	XRCAs > 1			
	XRCAs < 1	0.07	0.11	0.44

Transport services				
Countries	XRCAs	1990	1995	2000
India	XRCAs > 1		1.18	
	XRCAs < 1	0.84		0.46
China	XRCAs > 1	1.87		
	XRCAs < 1		0.74	0.52
Indonesia	XRCAs > 1			
	XRCAs < 1	0.10		

Table 9.8   Continued

Transport services				
Countries	XRCAs	1990	1995	2000
Malaysia	XRCAs > 1	1.11		
	XRCAs < 1		0.84	0.90
Singapore	XRCAs > 1			
	XRCAs < 1	0.62	0.66	0.85
Thailand	XRCAs > 1			
	XRCAs < 1	0.74	0.66	1.01
Philippines	XRCAs > 1			
	XRCAs < 1	0.27	0.12	0.92

Travel services				
Countries	XRCAs	1990	1995	2000
India	XRCAs > 1	1.03	1.18	
	XRCAs < 1			0.56
China	XRCAs > 1		1.41	1.68
	XRCAs < 1	0.90		
Indonesia	XRCAs > 1	2.53	2.83	2.98
	XRCAs < 1			
Malaysia	XRCAs > 1	1.28	1.01	
	XRCAs < 1			0.92
Singapore	XRCAs > 1	1.06		
	XRCAs < 1		0.77	0.67
Thailand	XRCAs > 1	1.97	1.60	1.68
	XRCAs < 1			
Philippines	XRCAs > 1			1.74
	XRCAs < 1	0.42	0.36	

Source: Computed from World Bank, *World Development Indicators,* CD-Rom (2002b).

up of IT training institutions and encouraging R&D by multinationals, there is likely to be impending competition that could directly affect India's comparative advantage in ICT services.

Table 9.9, adapted from Tschang (2003), summarizes the relative competencies of Indian and Chinese firms. It is evident that while Indian software firms possess strong capabilities in process maturity and management skills, Chinese firms are stronger in R&D and product branding. This implies that in order to gain from the growth in the PRC's software industry, Indian firms need to set up their operations in the PRC and cooperate with the software firms there on a long-term basis. Certain top Indian IT firms have already adopted this strategy of engagement, NIIT has already established centres in the PRC to train IT professionals in English and Mandarin courses. Infosys

Table 9.9 Comparison of capabilities of Indian and Chinese software firms

Aspect	India	China
Software processing	Strong, climbing up the value chain	Weaker than India at the organizational level
Management	Strong in many of the top firms	Weak
Technology	Weak in university-based R&D, strong in commercial technology	Strong focus on R&D, and linkages between universities and firms
Revenue model	Export of services	Product sales, with systems integration
Individual technical skills	Strong	Strong
Product marketing	Weak	Weak

Source: Tschang (2003).

has established facilities in Shanghai to tap the domestic market. Satyam and Tata Consultancy Services (TCS) have also set up its operations in the PRC. It is estimated that by 2004, 60 per cent of the top twenty-five Indian software and application development companies will have a direct presence or a Jv with Chinese firms (Gartner Research, 2002). This strategy of competition coexisting with cooperation on a long-term basis is likely to be adopted by most Indian and ASEAN firms interested in venturing into the PRC.

4   Concluding remarks on Asian regionalism

In an increasingly globalized world, decisions about production, investment and trade are closely interlinked and often cannot be made independently of one another. In the context of international production systems, market-driven (as opposed to institutional-driven) regional integrative initiatives are increasingly viewed as effective tools to promote trade, FDI and techno-logical progress:

> From ASEAN's perspective, this implies the need for more aggressive and urgent steps to deepen regional economic integration and reduce the extent of fragmentation that currently exists among ASEAN markets. (ASEAN–China Expert Group, 2002)

In relation to this, mention should be made of the proposed ASEAN–China Free Trade Area (ACFTA) first mooted by Chinese Premier Zhu Rongji during the ASEAN–China Summit in November 2001. After a series of negotiations, the so-called ASEAN–China Closer Economic Partnership Framework Agreement was given concrete shape during the ASEAN Summit in

Cambodia in November 2002. A key feature of the ACFTA agreement is the 'early harvest' clause which commits ASEAN and the PRC to reduce their respective tariffs for certain agricultural products within three years. These 'early harvest' products are mainly those that represent about 10 per cent (or more than 600) of all tariff lines in the Harmonized System (HS) of tariff classification.[11] Tariff reduction/elimination for goods that are not included under the 'early harvest' programme are to be negotiated through the ACFTA, with negotiations to be completed by June 2004. The timetable for the formation of the ACFTA in goods for the older ASEAN members (ASEAN-5 plus Brunei) is 2010, while that for the others (i.e. Cambodia, Myanmar, Laos, the PDR and Vietnam) is 2015.

The framework agreement also commits both parties to commence negotiations for the liberalization of services and investment by early 2003. The framework agreement identified five priority areas for economic cooperation apart from trade liberalization and facilitation measures: agriculture, HRD, ICT, investment and the Mekong River basin development. It agrees to implement capacity building programmes and provide technical assistance for newer ASEAN members to help them catch up with the ASEAN-6 members and increase their trade and investment cooperation with the PRC.

The ACFTA is a significant development in Asian regionalism, not only because it is the first such agreement that the PRC has entered into since becoming a WTO member, but also because it is going to be one of the largest FTAs ever negotiated, involving about 1.7 billion people, over US$ 2 trillion in aggregate GDP and US$1.2 in total trade spanning eleven diverse and heterogeneous economies (in terms both of their size and levels of development). The ACFTA will invariably offer first-mover advantages to businesses from both the PRC and ASEAN into one another's markets. Another big benefit of an ACFTA will be to reduce transactions costs and ensure the procurement of parts and components can be done in the region efficiently, hence benefiting all countries involved in the regional production network. The creation of the ACFTA also effectively raizes the costs of engaging in conflict among the countries involved and offers more systematic procedures and avenues to negotiate areas of dispute, thus possibly contributing to greater regional stability.

While the ACFTA ought to speed up the growing mutual interdependence between ASEAN and the PRC, its impact on individual ASEAN member economies is likely to be felt differentially depending upon the extent to which its economic structure and composition of trade complements or competes with that of the PRC. Without getting into details about the likely impact of the ACFTA, which is well beyond the scope of this chapter, simulation results by Roland-Holst and van der Mensbrugghe (2002) using a global forecasting model leads them to conclude that there is likely to be little enthusiasm for an ACFTA arrangement outside East Asia, and that the ACFTA offers a real incentive paradox, where China's participation is critical to the benefits enjoyed by other regional partners, but they cannot provide the depth and diversity of demand and supply that China needs to maintain stable terms of trade.

Differential potential effects of the ACFTA may well act as a roadblock preventing its full implementation. Nonetheless, an immediate positive side effect of the proposal is that it appears to have provided an impetus for ASEAN countries to hasten the process of intra-ASEAN integration. It has also had further 'domino effects', with the other major economic powers in Asia (Japan, India and Korea), also seeking trade pacts with ASEAN. In addition, the US President, George W. Bush, launched the Enterprise for ASEAN Initiative (EAI) during the APEC Summit in October 2002 to strengthen bilateral trade linkages with ASEAN (Lien, 2002). All of this in turn has offered ASEAN the potential to act as a hub, with the consequent benefits of being one.

ASEAN needs to encourage and act on such courtships in parallel with the implementation of the ACFTA for their own sake and also to act as buffers against the PRC's dominance in the South-East Asian region. At the same time, it is imperative that ASEAN maintain its cohesion and reinvigorate efforts to foster more intensive intra-ASEAN economic integration. Failure to do so could lead to a loss of hub status as the larger economic powers come to view ASEAN as a body that is disjointed and uncoordinated. There was a growing perception that this was the case during the height of the East Asian crisis in 1997–8 (Chang and Rajan, 1999, 2001); ASEAN has done remarkably well since then to rebuild its image in this regard. Greater efforts need to be made to deepen intra-ASEAN integration; current extra regional initiatives should not distract ASEAN from furthering its own regional integration under AFTA and the ASEAN Investment Agreement (AIA) (Kesavapany, 2003).

Some individual ASEAN members have aggressively sought to form bilateral trade pacts with extra regional countries separately from ASEAN. In particular, Singapore has gained first-mover advantage over other ASEAN members by seeking out its own bilateral trade pacts with a number of countries in Asia and elsewhere (Rajan, Sen and Siregar, 2001; Rajan and Sen, 2003b). For instance, while there are ongoing discussions on an ASEAN-Korea FTA, there have simultaneously been separate negotiations between Korea and Singapore on a bilateral basis. The same is true with regard to India and ASEAN wherein a Framework Agreement for Comprehensive Economic Cooperation (CEC) was signed in October 2003 on the one hand and negotiations between India and Singapore are ongoing, on the other. The formation of an India–Singapore Comprehensive Economic Cooperation Agreement (CECA) was proposed during the Indian Prime Minister's visit to Singapore, 2000, the scope of which has been studied by a Joint Study Group (JSG).[12] The study group has now tabled its recommendations, and negotiations on the CECA are ongoing. This agreement is expected to be as comprehensive as a FTA, covering trade in goods and services as well as trade-generating investments. The Comprehensive Economic Perspective (CEP) is expected to be fully operationalized by early in the next decade. The Framework Agreement for creation of an India–Thailand FTA within a decade has also been signed recently.

Both the PRC and India are now much more focused on opportunities for mutual rather than zero-sum gains. There are signs of intensified business and economic interactions between them, as there are in bilateral cultural and political ties (Nagpal, 2003). There has in fact been a serious suggestion regarding the possible formation of a bilateral FTA at some stage (Li Wei, 2003). As direct bilateral ties are fortified, the need for third countries to act as middlemen appears to be fast diminishing. Growing emphasis is being placed in some circles on pan-Asian regional integration involving Japan, ASEAN, China, India and Korea (JACIK) (Kumar, 2002). This is a potentially important initiative that ought to be further explored.

Appendix

Table 9A.1 Classification of commodities according to relative factor intensities (Garnaut and Anderson, 1980)

Unskilled labour-intensive goods	SITC code	Technology-intensive goods	SITC code
Textile yarn, n.e.s.	65	Medicinal and pharmacy products	54
Textile yarn	651	Fertilizers, manufactures	56
Cotton fabrics, woven	652	Explosives and pyrotechnic	57
Fabrics, woven of man-made fibres	653	Artificial resins and plastic materials	58
Other textile fibres	654		
Total	**651–654**	Chemical material and products	59
Special textile fabrics	657	Automatic data process	752
Glass	664	Parts, n.e.s and accessories	759
Glassware	665	Telecommunication equipment	76
Pottery	666		
Total	**664–666**	Electrical machinery and parts thereof	77–775
Sanitary, plumb fixtures	81		
Furniture and parts	82	Professional, scientific and controlling instruments	87
Travel goods	83		
Apparel and clothing accessories	84	Photographic apparatus – watch clock	88–885
Footwear	85	**Physical capital-intensive goods**	**SITC code**
Misc. jewellery, art, antiques	89–896–897	Organic chemicals	51
Baby carriages, toy	894	Inorganic chemicals	52
Human capital-intensive goods	**SITC code**	Iron and steel	67
Essential oils	55	Non-ferrous metals	68
Rubber manufactures	62	Power generating machinery	71
Paper, paperboard	64	Machinery specialized	72
Metal manufactures, n.e.s.	69	Metalworking machinery	73
Household electric and non-electric equipment	775	General industrial machinery and equipment, n.e.s.	74
Road vehicles	78	Office machines	751
Other transport equipment	79		
Watches and clocks	885		
Works of art and jewellery	896–897		

Source: Garnaut and Anderson (1980).

Notes

1. This chapter draws partly on Rajan (2003a,b) and Srivastava and Sen (2004). The authors are grateful to Mukul Asher, Rahul Sen and an anonymous referee for useful comments and suggestions on an earlier draft. This chapter was completed while the second author was a Visiting Freeman Foundation Scholar at the Department of Economics, Claremont McKenna College (CMC). He is grateful for the generous support provided by the Freeman Foundation as well as for the excellent research facilities made available to him at the Lowe Institute of Political Economy, CMC. The usual disclaimer applies.
2. Note that the terms PRC and China are used interchangeably throughout this chapter, as the analysis is restricted to Mainland China.
3. For details of the Southeast Asian financial crisis, see Rajan (1998).
4. McKibbin and Woo (2002) model the impact of the PRC's WTO accession as a reduction in the risk premium demanded by export-oriented investors as the PRC becomes a more reliable supplier to international markets.
5. This is even more so in the case of the other emerging Asian giant, India (Rajan and Sen, 2002, 2003a).
6. Also see Wei (1999) who makes a similar argument using a gravity model. If one considers Hong Kong and the PRC together, the improvement in the PRC's rankings would be more impressive, as Hong Kong rose from 2 to 4.
7. Of course, this argument runs both ways. As trade barriers in the PRC continue to decline and infrastructural and communications facilities improve further, FDI may move from some ASEAN countries to the PRC, and the ASEAN markets will be served from the PRC in the face of competitive pressures and falling margins.
8. The Indian official data puts bilateral trade in 2001–2 at US\$ 3000 million, substantially lower than the PRC's figures.
9. 'White goods' include large household appliances such as refrigerators, stoves, air conditioners and washing machines.
10. The results must be interpreted with some degree of caution, however, as the Garnaut–Anderson classification is only based on the 3-digit product level which does not adequately differentiate between the final good and its parts and components.
11. The 'early harvest' products belong to the following categories: Live animals, Meat and edible meat offal, Fish, Dairy produce, Other animal products, Live trees, Edible vegetables, and Edible fruits and nuts (MTI, 2002).
12. See Mehta (2003), Sen (2002) and Mohanty (2003) for in-depth discussions on India–Singapore economic relations. See Asher and Sen *et al.* (2004) (2003) for an exploration of ASEAN–India economic relations.

References

Adhikari, A. and Y. Yang, 'China's Increasing Openness: Threat or Opportunity?', ADB, Manila (23 February 2002).

ASEAN–China Expert Group on Economic Cooperation, 'Forging Closer ASEAN-China Economic Relations in the 21st Century' (October 2002).

ASEAN FDI Database, ASEAN Secretariat, Jakarta (2002).

ASEAN Trade Statistics Database, ASEAN Secretariat, Jakarta (2002), http://www.asean sec.org.

Asher, M., R. Sen and S. Srivastava, 'ASEAN–India: Emerging Economic Opportunities', in F. Grare and A. Mattoo (eds), *Beyond the Rhetoric: The Economics of India's Look-East Policy* (New Delhi: CSH-Manohar, 2003).

Asian Development Bank (ADB), *Key Indicators of Developing Asian Pacific Countries*, XXXIII (Manila: ADB, 2002).

Balassa, B. and M. Noland, 'The Changing Comparative Advantage of Japan and the United States', *Journal of the Japanese and International Economy*, 3 (1989): 174–88.

Bhagwati, J., 'The Global Age: From a Sceptical South to a Fearful North', *The World Economy*, 20 (1997): 259–83.

Bhaskaran, M., 'China as Potential Superpower: Regional Responses', *Deutsche Bank Research Report* (15 January 2003).

Chang, L.L. and R. Rajan, 'Regional Responses to the Southeast Asian Crisis: A Case of Self-Help or No Help?', *Australian Journal of International Affairs*, 8 (1999): 261–81.

Chang, L.L. and R. Rajan, 'The Economics and Politics of Monetary Regionalism in Asia', *ASEAN Economic Bulletin*, 18 (2001): 103–18.

Fernald, J., H. Edison and P. Lougani, 'Was China the First Domino? Assessing Links between China and the Rest of Emerging Asia', *Journal of International Money and Finance*, 18 (1999): 515–36.

Francois, J. and D. Spinanger, 'With Rags to Riches but then When?', Paper presented at the Fourth Annual Conference on Global Economic Analysis, Purdue University, Indiana (27–29 June 2001).

Garnaut, R. and K. Anderson, 'ASEAN Export Specialization and the Evolution of Comparative Advantage in the Western Pacific Region', in R. Garnaut (ed.), *ASEAN in a Changing Pacific and World Economy* (Canberra: ANU Press, 1980).

Gartner Research, 'Comparison: Indian and Chinese Software Services Markets', *Gartner Research Report*, M-16–1762 (May 2002).

Kesavapany, K., 'ASEAN's Contribution to the Building of an Asian Economic Community', RIS Discussion Paper 50, Research and Information Systems for the Non-Aligned and Developing Countries (RIS), New Delhi, India (2003).

Kumar, N., 'Towards an Asian Economic Community-Vision of Closer Economic Cooperation in Asia: An Overview', RIS Discussion Paper 32, Research and Information Systems for the Non-Aligned and Developing Countries (RIS), New Delhi, India (2002).

Kwan, C.H., 'The Rise of China and Asia's Flying-Geese Pattern of Economic Development: An Empirical Analysis Based on US Import Statistics', NRI Papers 52, Nomura Research Institute, Tokyo (2002).

Lall, S., 'Assessing Industrial Competitiveness: How Does Singapore Fare?', in R. Rajan (ed.), *Sustaining Competitiveness in the New Global Economy: A Case Study of Singapore* (Cheltenham: Edward Elgar, 2003).

Lall, S. and N. Albaladejo, 'The Competitive Impact of China on Manufactured Exports by Emerging Economies in Asia', Paper prepared for UNIDO, Queen Elizabeth House, University of Oxford (2001).

Li Wei, 'A Road to Common Prosperity – Examination of an FTA between India and China', RIS Discussion Paper 49, Research and Information Systems for the Non-Aligned and Developing Countries (RIS), New Delhi, India (2003).

Lien, J., 'Bush Targets FTAs with More ASEAN Nations', *Business Times*, Singapore (28 October 2002).

Martin, W. and E. Ianchovichina, 'Implications of China's Accession to the World Trade Organisation for China and the WTO', *The World Economy*, 24 (2001): 1205–19.

Mattoo, A., 'China's Accession to the WTO: The Services Dimension', Policy Research Working Paper 2932, The World Bank (2002).

McKibbin, W. and W.T. Woo, 'The Consequences of China's WTO Accession on its Neighbors' (2002), mimeo.

Mehta, R., 'Economic Co-operation Between India and Singapore: A Feasibility Study', RIS Discussion Paper 41, Research and Information Systems for the Non-Aligned and Developing Countries (RIS), New Delhi, India (2003).

Ministry of Trade and Industry (MTI), 'China's Rising Investment in Southeast Asia: How ASEAN and Singapore Can Benefit', *Annual Report*, Singapore (2001): 99–120.

Ministry of Trade and Industry (MTI), 'Foreign Direct Investments to China and Southeast Asia: Has ASEAN Been Losing Out?', *Economic Survey of Singapore*, 3rd Quarter, Singapore (2002): 96–115.

Mirza, H., 'Reviving FDI Inflows in Southeast Asia', University of Bradford School of Management (2001), mimeo.

Mohanty, S., 'Possibility of Closer Economic Cooperation Between India and Singapore', RIS Discussion Paper 45, Research and Information Systems for the Non-Aligned and Developing Countries (RIS), New Delhi, India (2003).

Nagpal, N. *'India Strategy: The Emergence of the Indian Exporter'*, Deutsche Bank Report, (25 April 2003).

Ng, F. and A. Yeats, 'Production Sharing in East Asia: Who Does What for Whom, and Why?', in L.K. Cheng and H. Kierzkowski (eds), *Global Production and Trade in East Asia* (Boston: Kluwer Academic, 2001).

Rajan, R., 'Liberalization and Foreign Capital Flows in the Presence of Uncertainty and Irreversibility: Theory and Policy Considerations', *Development and International Cooperation*, 10 (1994): 75–98.

Rajan, R., 'Economic Collapse in Southeast Asia', *Policy Study*, The Lowe Institute of Political Economy (Claremont, California, July 1998).

Rajan, R., 'Implications of the Emergence of the PRC as an Economic Power for ASEAN: Threat, Opportunity, or Both?', Unpublished report for the Asian Development Bank (April 2003a).

Rajan, R., 'Emergence of China as an Economic Power: What Does it Imply for Southeast Asia?', *Economic and Political Weekly*, 38 (28 June 2003b): 2639–44.

Rajan, R. and R. Sen, 'A Decade of Trade Reforms in India: How it Compares with East Asia', *World Economics*, 3 (2002): 1–14.

Rajan, R. and R. Sen, 'India's Decade Long Trade Reforms: How Does it Compare with its East Asian Neighbors?', in R. Rajan (ed.), *Economic Globalization and Asia: Essays on Finance, Trade and Taxation* (Singapore: World Scientific Press, 2003a).

Rajan, R. and R. Sen, 'The Japan–Singapore Trade Pact: A "New Age" Economic Partnership Agreement for the New Millennium', in P. Davidson, *Trading Arrangements in the Pacific Rim* (New York: Oceana Publications, 2003b).

Rajan, R. and R. Siregar, 'Private Capital Flows in East Asia: Boom, Bust and Beyond', in G. de Brouwer (ed.), *Financial Markets and Policies in East Asia* (London: Routledge, 2002).

Rajan, R., R. Sen and R. Siregar, *Singapore's Attraction to Free Trade Areas: Bilateral Trade Relations with Japan and the US* (Singapore: Institute of Southeast Asian Studies, 2001).

Roland-Holst, D. and D. van der Mensbrugghe, 'China and the WTO: Beginning of the End for East Asian Regionalism', Unpublished report, Asian Development Bank Institute (2002).

Sarma, A. and P. Mehta, 'Indo-ASEAN Trade Prospects: A Study of Trade Complementarity', in F. Grare and A. Mattoo (eds), *'Beyond the Rhetoric: The Economics of India's Look-East Policy'* (New Delhi: CSH-Manohar, 2003).

Sen, R., 'Singapore–India Economic Relations in the Context of their Globalization Strategies', Unpublished PhD Thesis, National University of Singapore (2002).

Sen, R., M. Asher and R. Rajan, 'ASEAN–India Economic Relations: Current Trends and Future Prospects', Public Policy Programme (PPP) Working Paper No. 54, National University of Singapore (2004).

Shafaeddin, S.M., 'The Impact of China's Accession to WTO on the Exports of Developing Countries', Working Paper 160, UNCTAD (2002).

Srivastava, S. and R. Sen, 'Competing for Global FDI: Opportunities and Challenges for the Indian Economy', *South Asia Economic Journal*, 5 (2004), forthcoming.

Tschang, T., 'China's Software Industry and its implications for India', *Development Centre Technical Paper*, 205, Paris: OECD (2003).

United Nations Conference on Trade and Development (UNCTAD), *World Investment Report 2002* (Geneva: UNCTAD, 2002).

Wattanapruttipaisan, T., 'The Newer ASEAN Member Countries and ASEAN–China FTA: Additional Market Access and More Challenging Competition' (June 2002), mimeo.

Wei, S.J., 'Can China and India Double their Inward Foreign Direct Investment' (November 1999), mimeo.

World Bank, *World Development Report* (New York: Oxford University Press, 2002).

World Bank, *World Development Indicators*, CD-Rom (2002b).

World Trade Organization (WTO), *International Trade Statistics Yearbook* (Geneva: WTO, 2000).

Wu, F., M.H. Toh, T.S. Poa, K.W. Seah and T.K. Lim, 'Potential of the Chinese (PRC) and Indian Tourism Markets for ASEAN', *Economic Survey of Singapore*, 2nd Quarter, Ministry of Trade and Industry, Singapore (2002a).

Wu, F., T.S. Pao, H.S. Yeo and K.K. Phua, 'Foreign Direct Investments to China and Southeast Asia: Has ASEAN Been Losing Out?', *Economic Survey of Singapore*, 3rd Quarter, Ministry of Trade and Industry, Singapore (2002b).

10
Foreign Investment, Foreign Trade and Related Issues: A Case Study for India and China

P.K. Vasudeva[1]

1 Introduction

The unprecedented build-up of foreign exchange reserves in India, to the tune of US$ 120 billion (1 August, 2004) after the payment of more than US$ 2 billion debt by the Reserve Bank of India (RBI), is seen as a sign of economic growth. In the early 1990s, when India's foreign exchange reserves were averaging close to US$ 5.5 billion, the country was in a balance of payment (BOP) crisis. The RBI's balance of payment statistics suggest that about US$ 1.3 billion of these reserves are on account of foreign direct investment (FDI) inflows during the year 2002–3. A healthy increase in FDI inflows in India in a global slowdown cannot detract from the fact that India accounts for an extremely small share of FDI inflows. China attracts 80 per cent of the FDI inflows in Asia against India's 5.5 per cent. China's membership at the World Trade Organisation (WTO) from November 2001 is likely to widen this gap.

Although FDI inflows have risen, however, they continue to be way behind China. India's share among the developing countries in terms of attracting FDI is only 1.7 per cent compared to China's 17 per cent. Besides China, India attracts significantly lower FDI than many other South East Asian countries such as South Korea, Thailand and Malaysia. In 2000, China attracted over US$ 44 billion FDI, Thailand over US$ 6 billion and South Korea around US$ 10.45 billion. The corresponding figure for India was US$ 3.19 billion.

The objectives of this chapter are first, to analyse why FDI inflows into India are poor (Sections 2–3); secondly, to formulate a strategy to enhance FDI inflows into India especially when China's FDI inflows are much more (Sections 4–8); thirdly, to find out the level of FDI inflows in the developing countries, and suggest measures for improvement in India (Sections 9–11).

2   FDI slippage

According to International Monetary Fund (IMF) Report (IMF, 2002), India's absolute attractiveness had improved compared to the previous survey in June 1999. However, after the international credit rating agency's revising India's long-term rupee debt to 'junk', there was a further blow to the country's efforts to bolstering FDI inflows. India slipped eight spots to fifteenth position in the index ranking of the Foreign Direct Investment Confidence Index (FDICI) released by the global management consulting firm A.T. Kearney (Kearney, 2002). The FDICI is constructed on the basis of the response received from the senior management managers (board-level positions) of *Fortune* 1000 companies. The main cause of this slippage is the simmering conflict with Pakistan over Jammu and Kashmir, which undoubtedly deters foreign investment, while fiscal deficit and poor infrastructure have further constrained India's attractiveness. According to the FDICI report India will now have to face a nearly 20 per cent decline in the likelihood of receiving FDI.

India's attractiveness has, however, improved significantly among non-financial services, where investment likelihood increased by 28 per cent over 2001. In the post-9/11 events, India's high-quality and lower-cost IT talents attracted more IT-related outsourcing services. In other telecoms and utilities, investors consider India as their twenty-fifth most attractive investment destination. Among investor nations, although India's ranking dropped the most, its position among Japanese investors and in the USA is holding steady. It should be a matter of grave concern to India that its FDI investments are going down rather than increasing.

One of the other main causes of India's poor FDI is a labour problem as the trade unions rule the roost. The Labour Commission Report (2002) suggested that a 'hire and fire' system for inefficient staff should be immediately implemented to improve FDI inflows.

3   Indian FDI statistics

In the case of India, FDI statistics are published by two official sources: (a) the Reserve Bank of India (RBI) and (b) the Secretariat for Industrial Assistance (SIA). The RBI presents a BOP statement in the *RBI Bulletin* and its *Annual Report* on a monthly and annual basis, respectively. SIA reports FDI inflows on both approval and actual basis in its monthly *SIA Newsletter* and *SIA Statistics*. Interestingly, the definition of FDI and computation of FDI statistics used by the RBI does not conform to the IMF guidelines; there are a number of discrepancies in the RBI projections:

- First, India excludes *reinvested earnings* (which are part of foreign investor profits that are not distributed to shareholders as dividends are reinvested in the affiliates in the host country) when estimating actual FDI inflows. According to the IMF guidelines, these reinvested earnings are a part of FDI inflows, and should be recorded as inflows on the capital account of the host country's BOP.

• Second, India does not include the proceeds of *foreign equity listings and foreign subordinated loans to domestic subsidiaries* which, according to the IMF guidelines, are part of inter-company loans (long- and short-term net loans from the parent to the subsidiary) and should be a part of FDI inflows.

• Third, India excludes *overseas commercial borrowings*, whereas, according to the IMF guidelines, financial leasing, trade credits, grants, bonds, etc. should be included in FDI estimates.

• Fourth, as per IMF standards, if a shareholding of 10 per cent or more is acquired eventually by a non-resident who entered initially through the portfolio route but holds investment aggregating over 10 per cent through the purchase of additional shares in subsequent transactions, those additional shares should be regarded as a part of FDI. However, in India some Foreign Institutional Investors (FIIs) hold well over 20 per cent of the equity in the form of American Depository Receipts (ADRs) and Global Depository Receipts (GDRs), but these are not a part of FDI.

The foregoing indicates that there is a lot of scope for improving India's FDI statistics if they are to be more consistent with IMF standards and therefore comparable with those of other countries. In an accounting sense, and abstracting from tax, depreciation and other issues, outward FDI flows by investor country ought to match inward FDI flows received by the investing country at the bilateral level. Table 10.1 highlights the discrepancy in reported FDI data among the major source countries (the USA, the UK, Japan and Germany) and the host country (India) for the period 1996–2000.

As is apparent from Table 10.1, when reported bilateral FDI data differences are computed, there is a clear distinction between countries for which India overvalues its inflows of FDI (the USA) and those for which it undervalues it (Japan and the UK).

4 Policy implications

The analysis suggests that the failure of India to adopt international guidelines on measuring FDI statistics implies that aggregate FDI data for India are not directly comparable to those of most other countries. For instance, in China reinvested earnings and intra-company loans together accounted for about 30 per cent of total FDI inflows during 1997 and about 51 per cent of total FDI inflows during 1998 (*World Investment Directory*, 2000, p. 113). Accounting for these components in FDI statistics would bring India's FDI figures much closer to those of China. This is especially true because official

Table 10.1   FDI data, India: SIA vs. OECD, 1996–2000

Investing partners	1996	1997	1998	1999	2000	Mean*	SD**
India's FDI: inward flows, by country – SIA data (US$ million)							
USA	267.58	709.81	332.23	420.62	320.87		
UK	51.09	91.41	53.55	91.97	57.19		
Japan	84.96	107.66	189.26	147.72	151.54		
Germany	133.51	156.67	151.94	45.99	74.32		
India's direct investment from abroad: outflows, by country – OECD data (US$ million)							
USA	262.00	267.00	80.00	−76.00	−67.00		
UK	171.61	280.33	341.06	250.81	275.34		
Japan	226.98	439.67	251.36	203.71	171.55		
Germany	101.66	100.92	292.21	255.80	178.79		
FDI: discrepancy statistics – author's calculation (per cent)							
USA	2.09	62.38	75.92	118.07	120.88	75.87	48.60
UK	−235.90	−206.67	−536.85	−172.69	−381.47	−306.72	151.30
Japan	−167.16	−308.40	−32.81	−37.91	−13.21	−111.90	125.60
Germany	23.86	35.58	−92.32	−456.24	−140.56	−125.94	199.40

Notes
* *Mean is the average FDI discrepancy from 1996 to 2000.*
** Standard deviation (SD) is the square root of the variance of FDI differences.

Sources: Secretariat for Industrial Assistance (SIA) *Newsletter* (January 1997–January 2001) and OECD (2000), *International Direct Investment Statistics Yearbook* (2000).

FDI figures for China may be somewhat inflated, and need to be interpreted with caution. For instance, while Hong Kong has been a major direct investor, part of the investments may be due to 'round-tripping' from the mainland as domestic (Chinese) investors try to take advantage of tax and tariff benefits extended to foreign investors. Exaggeration of FDI figures by each region in China may also be done for political purposes (one-upmanship among states/cities within China).

Thus, according to the International Financial Corporation (IFC) *World Business Environment Survey* (2002) (WBES), the FDI gap between India and China is not nearly as large as may be suggested by official figures. According to the WBES report, if FDI figures are adjusted for both 'round-tripping' in case of China and underestimation of FDI inflows in case of India, the difference in terms of the ratio of adjusted FDI to GDP is quite close, only about 15 per cent during 2000. This adjustment takes account of nearly 50 per cent of total FDI inflows round-tripped to China during 1999 and 2000 which reduces FDI net inflows from $ 40 billion to $ 20 billion, and also takes into account India's adoption of a standard computation of FDI, which raises the latter's net FDI inflows from US$ 2–3 billion a year to about US$ 8 billion

Table 10.2 Relative market sizes of India and China and purchasing power, 2000

Countries	India	China	India's share to that of China (per cent)
Real GDP (US$ billion)	467	1,040	0.45
GN, PPP (current international $ billion)	2,375	4,951	0.48
GNP per capita, PPP (current international $ billion)	2,340	3,920	0.59
FDI net inflows (per cent of GDP)	0.5	3.6	13.90
Adjusted FDI net inflows (per cent of GDP)	1.7	2	85.00

Comparison between measured and adjusted FDI of India and China, 2000

	India		China	
	Measured FDI*	Adjusted FDI**	Measured FDI*	Adjusted FDI**
FDI net inflows (current US$ billion)	2.3	8.0	39.0	20.0
FDI net inflows (per cent of GDP)	0.5	1.7	3.6	2.0

Notes
* Figures published by official sources.
** Based on IFC's *World Business Environment Survey* (2002).

Sources: Calculated from World Bank, *World Development Indicators* (2002); and IFC, *World Business Environment Survey: Economic Prospects for Developing Countries* (March 2002).

(Table 10.2). China's cumulative figures remain far higher than India's by virtue of the fact that China liberalized its trade and investment regime a decade before India did.

If officially published figures are incorrect, it contributes to flawed perceptions about India attracting 'too little' FDI among foreign investors. Given the 'herd mentality' of investors, this in turn could dampen confidence in the country on the part of other prospective investors, trapping India in self-fulfilling low investment equilibrium. Therefore, correct signalling through proper dissemination of data is required to ensure that perceptions are not too out of line with reality. India urgently needs to update its data dissemination standards to global standards, for its own sake and as a policy instrument for attracting global FDI. Some of the possible ways to improve data coverage may be as follows:

- The *indirect ownership* in subsidiaries, associates and branches ought to be included so that total and reinvested earnings are not understated. When a direct investor decides to invest in his subsidiary abroad by borrowing on the subsidiary's local market, the flow does not appear in the balance of payments.

- An *offsetting entry for reinvested earnings* (with opposite sign) could be included in current account flows that are recorded under direct investment income.
- Evaluating *project costs* vs. *equity investment* for India would be very useful in comparing India's FDI flows pre- and post- the Asian crisis and with those of other economies in Asia. India reports approvals on equity only, while South East and East Asian countries take project costs, which are usually higher than the value of foreign equity by three to four times and hence the differences are even more exaggerated.
- The FDI data does not give the classification for *NRI (non-resident Indian) investments* by country of origin. If such data could be disseminated, it would be possible to trace NRI investment from the different source that are available.
- *Actual FDI inflows* are available only for the top five investor countries from 1996. It would be more useful to have continuous time series trend for actual inflows by other source countries and across industries.[2]

The fact that India's FDI is somewhat higher than the official numbers since they are not in line with IMF standards has been known for a while. However, it is only now that the revised numbers are kicking in. The chief economist of the IFC, Guy Peffermann, pointed out in 2002 that India's annual foreign investment inflows were much higher than the official estimate of US$ 2–3 billion as they did not include reinvested earnings, subordinated debt and overseas commercial borrowings. With such inclusions as per IMF standards, overall FDI went up threefold, to US$ 8 billion in 2000.

5   FDI approvals and their composition

India's actual FDI inflow, as estimated by four different agencies for 1991–2000, is shown in Table 10.3. The IMF's and the *World Investment Report*'s estimates of the cumulative inflow during the 1990s are roughly the same – about US$ 17 billion. The *Economic Survey of India* estimate is about US$ 22 billion, while that by the RBI is US$ 17.3 billion. The difference between the last two estimates is mainly on account of ADR/GDR inflows. While the *Economic Survey of India* classifies them as FDI, the RBI records them under foreign portfolio investment.

As there has been a gradual improvement in the actual inflow from a low base, and a slowdown in approvals after 1997, there is an increase in the ratio of the actual to approved FDI since the mid-1990s. On average, it is a little over one-third in the 1990s. India's share in world foreign investment increased from 0.5 per cent in 1992 to 2.2 per cent in 1997. Approved FDI rose from about Rs 500 crore in 1992 to about Rs 55,000 crore in 1997

Table 10.3 Alternative estimates of actual FDI, 1991–2000

Year	Economic survey (Rs crore)	RBI (Rs. crore)	International financial statistics (million) $	World investment report (million) $
1991	351	316		155
1992	675	965	276.5	261
1993	1,787	1,836	550.1	586
1994	3,289	4,126	973.3	947
1995	6,820	7,172	2,143.6	2,144
1996	10,389	10,015	2,426.1	2,591
1997	16,425	13,220	3,577.3	3,616
1998	13,340	10,358	2,634.7	2,614
1999	16,868	9,338	2,168.6	2,154
2000	19,342	10,686	2,315.1	2,315
Total	89,286	68,034	17,065.3	17,080

Sources: *Economic Survey of India* (various issue); RBI, *Handbook of Statistics on Indian Economy* (2001); IMF, *International Financial Statistics*, CD-ROM; UN, *World Investment Report* (various issues).

Table 10.4 Share of FDI, 2001 (per cent)

Country/region	Share
USA	20.4
Mauritius	11.9
UK	6.4
Japan	4.0
South Korea	3.9
Germany	3.4
Australia	2.7
Malaysia	2.3
France	2.1
Netherlands	1.9

Note: In addition to the countries, external commercial borrowings and NRIs contributed 17.2 and 3.9 per cent, respectively, of FDI approvals.

Source: *Handbook of Industrial Policy and Statistics* (2001).

(*Economic Survey of India*, 2001–2). Cumulative approved foreign investment during 1991 and 2000, in dollar terms, is about US$ 67 billion – at an average exchange rate of Rs. 40 to a dollar. A fifth of it is from the USA (Table 10.4). Mauritius is the second largest source; reportedly a conduit for

Table 10.5   Sectoral distribution of FDI approvals, 1991–2000

Sector	No. of approvals	Approved investment (Rs billion)	Share (per cent)
Power and fuel	541	634,531.2	25.7
Telecoms	579	458,845.0	18.5
Services sector	790	152,389.0	6.2
Chemicals (other than fertilizers)	809	123,016.2	5.0
Food processing	648	87,574.9	3.5
Transport sector	722	184,467.6	7.5
Metallurgical industries	304	143,796.8	5.8
Electric equipment (including software)	2,491	245,791.5	10.0
Textiles	548	33,617.8	1.4
Paper and paper products	111	31,580.6	1.3
Industrial machinery	530	22,438.5	0.9
Others	2,404	348,976.2	14.2
Total	**11,965**	**247,025.3**	**100.0**

Note: Data are for the period, August 1991–March 1998.

Source: *Handbook of Industrial Policy and Statistics* (2001).

many US-based firms as India has a tax avoidance treaty since 1982. In Asia, South Korea has emerged as a new source of foreign investment.

A quarter of the approved FDI is for power generation (Table 10.5), followed by telecoms (mobile phone firms) at 18.5 per cent and electrical equipment (mainly software) at 10 per cent. While the proportion of projects with investment up to Rs 5 crore is high, their share is less than 5 per cent in value. At the other end of the distribution, larger projects with Rs 100 crore and above account for over two-thirds of the total value of approvals. Evidently, very little of the FDI has gone to augment exports that are mostly from-laboured intensive unregistered manufacturing.

6   The IMF report on FDI

IMF, which had projected a 5.5 per cent growth for India in April 2002, scaled it down to 5 per cent for the financial year 2002–3 in the face of the sluggish recovery of the economy and drought (IMF, *World Economic Outlook*, 25 September 2002): 'In India cyclic recovery is under way, although agriculture has been negatively affected by a poor monsoon, and the regional security situation and higher oil prices are sources of risk.' The IMF has forecast low growth not only in India but the entire South Asian region, which is now expected to post an average 4.8 per cent growth in 2002–3 against the earlier projections of 5.2 per cent. The report said that the tense situation in Jammu and Kashmir and the drought in several parts of the country due to poor monsoons had hit farm production, which was expected to face a shortfall of several million tones. Even the RBI brought down the growth projections of 6–6.5 per cent, announced in April 2002, to 5 per cent.

Though the IMF praised India for the 'significant progress' made in its disinvestments programme and the opening up of the oil sector, the report was critical of the slow progress of economic reforms: 'A large unfinished agenda remains, including further opening up to trade and foreign investment, removing restrictions on agricultural and industrial activity and in strengthening the financial system.' However, it forecast a higher growth for 2003 at 5.7 per cent. The IMF urged India to reduce its average tariff rate to 12 per cent from the current average rate of about 30 per cent and also to remove other barriers and red tape. 'Its average bilateral trade flow would then increase by about 44 per cent.'

The report found that between 1980 and 2000 India's trade openness had increased by about 50 per cent compared to about 150 per cent for China over the same time frame. India's share of world export then increased to just 0.7 per cent from 0.5 per cent in twenty years while China's share of trade more than tripled over the same time period, to almost 4 per cent.

7   The RBI on foreign investment inflows

The *RBI Report* (2003) stated that after recording an annual inflow of over US$ 5 billion for three consecutive years, Indian foreign investment inflows dipped to US$ 3.6 billion in 2002–3. This includes both FDI and portfolio investment by FIIs. After recording the highest growth in 2001–2 since liberalisation, FDI dipped to US$ 2.6 billion in 2002–3 from a high of US$ 5.3 billion in 2001. This includes equity acquisition, inflows by NRIs and those cleared by Secretariat for Industrial Assistance (SIA)/Foreign Investment Promotion Board (FIPB) inflows and money brought in by off-shore funds and other inflows amounted to only US$ 979 million during the year, with the majority (US$ 600 million) coming by way of ADR/GDR. FII inflows (as per the RBI definition) amounted to only US$ 377 million during the year.[3]

Interestingly, according to the Department of Industrial Policy and Promotion's *Annual Report* for 2002–3 released in April, India had recorded the highest-ever FDI realisation rate inflows to approval ratio of 191.1 per cent in rupee terms during 2002. Total FDI inflows during 2002 were US$ 4.4 billion (Rs 21,286 crore) including ADRs/GDRs and advance pending issue of shares. Net inflows of ADRs/GDRs during 2002 were Rs 18,195.6 crore, which is 8.5 per cent higher in rupee terms compared to 2001. Interestingly, this growth was achieved at a time when global FDI flows were showing a sharp fall (Table 10.6).

Table 10.6   Investment inflows, 1997–2003 ($ billion)

Year	FDI	Portfolio	Investment total
1997–8	3.6	1.8	5.4
1998–9	2.5	−0.1	2.4
1999–2000	2.2	3.0	5.2
2000–1	2.3	2.8	5.1
2001–2	3.9	2.0	5.9
2002–3	2.6	0.9	3.6

Source: RBI Report (2003).

Policies in the post-reform period have emphasized greater encouragement and mobilization of non-debt-creating private capital inflows for reducing reliance on debt flows as the chief source of external resources. Progressively liberal policies adopted have led to increasing inflows of foreign investment, in terms of both FDI as well as portfolio investment. A disaggregated time series profile of foreign investment inflows is given in Table 10.7. At a more micro level, a monthwise illustration of foreign investment inflows for the first seven months of 2001–2 and 2002–3 are given in Table 10.8.

Annual aggregate foreign investment inflows varied between US$ 4 billion and US$ 6 billion during the period 1993–4 to 2001–2 (except for 1998–9). The average volume of foreign investment inflows during the period is estimated to be roughly US$ 4.9 billion (US$ 5.2 billion excluding 1998–9). Inflows during April–October 2002 were around 53 per cent of the inflows during the period 1993–4. The reduced volume of inflows is attributable to heavy outflow of portfolio investment during 2002.

FDI inflows are an indicator of the foreign investor community's long-term stake in the host economy. A time series profile of FDI inflows into selected Asian host economies is given in Table 10.9. In 2001, the developing economies of Asia accounted for around 14 per cent of total global FDI inflows. China has been the largest recipient of FDI inflows among the developing economies of Asia, with its share in total FDI of these economies increasing from 43 per cent in 1996 to almost 46 per cent in 2001. India is, though, way behind China in attracting FDI inflows, which rose from 2.7 per cent in 1996 to 3.3 per cent in 2001.

Against this subdued backdrop, the spurt in FDI inflows in India in 2001–2 is remarkable, for several reasons. First, in terms of overall trends in FDI inflows into emerging markets of developing Asia, 2001 was hardly encouraging, but even then the Indian economy received its highest FDI inflows in the post-reform period, surpassing the previous high of 1997–8. Second, the major part of 2001–2 was characterized by a synchronized slowdown in the global economy, which dampened investor sentiments and tightened international

Table 10.7 Foreign investment inflows, 1991–2002

	1991–2	1992–3	1993–4	1994–5	1995–6	1996–7	1997–8	1998–9	1999–2000	2000–1	2001–2
(A) Direct investment	**129**	**315**	**586**	**1,314**	**2,144**	**2,821**	**3,557**	**2,462**	**2,155**	**2,339**	**3,904**
a SIA/FIPB	66	222	280	701	1,249	1,922	2,754	1,821	1,410	1,456	2,221
b RBI	–	42	89	171	169	135	202	179	171	454	767
c NRI	63	51	217	442	715	639	241	62	84	67	35
d Acquisition of shares*	–	–	–	–	11	125	360	400	490	362	881
(B) Portfolio investment	**4**	**244**	**3,567**	**3,824**	**2,748**	**3,312**	**1,828**	**–61**	**3,026**	**2,760**	**2,021**
a GDRs/ADRs**	–	240	1,520	2,082	683	1,366	645	270	768	831	477
b FIIs**	–	1	1,665	1,503	2,009	1,926	979	–390	2,135	1,847	1,505
c Offshore funds and others	4	3	382	239	56	20	204	59	123	82	39
Total (A) + (B)	**133**	**559**	**4,153**	**5,138**	**4,892**	**6,133**	**5,385**	**2,401**	**5,181**	**5,099**	**5,925**

Notes

* Relates to acquisition of shares of Indian companies by non-residents under Section 5 of the Foreign Exchange Management Act (FEMA) (1999). Data on such acquisitions have been included as part of FDI since January 1996.

** Represents the amount raised by Indian corporate through GDRs and ADRs.

** Represents fresh inflow of funds by FIIs.

Source: RBI.

Table 10.8 Monthly foreign investment inflows, 2002

	Apr	May	Jun	Jul	Aug	Sep	Oct	Apr–Oct 2001	Apr–Oct 2002
(A) Direct investment	**174**	**491**	**400**	**154**	**234**	**233**	**298**	**2,049**	**1,984**
a SIA/FIPB	36	212	56	70	177	71	220	1,240	842
b RBI	56	260	37	22	31	39	64	501	509
c NRI	–	–	–	–	–	–	–	30	–
d Acquisition of shares*	82	19	307	62	26	123	14	278	633
(B) Portfolio investment	**273**	**107**	**2272**	**43**	**233**	**2131**	**108**	**1,245**	**2251**
a GDRs/ADRs	–	20	–	–	–	–	117	477	137
b FIIS**	–73	87	–272	43	–33	–131	–9	729	–388
c Offshore funds and others	–	–	–	–	–	–	–	39	–
Total (A) + (B)	**101**	**598**	**128**	**197**	**201**	**102**	**406**	**3,294**	**1,733**

Notes

* Relates to acquisition of shares of Indian companies by non-residents under Section 5 of FEMA (1999). Data on such acquisitions have been included as part of FDI since January 1996.

* Represents the amount raised by Indian corporate through GDRs and ADRs.

** Represents fresh inflow of funds by FIIs.

Source: RBI, *Foreign Direct Investment Report* (2002).

Table 10.9 FDI inflows, selected Asian economies, 1996–2001

	1996	1997	1998	1999	2000	2001
World	386,140	478,082	694,457	1,088,263	1,491,934	735,146
Developed economies	219,908	267,947	484,259	837,761	1,227,476	503,144
Developing economies	152,685	191,022	187,611	225,140	237,894	204,801
Asia	93,331	105,828	96,109	102,779	133,707	102,066
South, East and South-East Asia	87,843	96,338	86,252	99,990	131,123	94,365
a China	40,180	44,237	43,751	40,319	40,772	46,848
b India	2,525	3,619	2,633	2,168	2,319	3,403
c Indonesia	6,194	4,677	−356	−2,745	−4,550	−3,277
d Korea	2,325	2,844	5,412	9,333	9,283	3,198
e Malaysia	7,296	6,324	2,714	3,895	3,788	554
g Philippines	1,520	1,249	1,752	578	1,241	1,792
g Singapore	8,608	10,746	6,389	11,803	5,407	8,609
h Thailand	2,271	3,626	5,143	3,561	2,813	3,759

Source: UNCTAD, *World Investment Report* (2002).

capital markets. But India received higher FDI inflows notwithstanding the rigidities in the global financial markets. Finally, 2001 saw the Indian economy grappling with exogenous shocks such as the Gujarat earthquake (January) and the terrorist attack on the Indian Parliament (13 December), quite apart from the calamitous attack on 11 September on the US World Trade Centre (WTC). The ability of the economy to overcome these shocks and attract record FDI inflows, points to the increasing attractiveness of India's country-specific attributes (strong macroeconomic fundamentals, expanding market, large pool of human resources, etc.), in securing FDI.

As part of the ongoing process of liberalizing FDI policies, the Planning Commission set up a Steering Committee on FDI in August 2001, to suggest measures for enhancing FDI inflows in India. The major recommendations of the Committee are given in Box 10.1. Other measures adopted during 2002 to encourage greater FDI inflows included permission for 100 per cent FDI in the development of integrated townships and regional urban infra-structure, the tea sector (including tea plantation), advertising and films, and permission to foreign firms to pay royalty on brand names/trade marks as a percentage of net sales in case of technology transfer.

In the line with more liberal policies pertaining to overseas investment by Indian firms, overseas direct investment (ODI) outflows from India have been exhibiting rising trends since the mid-1990s. Aggregate outflows rose from US$ 0.2 billion in 1995–6 to roughly US$ 1.2 billion in 2000–1. In 2001–2, the actual outflows declined to around US$ 0.9 billion. However, the previous year witnessed a sharp rise in volume of approved investment,

Box 10.1   Major recommendations of the Steering Committee on FDI set up by the
Planning Commission, August 2001

The Steering Committee on FDI set up by the Planning Commission in August
2001 has submitted its report, which is currently being considered by the
government. The main recommendations of the Committee are:

- To enact a Foreign Investment Promotion Law incorporating and integrating
  relevant aspects for promoting FDI.
- To urge States to enact a special investment law relating to infrastructure for
  expediting investment and removing hurdles to production in infrastructure.
- To empower the Foreign Investment Promotion Board (FIPB) to grant initial
  central-level registrations and approvals wherever possible, for speeding up
  the implementation process.
- To empower the Foreign Investment Implementation Authority (FIIA) to
  expedite administrative and policy approvals.
- To disaggregate FDI targets for the Tenth Plan in terms of sectors and relevant
  administrative ministries/departments, to increase accountability.
- To reduce sectoral FDI caps to the minimum and eliminate entry barriers.
  Caps can be taken off for all manufacturing and Mining activities (except
  defence), eliminated in advertising, private banks and real estate and hiked
  in telecoms, civil aviation, broadcasting, insurance and plantations (other
  than tea).
- To overhaul the existing FDI strategy by shifting from a broader macro-
  emphasis to a targeted sector-specific approach.
- Informational aspects of the FDI strategy require refinement in the light of
  India's strengths and weaknesses as an investment destination and should
  use IT and modern marketing techniques.
- The Special Economic Zones (SEZs) should be developed as internationally
  competitive destinations for export-oriented FDI, by simplifying laws, rules
  and procedures, and reducing bureaucracy on the lines of China.
- Domestic policy reforms in power, urban infrastructure and real estate, and
  de-control/de-licensing should be expedited to attract more FDI.

Source: Based on *Economic Survey of India* (2002–3).

---

which shot up from US$ 1.4 billion in 2000–1 to US$ 3 billion in 2001–2.
The increase in approvals was largely on account of higher approvals sought
for foreign equity investment, which also explains the lower materialization
of actual outflows compared to approvals, since the global equity markets
suffered from a sharp erosion in confidence, particularly after 11 September.
During the first half of 2002, actual outflows at US$ 0.4 billion, were around
40 per cent of the total approvals, worth US$ 1.1 billion. In 2002, the bulk
of India's overseas corporate investments were in the manufacturing sector,
followed by non-financial services. Sudan accounted for the largest share of
investment approvals in 2002 (US$ 0.75 billion), followed by the USA,
Mauritius and Singapore.

8   The role of FDI and FII

William Casey in *Beyond the Numbers: Foreign Direct Investment in the United States* (2002), has analysed the economic and non-economic costs that can arise if a country opens its borders to FDI. Casey suggested that FDI could accelerate economic problem in the following ways:

- Replace good jobs with bad
- Reduce real wages
- Transfer jobs back home because of a high import propensity
- Cause deterioration in the host country's trade balance
- Transfer technology back home, compromising the host country's technological secrets
- Time property acquisition in the host country to take advantage of fire-sale opportunities presented by exchange rate distortion.

Add to this the cultural and social tensions that may arise with local labour working for foreign companies and the problems of flexible accumulation of capital and capital flows, controlled by an increasing number of electronic networks. Technical changes and efficiencies of scale can make purely national markets relatively inefficient, thereby compelling businesses to spread across borders. The fiscal sacrifice involved in permitting the free entry of FIIs and FDI flows will be worth all the trouble only if a constant vigil is exercised to oversee the way the FIIs act and deploy their funds within India.

9   China and India: similar challenges

China and India – both vast countries with huge populations, have some common features. Why is China progressing so much faster than India? According to the UNDP *Human Development Report* (2002), China took an early lead in market reforms and spent much more than India on health and education. The report said that China enjoyed the fastest sustained economic advance in human history, averaging real per capita growth of 8 per cent a year over the 1990s. Its per capita income was US$ 3,976 in PPP terms. In India, however, real per capita income grew at a modest average of 4.4 per cent, reaching $ 2,358 in 2001. The proportion of people living on less than US$ 1 a day declined in China from 33 per cent in 1990 to 16 per cent in 2000, and in India from 42 per cent in 1993–4 to 35 per cent in 2001. China had been able to integrate with the global economy at a 'phenomenal' pace and was how the largest recipient of FDI among developing countries, with annual investment rising from almost zero in 1978 to about US$ 52 billion in 2002. In India, FDI also increased, but at much lower levels: from US$ 129 million in 1991 to US$ 4 billion in 2002. China also enjoyed much more success in export growth. The report noted that 'China's exports reached US$ 320 billion in 2001, compared to India's US$ 35 billion. China had particular success in moving from labour-intensive to technology-intensive exports'. China also boasted more social investments than India.[3]

Though the actual FDI inflow in India in the 1990s increased significantly, it was modest compared to many Asian economies and paled into insignificance in comparison with China. UNCTAD's (*World Investment Report*, 2001) ranking of countries in terms of foreign investment (relative to the size of the economy) for the period 1998–2000 was 119 for India, and 47 for China. The ranking in 1988 was 121 and 61, respectively (*New York Times*, 28 August 2002). It shows that even at the start of the reforms, China's ranking was way ahead of India's and China moved up the rankings much faster than India in the 1990s. However, it is well known that a large share of the investment inflow in China represents 'round tripping' – recycling of domestic savings via Hong Kong to take advantage of tax, tariffs and other benefits offered to non-resident Chinese. This is estimated to be in the range of 40–50 per cent of total FDI (IFC, *Global Financial Report*, 2002). The IFC's study of the business environment, in fact, places India marginally ahead of China, from the viewpoint of foreign investors (IFC, 2002). The study also found that the quantum of FDI inflow in China and India, as a proportion of their respective FDI, was roughly comparable. Thus, the widely held view of China's ability to attract enormous foreign capital needs to be judged with considerable circumspection.

10   FDI inflow constraints

It is typical of the Indian government to concentrate on peripheral matters instead of trying to resolve underlying problems. A good example of this relates to foreign companies wanting to test market their products in India before setting up manufacturing facilities. The Board has openly stated that India cannot turn down foreign investments, as there are so many other attractive investment destinations for foreign investors, including China, Russia, South America and a fast-improving South East Asia. It may be better to let the investors decide the timing of their investments, rather than force them to set up shop or leave. However, despite this reasoning within the Board (dominated by the Industry Ministry in the past, and likely to be led by the Finance Ministry in future) there are periodic discussions on plugging the test-marketing route. FDI in wholesale cash-and-carry forward is permitted, but not in retail trading under existing norms. Marks & Spencer, a leading UK retail chain, and Shoprite, a large South African grocery chain supermarket, have come in, as franchisee, while the retail chain German Metro AG operates its chain in the cash-and-carry format. Thus, while retail trading is not permitted under the FDI statutes, it has not stopped foreign investors from entering.

The Government of India should look at the possibility of opening up the sector, letting foreigners do their business without having to resort to such methods. FDI in retail trading is not permitted for political reasons, stemming from the trader lobby's pressure. This lobby has said that foreign retail chains will wipe out every grocer's shop from Kashmir to Kanya Kumari. Such fears are, in part, fuelled by statistics; the Indian retail sector is estimated to be worth $ 180 billion, of which the organized sector currently accounts for just 2 per cent but is estimated to reach 10 per cent over a decade – roughly a $ 3 billion market business over a ten-year timeframe.[5]

11 Conclusion

India accounts for an extremely small share of FDI inflows. China attracts 80 per cent of the FDI inflows in Asia against India's 5.5 per cent. India also attracts significantly lower FDI than many South Asian countries like South Korea, Thailand and Malaysia. From Standard and Poors, FDICI, IMF, Labour Commission, RBI and UNCTAD reports the main reasons of India's share of declining FDI have been found to be: (1) terrorism in Jammu and Kashmir and communal riots; (2) the fiscal deficit; (3) poor infrastructure; (4) severe drought due to shortfall of rains; (5) high trade barriers, which the IMF think need to be slashed by 12 per cent; and (6) poor labour reforms and lack of a hire and fire attitude, a major anti-growth element from the investors view point.

India's economic reforms began only in 1992 as compared to China, which began to liberalize twenty years earlier. However India should catch up if the present economic liberalization continues and drought can be combatted. India's attractiveness has improved significantly in the non-financial services area where investment increased by 28 per cent in 2001. India's high-quality and lower-cost IT talents have attracted significant IT-related outsourcing services. The principal determinants of FDI inflows are the openness of the economy, aggressive marketing in exports and FIIs' permission to invest: India must develop all of these.

Notes

1. I thank Mr Andrew Sumner, Development Studies Subject Area Leader, University of East London for reviewing this chapter and giving positive and useful suggestions.
2. Sadhana Srivastava, *Economic and Political Weekly* (15–21 February 2003).
3. Gayatri Nayak, *Economic Times* (24 June 2003).
4. *The Financial Express* (24 June 2003).
5. Jayanthi Iyengar, *The Hindu Business Line* (June 2003).

References

Kearney A.T., Global Management, *Foreign Direct Investment Confidence Index (FDICI) Report* (2002).
Bhattacharya, R. and F. Flatters, 'Ghana's Trade Policies: Exemptions from Import Duty', Paper Prepared for the Sigma One Corporation (September 1999).

Casey, W., *Beyond the Numbers: Foreign Direct Investment in the United States* (June 2003).

Economic Survey of India, Government of India Publications (2001–2).

Economic Survey of India, Government of India Publications (2002–3).

Global Development Finance Report, *Country and Summary Data* (2001).

International Financial Corporation, *Global Financial Report* (2002).

International Monetary Fund, *World Economic Outlook Report* (25 September 2002).

Labour Commission Report, Government of India Publications (2002).

Ministry of Commerce Report, *Exim Policy of India 2002–2007*, Government of India (2002).

RBI, *Foreign Direct Investment Report* (2002).

RBI, *Reserve Bank of India Report* (2003).

UNCTAD, *World Investment Report: Incentives and Foreign Direct Investments*, TD/B/ITNC/Misc. 1 (Geneva: United Nations, 2002).

United Nations Development Programme (UNDP), *Human Development Report* (2002).

World Business Environment Survey: Economic Prospects for Developing Countries (March 2002).

World Development Indicators (2001).

World Investment Directory (2000): 113.

11
Foreign Direct Investment in the Primary Sector of Mexico

Dale Colyer

1 Introduction

Historically, foreign direct investment (FDI) in Mexico's primary sector (agriculture, forestry, fisheries and minerals (including petroleum)) was constrained and discouraged due to constitutional, legislative and procedural restrictions which prohibited or limited foreign ownership of natural resources and engagement in economic activities that involved the use of such resources. This was due, in part, to Mexican distrust of and apprehension about the economic power of the USA, its much larger and economically more advanced northern neighbour. However, after the debt crisis and default in 1982, the government of Mexico began to shed autarkic policies, turn away from statism and open its economy to international economic forces. The reforms undertaken have included reinterpretations of legal requirements, the passage of new laws, negotiation of treaties and a constitutional amendment, all of which made FDI easier and more attractive. As a consequence, foreign investments in the economy and the primary sector grew rapidly in the late 1980s and early 1990s, although the economic crisis that erupted in December 1994 dampened some of the enthusiasm and slowed investment activities. Mexico joined the General Agreement on Trade and Tariffs (GATT) in 1986 and the Organization for Economic Cooperation and Development (OECD) in 1994. The trade and investment conditions of those organizations require that more open economic policies be followed. The approval and implementation of the North American Free Trade Agreement (NAFTA) in 1994 also had provisions for enhancing investment and provided a boost to FDI in Mexico, which continues to have a positive influence on investment activities. It should be noted, however, that Mexico has not opened all primary sector activities to foreign investment. Petroleum and forestry, to some extent, continue to be activities reserved for Mexican ownership and exploitation, while there are restrictions on the amount of foreign involvement in mining and some agricultural activities. However, 100 per cent foreign ownership is permitted in other agricultural activities including cattle ranching. Section 2 considers the pre-reform situation; Sections 3–5 the effects of reform, liberalization and NAFTA entry. Section 6 briefly concludes.

2   Pre-reform legal and policy frameworks

The legal framework that underpins FDI in Mexico is based on its Constitution, adopted in 1917 after the Mexican Revolution (see Table 11.1 for the evolution of factors affecting FDI in Mexico). Among the constitutional provisions are those that prescribe state ownership of minerals including petroleum, natural gas and so on. The most salient provision affecting foreign investment is the following, from Article 27 of the 1917 Constitution:

> Only Mexicans by birth or naturalization, and Mexican concerns, have the right to acquire ownership of lands, waters and their appurtenances, or to obtain concessions for the exploration of mining, water or mineral fuels in the Republic of Mexico. (From a translation in Whiting, 1992, p. 244)

Although the Constitution seemed to prohibit any foreign ownership, the clause 'and Mexican concerns' was interpreted to mean that a foreign entity that was legally located in Mexico could own any resource that individual Mexicans could own and, thus, carry out economic activities, such as mining and farming, that individual Mexican citizens could perform – Article 27 allows the state to grant foreigners the same rights if they agree to 'consider themselves nationals with respect to such property, and bind themselves not to invoke the protection of their governments in matters relating thereto' (Article 27, Section I). Rubio (1993, p. 245), in referring to the ownership and exploitation of minerals, points out that Article 27 further states 'the nation will carry out their exploitation according to Regulatory Law' and that use of the word 'nation' instead of 'state' implies that the private sector can be involved in mining, drilling, and production of minerals, oil, gas and so on. This includes foreign entities that are considered Mexican because they are located in Mexico. The oil industry, for example, was not nationalized until 1938, some twenty years after the adoption of the Constitution. The oil industry, however, has become a symbol of nationalism and a 1958 amendment to the regulatory law for oil continues to prohibit any private exploitation of the resource, although secondary petrochemical activities have been opened to the private sector.

Until 1993, foreign investments were regulated under the 1973 'Law to Promote Mexican Investment and to Regulate Foreign Investment' (Whiting 1992; Newman and Szterenfeld 1993; Fedorowicz *et al.*, 1994; World Bank, 1994, 1995). This law was part of a large and complex set of policies related to Mexico's 1950–81 import substitution industrialization policy that, among

Table 11.1 Evolution of Mexican laws, regulations, procedures and factors affecting FDI

1917	Article 27, Constitution of the United States of Mexico – Restricts ownership of mineral resources to the state – Restricts ownership of natural resources to Mexican citizens and entities
1920	Land Reform Activities: expropriations of land and the distribution of use rights to *ejidos*
1922	Title remained with the state so that *ejidatarios* could not sell or mortgage the land – Prohibition of foreign ownership of land in restricted zones (100 km of borders and 50 km of coastlines; could obtain control of land for limited use through real estate trusts)
1937	Nationalization of petroleum enterprises (established a monopoly for PEMEX)
1957	Petroleum law restricted all oil exploration and production to PEMEX
1960s	*Maquila* programme established to attract manufacturing for export to areas along border – incentives provided and programme later expanded to cover all of Mexico
1973	Law on Mexican Investment and Regulation of Foreign Investment – Prohibited foreign investment in many economic activities and restricted ownership to less than 50 percent where permitted – Required prior approval and registration of foreign investments, a process that was made difficult due the red tape and time required for approval
1970s	Encouragement of US firms to establish *maquiladoras* on the US–Mexican border – these could import inputs without tariffs if the processed products were then exported
1982	Economic crisis brought on by the default by Mexico in its international debt obligations
1984–	Reforms in Mexican policies: market orientation, privatization, internationally open – Changes in attitude that made approval of foreign investments easier and quicker – Revisions in ownership rules that allowed up to 100 percent control in some activities – Easing of restrictions on FDI in the primary sector, except for oil and forestry – Privatization of public enterprises with foreign investments (purchases) permitted
1986	Mexico joined GATT, which led to further liberalization of international activities
1989	New regulations promulgated for the 1973 Foreign Investment Law (codified the changes made in revised rules and executive decrees between 1984 and 1989)
1991	Amendment to Article 27 of the Constitution to permit private ownership of *ejido* lands

Table 11.1   Continued

1992	A New Agrarian Law to carry out reforms in the agricultural sector – Allowed *ejidos* and farmers to enter into long-term JVs, rent land and so on
1993	Passed a new law regulating foreign investment (incorporated changes made previously) – Continued prohibition on private activities in oil and basic petrochemicals – Forestry, gas distribution and thirty-two other activities reserved for Mexicans – Minority foreign investment permitted in other activities including mining – Majority ownership, with prior approval, permitted in fifty-eight, others including agriculture – 100 per cent foreign ownership permitted in all other activities – Registration and approval to be automatic for investments meeting criteria with respect to size, location, environmental conditions, foreign funds flow requirements and when financed from abroad
1994	NAFTA agreements approved and implemented starting in January 1994 – Liberalized investment requirements between Canada, the USA and Mexico – Mexico joined the OECD and agreed to abide by OECD Codes of Liberalization, with negotiated exceptions
1996, 1998, 1999, 2001	Investment law modified to clarify and enhance opportunities

other things, promoted the development of domestic industries through high tariffs and protectionism, incentives, credits and tax breaks for priority investment areas, regulation of business entry and operations, restrictions on foreign investments and expansion of parastatal enterprises (World Bank, 1994, p. 1).[1] The 1973 Law prohibited foreign investment or involvement in some primary areas, restricted such activities in the other areas to less than 50 per cent ownership and required registration and prior approval of foreign investment activities, a red-tape encrusted process that was cumbersome and time-consuming. Firms receiving concessions for mining operations could not have more than 39 per cent foreign ownership. Since the minerals are owned by the state, mineral exploration and mining are allowed under 'trusts' for a limited number of years. While the interpretation of the law varied with each presidential Administration, the tendency was to discourage most investments in the primary sector. It had less effect on the manufacturing sector, where FDI was more common and even encouraged, especially for the *maquiladoras* along the US–Mexican border – factories that import materials duty free from the US for manufacturing or assembly and that are re-exported to the US.

In addition to the laws regulating foreign investment, the Mexican land tenure system played a very important role in limiting FDI in the primary sector. There are three types of land ownership in Mexico: privately owned land, communal land, and '*ejido*' land. The last category has been the most dominant and consists of lands expropriated and redistributed under Mexico's land reform laws. The title to such land remained with the state, but use rights were distributed to the members of particular population groups denominated as *ejidos*. In farming communities, the rights to use particular parcels were usually well identified but this was not the case for most forest and wildlands. Communal lands are those belonging to certain indigenous groups, that is, to communities that had a pre-Hispanic history of communal land ownership and operation, although some of these population groups operate as *ejidos* rather than communal societies (World Bank, 1995). Restrictions on private land ownership limited the size of holdings, with the size limits varying with respect to the area of the country and type of operation. The users of *ejido* land did not own the land they used and could not sell it. Thus, there was no opportunity for foreigners to acquire such land even if it had been allowed. Furthermore, there were restrictions on contracting with the *ejidos*, generally limited to one year, which discouraged indirect investment in farming.

Another land-related issue that affects FDI is a prohibition of foreign land ownership in restricted zones, areas within 100 km of the borders and 50 km of coastlines. These, however, have little impact on foreign investments in the primary sector. Furthermore, control of land by foreign firms in these zones can be achieved through trust arrangements (Secretaria de Economiá, 1998). The uses permitted under the trust arrangements include those for 'establishments engaged in the production, transformation, packaging, conservation, transportation or storage of agricultural, ranching, forestry and fishing products' (1998, p. 7). The Mexican government maintains a National Foreign Investment Registry and a National Foreign Investment Commission, which acts on applications for foreign investment activities, but encourages these and other types of foreign investments.

3 Reforms and FDI

Economic growth and development under the import substitution policies during the 1950s, 1960s and 1970s were impressive, with growth in gross national product (GNP) averaging 6.5 per cent per year (World Bank, 1994, p. 1). This situation, often referred to as the 'Mexican economic miracle', was originally sustained by agricultural exports and, when those began to lag, oil exports enabled the process to continue. Mexican officials, like many others throughout the world, expected the oil bonanza to continue indefinitely and to accelerate the development process; both the government and private sectors borrowed heavily during the 1970s, a petro-dollar-influenced era of easy money. When world oil and other commodity prices declined in the early 1980s, the country found that it was not able to fulfil its debt obligations and defaulted in 1982, a situation that preceded the international debt crisis and a faltering of many other economies throughout the world. The crisis revealed weaknesses and inefficiencies in the Mexican economy that had been hidden by protection and subsidization policies: Mexican industries had not been subject to the discipline of international markets and, thus, were at a competitive disadvantage – that is, they were high-cost industries. The decline in oil revenues also made it difficult for the government to maintain subsidies without incurring large deficits and causing inflation to accelerate.

The default and resulting economic crisis together with pressures from international financial organizations (IFIs), caused a realization by Mexican officials that the weaknesses in the economy could not be cured by a continuation of the past import substitution and nationalistic policies of extensive governmental intervention, regulation and involvement in the economy. This led to reversals of many of those policies through a liberalization that included greater dependence on market forces and the private sector, privatization of many state-owned enterprises (SOEs), reductions in tariffs and non-tariff barriers (NTBs) to open the economy to international competition, and a more friendly approach to attract foreign investment in most, but not all, areas of the economy (OECD, 1999).

The early reforms that affected FDI were achieved primarily by a change in attitudes and interpretations of the 1973 Law that regulated foreign investment. These reforms reduced red tape and made it easier for proposed foreign investments to gain approval and registration with the regulatory agency in the Department of Commerce and Industrial Development (Secretaria de Comercio y Fomento Industrial – SECOFI). As indicated by the World Bank (1994, pp. 12–13), the Mexican government progressively eliminated impediments to foreign investments and took other actions to integrate the Mexican economy into global markets. Among the measures to facilitate these processes were provisions for financing; improvements in the structure of foreign liabilities that let foreigners share risks; inducements to improve technology, management and marketing; strengthening the competitive position of the domestic economy; and allowing majority foreign ownership for selected economic activities. These measures were implemented by issuing guidelines and through general resolutions issued during the years 1984–8.

In 1989, the government of Mexico promulgated new regulations under the 1973 Law regulating foreign investments. While generally liberalizing the regulation of FDI, the new rules also provided for a continuation of the government's presence in some economic activities (World Bank, 1994, p. 13). Of some 754 economic activities, twelve, including energy and basic petrochemicals, were reserved for the state; thirty-four, including forestry and gas distribution, were reserved for Mexicans; thirty-seven were permitted to have minority foreign ownership including mining (up to 30 per cent) and secondary petrochemicals (up to 40 per cent); and fifty-eight, including agriculture, could with prior approval have a majority of foreign ownership. Foreign ownership could be up to 100 per cent in the other, unrestricted activities, which consisted primarily of manufacturing and processing.

While foreign ownership still had to be approved and registered, approval was to be automatic when the following conditions were met: (1) The fixed investment was less than US$ 100 million; (2) the investment was financed from abroad; (3) the activity was located outside of the three largest cities, Mexico City, Guadalajara and Monterrey; (4) the foreign exchange flows were balanced over the first three years; (5) the investment created jobs and included training and development; and (6) the investment was environmentally safe. While the unrestricted activities are not in the primary sector, many are processors of primary products (food, tobacco, leather, textiles) and can result in indirect investment through the provision of credit, inputs, or technical assistance. Some specific examples will be discussed in Section 4.

Subsequently, a 1991 amendment to Article 27 of the Constitution and a 1992 Agrarian Law altered the land tenure situation by allowing farmers and others (e.g., foresters) in *ejidos* to acquire ownership of the land to which they had use rights, permitting foreigners to own land and allowing joint ventures (Jvs), with up to 49 per cent foreign ownerships, between businesses and farmers or *ejido* communities (World Bank, 1994, p. 14; Bonilla and Viatte, 1995, pp. 21ff.).[2] The new tenure rules also allowed farmers to mortgage or sell their land. In addition, the foreign investment chapter in the NAFTA agreement, which went into effect in January 1994, and the OECD Codes of Liberalization, which Mexico joined in May 1994, requird freer flows of capital between countries participating in those agreements (Poret, 1995). It is anticipated that PROCAMPO, the recently introduced Mexican agricultural program, which reduces government intervention and subsidization of the sector, will help make the sector more competitive and attractive to foreign investors.

As a way to consolidate and codify the revisions to the guidelines and procedures affecting FDI implemented under the economic liberalization program, a new law regulating foreign investment was enacted in 1994 (Houde, 1994; World Bank, 1994). This law also incorporates the provisions of the foreign investment chapter in the NAFTA agreement. Thus, an almost completely new legal framework for regulating foreign investment has been developed to accompany the remarkable shift from an anti-international set of policies to one that is open and attractive to foreign investment. It should be noted, of course, that some primary economic activities, including petroleum and forestry, are still excluded. Some analysts believe that the liberalization process will not be complete or adequate until the restricted sectors also are incorporated into the liberalized sectors and that once NAFTA and related agreements are fully in place, Mexico must also move to liberalize those activities (Rubio, 1993). Since 1994, the foreign investment law has been amended periodically to clarify issues and to further improve the climate for foreign investment (Secretaria de Economiá, 2003b).

4   Effects of liberalization on FDI

Mexican economic reforms and revised attitudes toward FDI produced a relatively rapid and large response from international investors. As can be seen from Figure 11.1, total FDI began to rise in the 1970s due in part to the encouragement of the *maquiladoras* on the US–Mexican border. However, the process was interrupted by the 1982 default and economic crisis, which caused investors to lose confidence in Mexico and reduce their investments, including those in the *maquiladoras*. This led to the economic liberalization era that began in 1984 when the pace of FDI was resumed and it has generally remained at much higher levels than in the pre-reform era. By the early 1990s, annual total FDI was nearly US$ 5 billion and the cumulative total was around US$ 40 billion in 1992 (World Bank, 1994, p. 14). In 1994, FDI in Mexico reached US$ 6 billion, although the economic crisis of December 1994 had a dampening effect on foreign investment (Burke and Edwards, 1995). Thus, FDI in the first quarter of 1995 fell to US$ 607 million, but recovered partially to US$ 1,607 million and US$ 1,537 million in the second and third quarters, respectively (Consulate of Mexico, 1995).

The majority (70 per cent) of the FDI in Mexico during the 1989–93 five-year period, as in the past, originated in the USA (Houde, 1994, pp. 10–11) followed by Great Britain with 5.2 per cent, France 5.1 per cent,

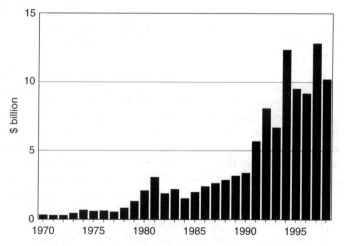

Figure 11.1   FDI in Mexico, 1970–99

Source: UNCTAD, *Yearbook of Statistics* (various issues).

Switzerland 5.0 per cent, Germany 4 per cent, Japan and Canada 2 per cent each and Spain 1.2 per cent. While total Asian FDI is still relatively low, there has been an increasing interest in manufacturing investments in Mexico by Asian countries, especially since the implementation of NAFTA.

In the pre-NAFTA years, the largest shares of FDI in Mexico were in the service and manufacturing sectors (including food processing), with around 40 per cent and 30 per cent, respectively (Houde, 1994, pp. 10–11). During the post-NAFTA period (1994–2001), the share of the manufacturing sector increased to nearly 50 per cent (Table 11.2). Thus, although the amounts invested in primary sector activities, where FDI is permitted, have risen, the proportions are small, about 1 per cent of the totals in the 1994–2001 period. They had been slightly less than 2 per cent of the total in the 1989–93 period and, thus, have fallen as a per centage of the total – that is, they have not risen as fast as in manufacturing and some other sectors.

FDI in agriculture, forestry and fisheries rose from only about US\$ 800,000 in 1984 to US\$ 64 million in 1990 (Nacional Financiera, 1994, p. 232). Although the investments totalled over US\$ 80 million in 1999 and 2000, they averaged only about US\$ 30 million per year in the years 1994–2001 (Comisión de Inversiones Extranjeras, 2003a). Data from the Mexican Secretariate of Economics indicates that, for 1999–2002, 28.9 per cent of the investments in the agricultural sector were in were crops, 70.3 per cent in livestock, 0.4 per cent in forestry and 0.3 per cent in fishing (Secretaria de Economiá, 2002a). Most of the investment in crops (25.9 of the 28.9 per cent) was for horticultural crops and flowers while most of that in livestock was for pork production (69.1 of the 70.3 per cent). Nearly all of these investments were from the USA, with 97.5 per cent of the total for the four-year period. This compares with 71.4 per cent from the USA in all sectors of the Mexican economy during those four years (Secretaria de Economiá, 2003a). The investments were concentrated in the states of Sonora and Sinoloa, with 65.1 and 24.0 per centages of the totals, respectively. It should be noted that a substantial portion of the investments in the manufacturing sector was for food and wood products processing (Bolling, Neff and Handy, 1998; Secretaria de Economiá, 2003a).

In the extractive (mining) sector, FDI increased from about US\$ 5.7 million in 1984 to US\$ 91 million in 1990, but averaged only slightly over US\$ 31 million during 1994–2001, with a high of US\$ 181 million in 2000 (Secretaria de Economiá, 2002b). During 2002, 59 per cent of the investments were in non-ferrous metals, 14.1 per cent in the extraction of precious metals, 10.3 per cent for ferrous metals, 7.4 per cent in non-metallic mineral extraction and 9.2 per cent in other mining activities. Unlike agriculture and manufacturing, the USA was not the largest source of investments. In 2002, Canada led with 42 per cent of the total while the USA had 37.9 per cent; thus, North America accounted for nearly 80 per cent of the total. However, during the four-year period, 1999–2002, Canada provided 69.2 per cent of

Table 11.2 FDI in Mexico, by economic sector, 1994–2002 (million $)

Sector	1994	1995	1996	1997	1998	1999	2000	2001	2002	1994–2002 (%)
Total	10,639.8	8,324.8	7,703.6	12,125.8	8,126.9	12,856.0	15,484.4	25,334.4	9,696.4	100.0
Agriculture	10.8	11.1	31.7	10.0	28.7	80.9	88.2	4.6	4.8	0.2
Mining	97.8	79.1	83.8	130.2	42.4	127.1	181.1	33.2	90.7	0.8
Manufacturing	6,187.0	4,848.7	4,706.1	7,282.9	5,100.0	8,750.2	8,865.1	4,798.7	4,092.9	49.5
Electricity and water	15.2	2.1	1.1	5.2	26.6	139.5	116.8	268.9	24.6	0.5
Construction	259.4	26.2	25.5	110.4	81.6	129.0	168.4	73.0	99.8	0.9
Wholesale and retail trade	1,250.7	1,008.6	726.8	1,899.4	938.3	1,196.9	2,175.9	1,542.2	1,126.5	10.8
Transport and communications	719.3	876.3	428.0	681.5	435.9	278.3	−2,371.9	2,912.9	750.3	4.3
Financial services	941.4	1,066.0	1,214.4	1,102.4	708.4	717.9	4,599.6	13,576.0	2,938.8	24.4
Other services*	1,158.2	406.7	486.2	903.8	765.0	1,436.2	1,661.2	2,124.9	568.0	8.6

Note: * Includes community and social; hotels and restaurants; professional, technical and personal services.

Source: Secretariat of Economics, Mexico, DF, www.economia.gob.mx.

the investment in mining, while the UK accounted for 18.6 per cent and the USA share was only 6.9 per cent. Under the 1993 Foreign Investment Law, opportunities are still limited to minority positions in mining but can be a majority in agriculture and up to 100 per cent in cattle ranching. Liberalization of the investment and agrarian laws also permits Jvs, with rental of land to, and other activities of, foreign controlled entities in Mexico.

Revisions encompassed in a 1991 constitutional amendment and the 1992 Agrarian Law have enabled farmers and *ejido* communities to rent land and to enter into longer-term contracts with non-*ejido* entities. This is resulting in new arrangements for producing agricultural products for processing. An example cited by Newman and Szterenfeld (1993), is of Gamesa, a Mexican firm purchased by Pepsi Cola's snack food producer, Sabritos, which has entered into contracts with an *ejido* to produce 5,000 acres of corn and beans. Through a set of complex arrangements Gamesa provides funding for tractors, irrigation and other investments required for production of the quality of products that Sabritos needs. Another example, also cited by Newman and Szterenfeld (1993), is Provamex, which is contracting with *ejidos* to produce broilers. Other foreign firms, such as Pilgrims Pride and Tysons, produce and process broilers in Mexico for the Mexican market, but also contract with producers for some of their broilers and help to finance those operations. Similarly, Green Giant and other vegetable processors have plants in Mexico and may provide seeds, technical assistance, supervision, credit and other inputs for contract producers.

5   Effects of NAFTA and other trade agreements

Mexico participates in NAFTA and a number of other regional and bilateral trade agreements. NAFTA appears to have had very significant effects on the trade and investment regimes of Mexico; the OECD (1999), for example, states that 'the North American Free Trade Agreement (NAFTA) has had a profound influence on the Mexican policy formulation given the scope and pace of policy reform involved' (p. 6). The success of NAFTA also led to the development of trade agreements by Mexico with other countries and groups of countries, including one with Central America (MERCOCEN). However, the influence of these agreements on investment is difficult to determine since the reform process was well established prior to the date that the NAFTA agreements were implemented. Trade and investment had also expanded and the trend continued subsequent to NAFTA implementation, although an economic crisis led to a temporary decline in some activities. Worth (1998, p. 81) maintains that the effects of NAFTA on FDI 'appear minor for the United States, Canada and Mexico'. However, Bolling and Jerado (2002, p. 26) find that 'NAFTA has fostered a positive synergy between trade and FDI in the North American processed food industry'.

US Department of Commerce data show that US FDI is much larger now than in pre-NAFTA years (BEA, 2003). The average FDI for the seven years prior to NAFTA's implementation was US$ 1,554 million while it averaged about US$ 4,473 in the first seven years after implementation (1994–2000). This difference is highly significant ($t = 4.979$, with a probability of 0.00016), but a regression analysis with a dummy variable for pre- and post-NAFTA periods, found the trend to be highly significant, but the dummy variable not statistically significant.[3] Thus, as in the case for agricultural trade (see Colyer, 2001), while FDI has continued to increase, it seems to follow the trend that was established when Mexico liberalized its trade regime in the early 1980s. While the additional reforms made during and following the NAFTA negotiations probably contributed to the continuation of the trend toward increased FDI, they did not materially affect the trend in the overall rate of foreign investment in Mexico.

Investments by the MERCOCEN countries in Mexico, while still small, has grown considerably since 1994, rising from only US$ 1.1 million in 1994 to over US$ 8.5 million in 2001 (Secretaria de Economiá, 2002c). However, relatively little of this was in the primary sector. Only three of 155 firms making investments (1.9 per cent) were in the primary sector, all in agriculture – two in crops and one in livestock.

6 Conclusions

FDI in the primary sector of Mexico has grown rapidly since liberalization of attitudes and laws have permitted investments in most economic activities, although investments in the primary sector are a relatively small proportion of the country's total FDI. The impacts of the movement toward market-oriented and internationally open policies have not been fully realized, especially those that affect land tenure and ownership in the *ejido* sector as well as liberalization of ownership limits in the private sector. These changes are expected to result in consolidation into larger and more efficient farm units, but this is a process that will evolve as land markets develop and as the institutional infrastructure changes to meet the requirements of a new set of economic conditions, a set that is very different from what existed under the import substitution and statist policies that existed prior to 1984. This process was interrupted by the 1994 economic crisis, but as economic recovery took place it resumed, although at a more moderate pace. FDI dropped sharply in the first quarter of 1995, but recovered during the second quarter and continued to increase in most of the following years.

The agricultural sector of Mexico is being transformed by the economic forces being unleashed under the NAFTA, other trade agreements and a moderate amount of FDI, as well as a continued process of liberalization of domestic economic policies initiated after the default of the early 1980s. The changes under NAFTA are being phased in over a fifteen-year period and their full impacts are yet to be felt. The comparative and competitive advantages of the agricultural economies of the signatory countries – Canada, Mexico and the USA – imply that a restructuring in productive activities will take place in the future due to changes in economic conditions. Mexico has cost advantages in the production of many fruits and vegetables, especially where advanced technologies may be supplied by foreign investors under Jvs or other arrangements. FDI thus can be expected to play an important role in the nature and extent of the restructuring of the agricultural sector during the next several years. This will include direct investments in the primary sector as well as in the industrial sectors supporting agricultural activities.

A similar set of conclusions applies to the mining sector and to other primary activities where foreign investments are permitted. If restrictions on foreign investment in petroleum and/or forestry are lifted, FDI can be expected to enter since many of the activities in those sectors are not being exploited in efficient and effective ways. The improvements in technology and management that FDI would induce would make those activities more internationally competitive. This is occurring to some extent in forestry processing and in secondary activities in petrochemicals.

Notes

1. See Hayami and Ruttan (1985), Gillis *et al.* (1992), or Whitaker and Colyer (1990) for discussions of the import substitution policy and its related dependency model.
2. The amendment to Article 27 of the Constitution ended land redistribution through agrarian reform, allowed corporate ownership of land, individualized *ejido* agrarian rights (they had been family rights), and permitted *ejiditarios* to privatise (and sell) their land holdings (Quintana, Bórquez and Aviles, 1998). Article 27 concerns land use and ownership and even the amended version, which deleted several paragraphs, is some seven pages long (Government of Mexico, 2001). Many provisions were modified by the amendment, but the primary effects were those cited by Quintana, Bórquez and Aviles.
3. The regression results were:

$$FDI = 204.6429 + 337.3393*time + 558.0536*dummy$$
$$(114.4078) \qquad (922.3851)$$

Standard errors are in parentheses; $R^2 = 0.8178$. To test whether the slope of the regression changed after NAFTA was implemented, an interaction term for the dummy and time trend was included in a modification of the regression, but the term was not statistically significant and caused the coefficient of the dummy variable to become negative and the time trend to become statistically non-significant.

References

Bolling, C. and A. Jerado, 'Investment in Agriculture and Food Processing', in S. Zahniser and J. Link (eds), *Effects of North American Free Trade Agreement on Agriculture and the Rural Economy*, WRS-02–1 (Washington, DC: US Department of Agriculture, July 2002): 22–6.
Bolling, C., S. Neff and C. Handy, *US Direct Investment in the Western Hemisphere Processed Food Industry* (Washington, DC: US Department of Agriculture, 1998).

Bonilla, J. and G. Viatte, 'Radical Reform in Mexican Agriculture', *The OECD Observer*, 189 (1995): 21–6.

Bureau of Economic Analysis (BEA), 'Direct Foreign Investment' (Washington, DC: US Department of Commerce), www.bea.gov/international/bweb/action.cfm, accessed 16 May 2003).

Burke, S. J. and S. Edwards, *August 1995: Latin America After Mexico: Quickening the Pace* (Washington, DC: World Bank, 1995).

Colyer, D. 'Impacts of NAFTA on US – Mexico Agricultural Trade', Paper presented at the Annual Meeting of the Northeastern Agricultural and Resource Economics Association, Bar Harbor, Maine (10–12 June 2001), http://agecon.lib.umn.edu.

Comisión Nacional de Inversiones Extranjeras, 'Informe Estadistico Sobre el Comportamiento de la Inversión Extranjera en Mexico (Enero-deciembre de 2002)' (Mexico, DF: Secretaria de Economiá, 2003).

Consulate of Mexico, 'México: Balanza de Pagos (Electronic Data Base)' (New York: Dirección General de Análisis Económico de la Secretaria de Relaciones Exteriores, 1995).

Fedorowicz, J., M. Bedward, J. Townsend and R. Reymont, *Business Mexico* (Chicago: Probus, 1994).

Gillis, M., D.H. Perkins, M. Roemer and D.R. Snodgrass, *Economics of Development*, 3rd edn (New York: W.W. Norton, 1992).

Government of Mexico, *Constitución Política de los Estados Unidos Mexicanos, actualizada hasta Reforma de 14.08.2001*, http://www.georgetown.edu/pdba/ Constitutions/Mexico/mexico.html (2001).

Hayami, Y. and V.W. Ruttan, *Agricultural Development: An International Perspective*, revised edn (Baltimore, MD: Johns Hopkins University Press, 1985).

Houde, M. 'Mexico and Foreign Investment', *OECD Observer*, 190 (1994): 10–13.

Nacional Financiera, *La Economiá Mexicana en Cifras*, 13th edn (Mexico, DF: Nacional Financiera, 1994).

Newman, G. and A. Szterenfeld, *Business International's Guide to Doing Business in Mexico* (New York: McGraw-Hill, 1993).

OECD, *Regulatory Reform in Mexico* (Paris: OECD, 1999).

Poret, P. 'Mexico and the OECD Codes of Liberalization', *The OECD Observer*, 189 (1995): 39–42.

Quintana, R., L. Bórquez and R. Aviles, 'Peasant Logic, Agrarian Policy, Land Mobility, and Land Markets in Mexico', Working Paper 21 (Madison, WI: Land Tenure Centre, University of Wisconsin, 1998).

Rubio, L. 'Mexico's Economic Reform: Energy and the Constitution', *The Energy Journal*, 14(3) (1993): 241–8.

Secretaria de Economiá, 'Regulations to the Foreign Investment Law and the National Foreign Investment Registry' (Mexico, DF: Secretaria de Economiá, 1998): 6–8.

Secretaria de Economiá, 'Inversión Extranjera Directa en Agricultura, Ganaderia, Caza, Sivilcultura y Pesca' (Mexico, DF: Dirección General de Inversión Extranjera, September 2002a).

Secretaria de Economiá, 'Inversión Extranjera Directa en Mineria y Extracción' (Mexico, DF: Dirección General de Inversión Extranjera, September 2002b).

Secretaria de Economiá, 'Inversión del MERCOCEN en México' (Mexico, DF: Dirección General de Inversión Extranjera, September 2002c).

Secretaria de Economiá, 'Inversión Extranjera Directa en la Industria de Madera' (Mexico, DF: Dirección General de Inversión Extranjera, January 2003a).

Secretaria de Economiá, 'Marco Juridico Nacional de la Inversión Extranjera en México' (Mexico, DF: Dirección General de Inversión Extranjera), http://www.economia.gob.mex/?P = 1195, accessed 14 May 2003b.

Whitaker, M.D. and D. Colyer, *Agriculture and Economic Survival: The Role of Agriculture in Ecuador's Development* (Boulder, CO: Westview Press, 1990).

Whiting, V.R. Jr., *The Political Economy of Foreign Investment in Mexico* (Baltimore, MD: Johns Hopkins University Press, 1992).

World Bank, *Mexico: Country Economic Memorandum: Fostering Private Sector Development in the 1990s,* Report, 11823-ME (Washington, DC: World Bank, 1994).

World Bank, *Mexico: Resource Conservation and Forest Sector Review,* Report, 13114-ME (Washington, DC: World Bank, 1995).

Worth, T. 'Regional Trade Agreements and Foreign Direct Investment', in M.E. Burfisher and E.A. Jones (eds), *Regional Trade Agreements and US Agriculture,* AER 771 (Washington, DC: US Department of Agriculture, 1998): 77–83.

12
The Impact of Culture on Investment in Emerging Markets

Richard Fletcher

1 Introduction

The purpose of this chapter is to highlight the cultural differences between emerging and developed markets overseas and the extent to which such cultural differences can impact on market selection for siting an investment, negotiating it, locating investment partners, managing an investment and withdrawal from an investment activity. This will be achieved by exploring aspects of culture in terms of its impact on investment in emerging markets (Section 2). This is illustrated by an analysis of the impact of culture on communication in such markets as far as investment activities are concerned (Section 3); the analysis is then compared with a research study on the topic undertaken in Thailand (Section 4). The chapter concludes by reviewing the impact of culture on investment in emerging markets in relation to each phase of the investment process (Section 5).

2 Background: cultural differences between developed and emerging markets

A working definition of 'culture' is that it is the way of life in a specific society (Fletcher and Brown, 2002, p. 2). There are a number of key cultural differences between developed and emerging markets that affect investment undertakings. These will be reviewed as appropriate in terms of both 'marketplace' and 'marketspace' (the term given to business undertaken via the Internet). They include time, space, familiarity and friendship, consumption patterns, business customs and adoption of innovation. They all have an impact on both negotiating investment approvals and operating in emerging markets.

Time

Although formally most cultures adopt a common model of time (the clock), *assumptions about time* are deep-seated and vary considerably between

developed and emerging markets, with the result that more time is needed
to transact business in emerging than in markets such as Australia. In many
emerging markets, the time taken to reach a decision is directly proportional
to the importance attached to it. In these circumstances, to hurry the decision sends a message that you do not consider the outcome important.
Cultures differ in temporal orientation, with some focusing on the past
when evaluating current events (Southern Europe), some focusing only on
the present as the past is gone and the future is too far away to contemplate
(Middle East) and others, such as Australia, being willing to plan forward
and establish realistic lead times. Finally, there is the difference between cultures where time is *monochronic* (time is linear, having a beginning and an
end and only one thing is done at a time), and time is *polychronic* (time is
cyclic and people do a number of things at the same time, such as seeing
several visitors in their office together). In terms of marketspace, because the
Internet saves time, it is more likely to be used in cultures where 'time is
money' and these are less likely to be found among emerging markets.

Space

From a cultural perspective, this is both *physical* and *abstract*. In the physical
domain, space can denote status, as indicated by the size of one's office in
Australia, for example. In many emerging markets, however, this is not the
case and it is not uncommon for senior executives to work in the middle of
a large room surrounded by others for whom they are responsible. Personal
proximity is another manifestation of culturally influenced physical space
and in emerging markets in middle eastern countries acceptable distances
are much closer than in Australia. Space is also abstract and refers to being
an 'insider' or 'outsider' as far as a group of persons is concerned and the
ease or difficulty of gaining 'insider' status. This is likely to much more difficult to achieve in emerging markets where the rights and obligations of
group members are more stringent.

Consumption patterns

These are reflected in attitudes towards *material possessions* and *dress*. In
some cultures, these are displayed in an ostentatious manner and in others
these symbols are understated. Issues that in Australia are deemed to be private, such as 'how much do you earn?', are not viewed the same way in some
emerging markets. Underlying differences in consumption patterns are differences in the hierarchy of needs. Figure 12.1 shows that that this hierarchy differs between the West and Asia, especially at the upper need level.
This hierarchy of needs will need to be taken into account in assessing the
market appeal of the output of any investment activity.

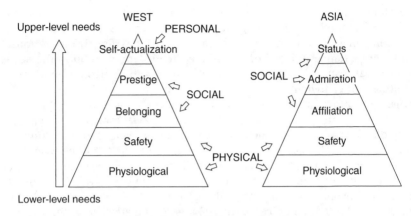

Figure 12.1   Hierarchy of needs between different cultural groups
Source: Schutte and Ciarlante (1999, p. 93).

Familiarity and friendship patterns

These vary as far as the speed with which friendships are formed, the obligations entailed and the degree of superficiality. In many cultures, these are not based on business opportunism as is often the case in Australia, for example. In many cultures in emerging markets, the degree to which the individual is a private person also varies, as does the way in which this privacy manifests itself and the expression of emotion The easy assumption of familiarity and back-slapping in Australia is regarded as an affront in many parts of Asia. Sensitivity to differences in respect of such matters is important in the negotiation and conduct of investment in emerging markets, especially when gauging the reaction to an offer or a statement. While an Australian might interpret a laugh or a smile as a sign of happiness, in some emerging markets it may indicate disappointment or annoyance.

In emerging markets, the marketspace perspective may be limited by the lack of necessary infrastructure, the dominance of English as the language used, the unemployment effects of disintermediation, the dependence of the medium on interactivity, and its 24-hour, 7 days a week attribute (24/7). While these are due to the level of development, they are also due to cultural factors such as reluctance to innovate, a focus on the past as opposed to the present or the future, collectivism, uncertainty avoidance and a high degree of dependency on context. Hall (1976) illustrates this by listing countries or groups in terms of where they fall along a continuum from high- to low-context cultures: in order lie Japan, the Arabic countries, Latin America, Spain, Italy, the UK, Australia, North America, Scandinavia, Germany and Switzerland. When this table is compared with rates of Internet adoption,[1] there is evidence that low-context countries are more likely to use the Internet than high-context countries, most of which are emerging markets.

In addition to operating at the individual level, culture also operates at the national, industry, and company levels, all of which can impact on investment overseas.

National culture

This involves dealings with governments and is reflected in the values on which laws and institutions are based. National culture also influences the way laws are applied, which can be more subjective in emerging markets than is the case in developed country markets. An example of national culture is the insistence on use of the national language in communication with government, despite it not being the most common language used in business (e.g. Malaysia).

Industry culture

This reflects the norms that prevail in the industry – its impacts on negotiations within the industry in the overseas country and its manifestations include credit policy (Prohibition of usury in Islamic countries), attitude to the environment, whether relationships are confined to specific business transactions or extend beyond them and the norms of negotiation.

Company culture

This is reflected in negotiations with commercial bodies in the overseas country – it is embedded in the basic pattern of assumptions developed by the firm and includes its code of ethics and attitude towards its employees. In many emerging markets, for example, the employer is considered to be responsible for the welfare of employees and the treatment of employees as a short-term expendable resource, as can happen in Western countries, is rejected.

3 Culture and communication in emerging markets

Different approaches have evolved for classifying countries according to their underlying cultural dimensions – the etic (culture-general) or emic (culture-specific) approaches. The findings of these studies have relevance for negotiating and managing investment operations in emerging markets.

The etic approach

The two most influential etic studies here have been by Hofstede (1991) and Trompenaars and Hampden-Turne (1997). Hofstede found four underlying dimensions:

- *Power distance* – the degree to which less powerful persons in a culture accept the existence of inequality and the unequal distribution of power as a normal situation.
- *Uncertainty avoidance* – the extent to which people in a culture feel threatened by uncertain or unknown situations.
- *Individualism/collectivism* – the extent to which people in a culture look after their own interests as opposed to cultures where people see themselves as being members of a group and as having a responsibility to look after the interests of that group.
- *Masculine/feminine* – in the former, it is material success and assertiveness that is stressed whereas in the latter the focus is on quality of life and caring for the weak.

Trompenars and Hampden-Turner found five underlying dimensions:

- *Universalism vs. particularism* – for the universalist, what is good and right can be applied everywhere, whereas for the particularist the obligations imposed by relationships are more important than general rules.
- *Individualism vs. communitarianism* – this is similar to the Hofstede individualism/collectivism dimension.
- *Neutral vs. affective* – in affective cultures, expression of emotion is viewed as natural whereas in neutral cultures it is repressed so as to give the impression of 'being in control'.
- *Specific vs. diffuse* – people in specific cultures get straight to the point whereas people in diffuse cultures discuss business only after relationships have been established.
- *Achievement vs. ascription* – in achievement-oriented cultures, status derives from what you have achieved rather than who you are in terms of factors such as age, kinship, education, connections, etc.

Using UN statistics, a comparison of the fourteen most developed with the fourteen least developed countries was undertaken with respect to the Hofstede and Trompenaars and Hampden-Turner dimensions; the results are shown in Table 12.1.

The significance of this analysis for investment in emerging markets can be summarized as follows:

- As emerging markets exhibit a much greater degree of power distance, relationships formed are more likely to be influenced by *hierarchy* and an egalitarian approach to management is unlikely to be successful.
- As such markets display a much greater degree of *collectivism*, cooperation rather than competition will characterize workplace relations and incentive

Table 12.1 Cultural comparison of developed with emerging markets

	Hofstede (developed*)	Hofstede (emerging**)	Trompenaars (developed***)	Trompenaars (emerging****)
Power distance	38	72		
Uncertainty avoidance	58	59		
Individualism	72	24		
Masculinity	59	47		
Universalism			89	61
Affective			43	45
Specific focus			83	69
Achievement			83	73

Notes
* Australia, Austria, Canada, Denmark, France, Germany, Britain, Italy, Japan, New Zealand, Spain, Switzerland, the USA.
** Africa West, Africa East, Costa Rica, Guatemala, India, Jamaica, Malaysia, Mexico, Pakistan, Panama, Peru, the Philippines, Thailand, Uruguay.
*** Australia, Austria, Canada, Denmark, France, Germany, Great Britain, Italy, Ireland, Japan, Norway, Spain, Switzerland, the USA.
**** Brazil, China, Czechoslovakia, Cuba, Ethiopia, Hungary, India, Indonesia, Mexico, Nigeria, the Philippines, Poland, Thailand, Russia.
Source: Fletcher and Melewar (2001, p. 11).

programmes should be based on reward for the group as opposed to reward for the individual.
- As these markets are *particularist* rather than universalist, the obligations imposed by relationships will be more important than general rules. This is likely to be important in negotiation of investment contracts.
- As emerging markets are *specific* as opposed to diffuse, it is necessary to establish relationships before business is discussed and the relationship established is likely to extend beyond the specific investment negotiation.

Many would share the view expressed by Abosag, Tynan and Lewis (2002) that, although these underlying dimensions of culture have some limitations and may not explain all behaviours in a specific market, they still constitute the best framework available for comparing cultural behaviours in a business context. However, the etic approach is based on the notion that underlying cultural differences between nations are a set of variables that can be applied uniformly and which cover all dimensions of difference between one culture and another. This is questionable, as these studies were all undertaken before the 1990s revolution in cross-border communication, the accelerated movement of peoples between countries, the rising level of globalization and the information revolution led by the Internet. This raises the issue as to whether their resulting dimensions are as relevant in the new millennium as when they were originally developed.

These approaches were also derived from large-scale surveys based on 'Western' cultural dimensions and evaluated according to 'Western' interpretation of measurement descriptors (i.e. very high; high; somewhat high; neither high nor low; somewhat low; low; very low). It is likely that the resulting measures do not cater for the reluctance of people in many cultures to provide information, to give accurate answers as opposed to what they think you would like to hear, or express definite opinions. In such circumstances, can the resulting scores truly reflect the extent of difference on these variables between respondents in one culture compared to another? The implied assumption in these studies, that all cultural variance can be explained by these dimensions, ignores the possibility that there might be dimensions that are unique to a particular culture of group of cultures. Hofstede in his subsequent research (1988) admitted this possibility when he and Bond examined the Chinese Value Survey and arrived at a fifth dimension of particular relevance to Asia–Confucian dynamism, subsequently referred to as long-term vs. short-term orientation.

For the most part, advocates of the etic approach identify cultural boundaries with political (i.e. geographic) ones. Although beguilingly convenient, such an approach ignores the fact that a number of different ethnic groups can exist within a political boundary (e.g. Malay, Chinese and Indian in Malaysia), that ethnic groups may flow across political boundaries (e.g. Chinese in South East Asia; Kurds in Iran, Iraq and Turkey); and that within a political boundary there can be distinctive cultural groups as evidenced by the increasing multiculturalism in Australia and the growing urban–rural divide in many developing Asian countries. Aligning cultural groups with national boundaries therefore provides a questionable basis for predicting cultural variables that may need to be taken into account in developing relationships with parties in emerging markets.

From a marketspace perspective, Park (2000) found using Hofstede's dimensions, that it was low-uncertainty-avoidance cultures rather than high-uncertainty-avoidance cultures that were more likely to adopt the Internet, because the Internet provides egalitarian access to communication networks and makes it possible for non-traditional power holders to access information previously denied to them. Park also found that individualistic cultures were more likely to adopt the Internet than collectivist cultures, and that feminine cultures were more likely to adopt the Internet because, owing to its anonymity, gender and ethnic identification were avoided. If the countries listed in the Economist Intelligence Unit Survey (1999), showing rates of Internet access at home, are compared with scores by countries on Trompenaar's dimensions, countries adopting the Internet tend to be universalist rather than particularist; individualist rather than communitarian; and achievement- rather than ascription-oriented. In addition, the comments in respect of both Hofstede and Trompenaars and Hampden-Turner point to a relationship between culture and Internet adoption that impacts on the way information is used, the credibility attached to information and the degree of trust exhibited in the Internet as a medium for information. Cultural differences play a role in the adoption of the Internet in emerging markets, and this could impact on investment activities where the Internet is involved, influencing both the selection of the emerging market if the Internet is involved in the delivery of the product/service and the promotion of the output of the investment activity.

The emic approach

Unlike the etic approach, which seeks dimensions of *cultural variability*, the emic approach is *culture-specific*. It endeavours to identify the idiosyncracies of individual cultures in order to understand what are effective negotiating behaviours to employ when dealing with executives. Advocates of this approach, such as Fang (1999) argue that an emic approach is necessary to discover the indigenous cultural values that underlie people's behaviour. Fang (1999, p. 67) modelled the business culture of China on the basis of three forces – the PRC condition, Confucianism and 'Chinese stratagems'. Although developed to describe Chinese culture, this framework can be applied to any culture to uncover its idiosyncracies and might be described as a local situation, social conventions/belief systems and negotiation strategy.

To discover the first of these forces – *condition* – it is necessary to examine the prevailing political ideology; the extent of economic planning and government involvement; the existing legal framework and its application; the state of technology in the market and the attitude towards innovation; the nature, equity and average level of income distribution; the magnitude of resource endowment, including infrastructure and capital; the exposure to international influences; and the rapidity of change in the society. These factors are a reflection of the *underlying culture*.

The second of these forces can be described as *religious underpinning and social mores*. In his discussion of Confucianism, Fang (1999) highlights several factors and these can also apply to other cultural groups: morality and trust; the role and obligations on the self in interpersonal relationships; the strength of family orientation; respect for age and hierarchy; the requirement to avoid conflict and create harmony; and the need to dignify rather than diminish the other party by saving face.

The third of these forces (categorized by Fang as '*Chinese stratagems*') can apply to other cultures, as all cultural groups have culturally influenced negotiation tactics and approaches to strategic thinking. In some societies, these may be based on winning by subtlety rather than confrontation, in others on winning by cooperation and in yet others by winning by direct confrontation. In all cases, these strategic approaches influence relationship formation and network creation. In manuals on negotiation (mostly based on research carried out in 'western' countries), negotiation strategies are based either on game theory (focus on maximizing the outcome for the individual party via manipulation resulting in a 'win–lose' or 'zero-sum' game) or on social exchange theory (relationships between the parties are cooperative and the aim is to maximize benefits for all those involved on a 'win–win' basis). Fang (1999) argues that in China both strategies are employed jointly, whereas in the 'West' the use of one strategy usually precludes the use of the other.

This reflects a characteristic of many Asian cultures that can complicate relationships between them and Western organizations. This characteristic, which can lead to accusations of unreliability and deception, has been tentatively labelled 'tolerance of ambiguity'. Although sometimes included with uncertainty avoidance, tolerance of ambiguity is different in that it reflects the common situation in many Asian cultures where a strong tendency towards one extreme of a bipolar dimension (such as individualism) does not preclude its opposite (collectivism). Further examples of this are:

- while in Chinese society the absence of a well-functioning legal framework stimulates behaviours that are indicative of collectivism such as *'guanxi'* and network formation the Chinese, with their focus on the family and money-oriented behaviour, also display *individualistic* traits.
- Asian cultures are characterized by a *situation-accepting* orientation (Leung, 1992), and people react in a flexible manner. Asian cultures also accept uncertainty and disorder as natural phenomena (Lamposki and Emden, 1996) and cope with situations on an individual or communal basis as circumstances require.
- Cultures in Asia are 'high-context'. Because the meaning is *contextual* the degree of commitment is likely to be qualified by the context and this often creates ambiguity. This results in the meaning attached to positives and negatives being different to that in the 'West'. In these cultures, a 'yes' may mean nothing more than 'I hear what you are saying' and 'no' may not mean a definite negative but rather 'it is under consideration'.
- The nature of *religion* in Asia. Apart from Islamic societies, Asian cultures are not monotheistic and can be influenced by a number of religions or gods. Confucianism deals with human relationships, Taoism with life in harmony with nature and Buddhism with people's immortal world (Fang, 1999) and Hinduism has many gods in its pantheon. These can be viewed more as philosophies than religions and in some cultures, people follow several philosophies.
- the *'yin–yang' principle*. This simultaneously reflects elements of both the female (water, weak, dark, soft, passive) and the male (fire, strong, bright, hard, active) in a situation.

There may well thus be a middle ground between the etic approach of global variables of cultural difference and the emic approach of viewing cultures in terms of their own idiosyncratic natures. In this alternative approach, it may be possible to apply the emic approach to individual cultures and then, on the basis of perceived commonalities, cluster cultures into groups. Such an approach would provide general guidance to firms when contemplating cross-border investment relationships without the shortcomings exhibited by the etic approach of ignoring unique cultural differences that may be of major importance. Although based on attitudinal dimensions rather than specifically on cultural differences, Ronen and Shenkar (1985), in their clustering of countries, point the way. They came up with the following clusters: Nordic; Germanic; Anglo; Latin American; Far Eastern; Arab and Near Eastern (the four countries that did not fit into any cluster were classified as 'independents').

4   Communicating in emerging markets

It should thus be apparent that culture is likely to impact on communication with others in emerging markets during the stages of negotiation, implementation, operation and cessation of an investment. It is therefore vital to examine the impact of culture on communication. As communication is basic to all commercial activities including investment, a traditional communications model was explored in terms of likely differences (as reported in the literature) in its application in developed as compared to emerging markets. For each element of the model (sender, medium, receiver, interference, feedback and environmental factors), these assumptions were compared to the results of a research study undertaken by the author in Thailand. This study on the impact of culture on communications is relevant to the promotion of the benefits of the investment to the wider group of stakeholders as well as promoting the output of the investment activity to consumers in the emerging market. The study in Thailand reports on the findings as they apply to both the upper/middle-income group, who are most likely to be involved in the investment negotiations, and the lower-income group who are likely to be the targets of communication about the macro benefits of the investment to the community. Figure 12.2 shows a typical communications model.

Sender-oriented

From the literature (Rogers, 1995; Thomas, 1996), it appears that the sender will need to tailor the message according to the cultural norms, as well as to the economic conditions and political constraints, operating in the emerging market. The message will need to be couched in terms of what investors in the emerging market both expect and can afford. From a cultural perspective, the message should be sensitive to social issues in the emerging market as well as to religious mores, ethical behaviours, morality and business customs, practices and hierarchies. The words used and situations

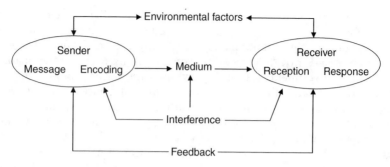

Figure 12.2 The communication process
Source: Griffin (1993, p. 11).

depicted in the message conveyed should, where appropriate, reflect tribal-ism and allegiance to ethnic affiliations. Furthermore, in many cultures in the developing world, being insistent or asking for the order is considered offensive. In these circumstances, messages should be more focused on information provision rather than on persuasion. The message must also be sent by someone who is both acceptable and credible in the receiving cul-ture. Such a sender may be an opinion leader or a respected figure (Hollows Foundation, 1999). Although important at both the knowledge stage and persuasion stage in the diffusion of the idea, this is most important at the persuasion stage.

Because of low literacy levels, the encoding of the communication relat-ing to the investment should involve the use of non-verbal stimuli such as photographs, show cards, sketches and pictures. Such non-verbal stimuli are useful in cases where the product class is new to the emerging market or the product represents a major shift in traditional use and its application is best illustrated rather than described. Non-verbal stimuli are often used in conjunction with verbal stimuli.

The research in Thailand (see the tables on pp. 256–8), showed that creators and senders of messages need to take into account a preference for local rather than foreign presenters and that presenters should be selected because of their accomplishments rather than their background. There is a preference for messages containing testimonials by both authority figures and glamorous people. The appeal of the message should be directed to the individual rather than to the group with which the person is associated and that appeals that focused on aesthetic rather than utilitarian issues were favoured. Overall, there was a degree of preference for non-verbal rather than verbal stimuli in promotional communication. Messages should also be directed more towards immediate satisfaction rather than long-term goals and focus more on conveying information rather than on persuasion. In a number of respects, these general findings concerning sender issues do not apply equally to both higher/middle-income customers and lower-income customers. If the target of the communication is the higher/middle-income group, they are perceived as being more likely to be motivated by messages where the presenter is a foreigner, where the emphasis is on verbal rather than non-verbal stimuli and where the appeal is to long-term goals rather than short-term satisfaction. Lower-income customers, on the other hand, prefer local presenters of messages and like messages containing testimonials. They prefer appeals directed to the group rather than to the individual, and they have a preference for non-verbal stimuli and for messages that offer short-term satisfaction.

Medium-oriented

The marketing infrastructure that most developed country companies would consider basic is often absent in emerging markets (Quelch and Austin, 1993). Regardless of whether the medium is a letter, outdoor signage, radio, TV or newspaper/magazine, some degree of infrastructure outlay by the recipient of the message is likely to be necessary in order to receive the communication. National infrastructure can also have an impact, as is the case when poor telecoms in emerging markets impede the use of the Internet. The cost of infrastructure may rule out use of some media for reaching customers in emerging economies.

Research such as that by Craig and Douglas (2000, pp. 92–3) shows that media usage is more restricted in the emerging markets than in other parts of the world. While this is mainly a reflection of stage of development, it does also indicate the way of life in that society. Emerging markets vary in both the availability of certain media and the extent to which that media is controlled by the government, and hence available for use by advertisers. Underlying this may be issues of protectionism, national sovereignty or fear that the local culture will be contaminated. The threat to national sovereignty is particularly an issue with media that crosses national boundaries, such as satellite TV or the Internet. Among advertising media, radio is the most popular for reaching audiences in small towns and rural areas. Although the use of colour TV is increasing in many urban areas of emerging markets, black and white TV is often in widespread use in rural areas. If complex messages need to be conveyed, then newspapers are used. However, literacy levels may restrict use of this medium, especially in countries where literacy rates are much lower for females than for males. Personal communication in emerging markets is very important for business-to-business (B2B) marketing, especially where demonstration and education in product usage is required. In addition, out-of-home media such as buses, cinemas and mobile unit are important. The medium employed is more likely to be the direct sales person.

The research in Thailand showed that although radio usage is high, it is less common than TV usage, which is very high. Internet use is modest by world standards, and newspaper readership is also below the level of most Western countries, although its use as a promotional medium is reasonably high. The same is true of public relations. Overall, magazine usage is only moderate and usage of direct mail is limited. Promotional offers are popular but the use of trade shows is very limited. Levels of personal selling are considered to be greater than in Australia. Differences in media usage are apparent between lower-income customers and upper/middle-income customers, with radio usage higher among the former group and Internet use lower. Magazine readership is lower with low-income customers, although there is little difference between the two groups in respect of newspaper readership. Publicity targeted at the upper/middle-income group is much higher and trade shows are more likely to be visited by this group. The same is true of direct mail.

Receiver-oriented

One of the factors that will impact on how the message is received is whether there is a general acceptance of marketing and the conventions associated with it. In emerging markets this is less likely to be the case because people, especially in rural areas, are less likely to have been exposed to marketing, while those in the former centrally planned economies (CPEs) have been raised in an environment in which marketing was frowned upon as one of the trappings of the capitalist West. The marketing conventions that are taken for granted in developed countries are often also absent in emerging markets.

Impacting on how the message will be responded to is the level of education and literacy that prevails among those receiving the message. Levels of both literacy and education in emerging markets are likely to be lower than in other markets. This will require a change in the content of the message (less sophisticated), in the balance between pictorial and verbal in advertisements and a change in the media used in favour of visual or aural. Another factor will be the extent of previous exposure to promotion. Whereas in developed markets exposure has been continuous for decades, in emerging markets exposure has been limited and promotion may still be a novelty in itself. This was found to be the case with public relations activity in China (Shao and Wong, 1996). As a result, instead of novelty approaches and attention-getting devices to attract the attention of a jaded audience, promotional content in emerging markets is likely to be more appealing if it is simple and direct. Another factor is that of emotional response. This has a cultural bias; as previously mentioned, emerging markets tend to value collectivism, accept power distance and are characterized as high context. The type of commercial, the spokespersons and the storyline are therefore likely to cause a different emotional response and will require any standard advertisement or promotional form to be adjusted.

One of the important issues in who receives the message is literacy rates, which are much lower for women than for men (in Africa, for example, 41 per cent of men and 60 per cent of women are illiterate) (Craig and Douglas, 2000). In these circumstances, if household purchasing decisions are made by women, then a different media focus is likely to be required as to both content and medium. In other emerging markets, household purchasing is often undertaken by men due to the prevailing religion (fundamentalist Islamic regimes such as Libya). This points to the need to target groups in emerging markets that can be influenced by word-of-mouth and others that cannot be reached as easily via conventional media and promotion.

The research in Thailand showed that overall, affording the equipment to receive a message is perceived as a possible problem, as is the adequacy and reliability of the existing infrastructure. There are indications that promotional messages, are often received in a group situation and that messages involving some appeal to group norms are likely to elicit a more favourable response. Familiarity with marketing concepts is regarded as being a definite factor in creating a more positive reaction to promotional messages, and literacy and education levels are likewise perceived to influence responses. Overall, messages containing emotional appeals are likely to be responded to more favourably than those simply based on rational appeals, which is the reverse of the earlier finding as far as the preferred content of the message is concerned. When the perception of likely responses by upper/middle-income customers is contrasted with likely responses by low-income customers, it appears that a number of the response factors above are much more likely to apply to lower-income customers.

Interference factors

Interference may disrupt communication to a greater extent in international than in domestic marketing because of the complexity of the international environment. The more important of these interference factors are socio-cultural, distribution channel-related and government controls. In societies where the cooperative movement is strong, such as in rural Indonesia, the opinions of other members of the cooperative can influence the message received (Towie, 1997). Socio-cultural factors in emerging markets include tribalism and allegiance to ethnic affiliations, and effective promotion in such circumstances must be directed to these powerful groups. Another factor is the conditions under which it is received. Because of the cost of communications infrastructure to receive the message in such markets, it may be received in a public rather than in a private setting. This may be around the village radio, in front of the communal TV set or at the local Internet café. This communal environment may result in the message received being influenced by the opinions of others.

The research in Thailand indicated that overall, sources of interference on the receipt of messages were mostly due to group influence, local or regional loyalties and government wishes and directives. Competitor activities were also viewed as impacting on customers' reaction to the messages they had received. This pattern was much stronger in all cases among lower-income customers, particularly as far as group influences and local and regional loyalties were concerned.

Feedback

Willingness to provide feedback, and the form the feedback is likely to take will be influenced by culture. Feedback is likely to be different when communicating in emerging markets and will be influenced by the greater degree of both collectivism and power distance in such markets. Collectivism is likely to result in feedback being more reflective of group opinion than that of the individual. It is also responsible for some of the reluctance by the individual to provide evaluative comment. Power distance may result in a reluctance to provide feedback at all, especially where the sender of the message is perceived to be of superior status to the recipient, or the product is perceived as 'Western' or sophisticated. In emerging markets, it is thus more likely that feedback will be reflected in purchasing activity than in evaluative comment.

The research in Thailand showed that feedback was not viewed as being easy to obtain, possibly due to a cultural reluctance to respond to questions posed by strangers. This reluctance to provide feedback was perceived as being greater among lower-income customers.

Environmental factors

The environment in which the communication of the message occurs is likely to impact on the communication process (Thomas, 1997). The environment in emerging markets is likely to be very different due to underlying cultural dimensions, and this impacts on political systems and economic behaviours. The research in Thailand showed that promotional activities were influenced by a flexible attitude to time and also by attitudes towards gender. Concern for privacy is another variable that was considered by respondents to influence communication. Overall, environmental factors are very important if communication is to be effective, and this importance is regarded as being greater in Thailand than in Australia, reflecting the high-context nature of the market. In most cases, this importance was viewed as being greater when targeting low-income segments of the market.

Overall, the study found that not only did the communications model operate differently in an emerging markets compared to developed markets, but that the model operated differently within an emerging market as between the upper/middle-income group and the lower-income groups.

5 Conclusion

In selecting emerging markets in which to invest, it is preferable to select on the basis of *cultural (ethnic) identity* rather than geographical boundaries, as several cultural groups are often located within the one political boundary. Although the temptation might be to invest in markets that are similar to Australia in terms of psychic distance, these are often likely to be mature markets which do not offer the same potential for investment as emerging markets that are psychically distant. Such markets are likely to be high context, which will need to be taken into account in evaluating opinions and information concerning them. Although using underlying dimensions derived from the etic approach is useful for short-listing emerging markets for investment consideration, a clustering approach may be preferable, and final selection should be based on an emic approach so all major cultural variables in the market are taken into account.

In negotiating for approval of the proposed investment in the selected emerging market, an approach that takes into account the interests of all *stakeholders* (not just shareholders) should be adopted, as this will be much more appealing to government officials due to the culturally influenced factors of nationalism and collectivism. Cultural sensitivity will be required (appreciation of attitudes towards time and space) and in these negotiations the natural cultural baggage of one's our self-reference criterion, should be compensated for. The factor of tolerance of ambiguity will need to be considered in interpreting what is said, and an understanding of attitudes towards formal (contractual) vs. informal (handshake) agreements appreciated.

In locating appropriate investment partners, it is important to tap into existing *networks* in the selected overseas market that will provide you with 'insider' status as far as the overseas market is concerned. Accessing such networks will require the cultural sensitivity which is a prerequisite for creating trust. In most emerging markets, trust is the essential ingredient of commercial relationships, and without it business will not take place. The need for trust is culturally influenced, and is a substitute for legal protection and regulation, which in many cases is either not trusted or is viewed as being corrupt. The Western approach of requiring protection via legal contracts is interpreted as lack of trust in the other party and is the wrong approach to take with a potential investment partner in an emerging market. In such markets, the obligations imposed by the creation of a relationship are viewed as being much more important than rules which in such markets are selectively applied and cannot be relied upon to deliver an unbiased outcome. In some cultures, the attitude towards technology and the existence of a past, present or future orientation needs to be taken into account in presenting your investment proposition to a potential investment partner, as culturally it is necessary to couch your proposal in terms which relate to the culture of the market in which you hope to invest.

In managing an investment operation in an emerging markets, attention needs to be paid to the *cultural norms* that prevail in that market. Emerging markets are usually characterized by paternalism, collectivism, hierarchy and low education levels. This means that employees view you as having a responsibility for their long-term welfare in return for which they provide you with their loyalty. They will respect a hierarchical structuring of the workplace and will be uncomfortable with informality and Western-based egalitarian approaches. They will favour reward systems that reward the team rather than the individual. In the firm's promotional approach, a stakeholder orientation should be adopted and money spent on promoting the benefits of the investment operation to the local community, among others. The cultural issues that came to light in the research on promotion in emerging markets should be taken into account in communicating with customers, to ensure that the messages conveyed receive the optimum attention.

Whereas in the 'West', it is normal to close operations when they no longer deliver competitive returns to shareholders, this is not the case in emerging markets which regard such actions as opportunistic and insensitive. It is expected that the overseas investor will take a long-term view and consider the interests of all stakeholders, including employees. In these cultures, the implied obligations due to network membership and established relationships outweigh short-term considerations or opportunism. In the author's experience, withdrawing from operations in an emerging market not only damages the firm's reputation but also that of the country with which the firm is associated. Culture impacts at all stages of the process and the display of cultural insensitivity at any stage carries a real prospect of damaging the success of the activity. Many of the cultural characteristics of emerging markets are also likely to inhibit the use of the Internet in connection with investment in these markets.

Note

1. A study by the Economist Intelligence Unit in December 1999 listed countries in terms of Internet access at home in descending order as follows: Norway, Singapore the USA, Sweden, Canada, Finland, Australia, Denmark, New Zealand, Netherlands, Britain, Switzerland, Austria, Taiwan, South Korea, Belgium, Germany, the UAE, Japan, Italy, Ireland, France, Spain, Poland, Brazil, South Africa, Russia, Mexico, China, Egypt, India.

References

Abosag, I., Tynan C. and C. Lewis, 'Relationship Marketing: The Interaction of Cultural value Dimensions', Academy of Marketing Annual Conference, Nottingham Business School (2–5 July 2002).

Craig, C.S. and S. Douglas, *International Marketing Research* (Chichester: John Wiley, 2000).

Fang, T., *Chinese Negotiating Style* (Thousand Oaks, CA: Sage, 1999).

Fletcher, R. and L. Brown, *International Marketing – an Asia-Pacific Perspective*, 2nd edn, (Sydney: Prentice-Hall, 2002).

Fletcher, R. and T.C. Melewar, 'The Complexities of Communicating to Customers in Emerging Markets', *Journal of Communications Management*, 6(1) (2001): 9–23.

Griffin, T. *International Marketing Communications* (Oxford: Butterworth-Heinemann, 1993).

Hall, E.T., *The Silent Language* (New York: Anchor Press, 1973).

Hall, E.T., *Beyond Culture* (New York: Anchor Press/Doubleday, 1976).

Hofstede, G., *Cultures and Organizations: Software of the Mind* (London: McGraw-Hill, 1991).

Hofstede, G., *Culture's Consequences*, 2nd edn (Thousand Oaks, CA: Sage, 2001).

Hofstede, G. and M.H. Bond, 'The Confucious Connection: from Cultural Roots to Economic Growth', *Organizational Dynamics*, 16(4) (1988): 4–21.

Hollows Foundation (1999), http://hollows.com.au.

Lamposki, K. and J.B. Emden, *Igniting Innovation: Inspiring Organizations by Managing Creativity* (New York: John Wiley, 1996).

Park, Leung, D.H., 'A Cross Cultural Analysis of Internet Connectivity', *Journal of Current Research in Global Business* (Fall 2000): 97–107.

Quelch, J. and J. Austin, 'Should Multinationals Invest in Africa?', *Sloan Management Review* (Spring 1993): 107–9.

Rogers, E.M., *Diffusions of Innovations*, 4th edn (New York: Free Press, 1995): 9, 194–6.

Ronen, S. and O. Shenkar, 'Clustering Countries on Attitudinal Dimensions: A Review and Synthesis', *Academy of Management Review*,10 (1985): 435–54.

Schutte, D. and Ciarlante, D., *Consumer Behaviour in Asia* (London: Macmillan, 1999).

Shao, A.T. and M.Y. Wong, 'Public Relations in China: a Status Report', *Journal of Asia-Pacific Business*, 1(4) (1996): 43–66.

Thomas, A.O., 'Advertising to Masses Without Mass Media', in D.M. Johnson and E. Kaynak (eds), *Marketing in the Third World* (London: Haworth Press, 1997): 75–88.

Towie, M., 'A Plant Investment with a Fresh Dividend', *Business Review Weekly* (24 March 1997): 52.

Trompenaars, F. and C. Hampden-Turner, *Riding the Waves of Culture*, 2nd edn (London: Nicholas Brealey, 1997).

Table 12A.1 Results of the Thai survey

	Positive(%)			Indifferent(%)			Negative(%)		
	Overall	H/Middle	Lower	Overall	H/Middle	Lower	Overall	H/Middle	Lower
Sender issues									
Local presenters more credible	47	25	70	36	46	26	17	29	4
Background vs. accomplishments of presenter	23.5	25	26	34	29	39	42.5	46	39
Promotion requires testimonials	19	25	13	45	46	44	36	29	43
Testimonials from authority figures	17	21	13	29	42	17	54	38	70
Testimonials from (glamour) figures	17	30	5	22	39	5	61	31	90
Couched in group rather than individual terms	19.5	13	26	31.5	33	30	49	54	44
Focus on abstract rather than specific concepts	31	26	36	29	35	23	46	39	41
Meaning influenced by context rather than specifics	29.5	29	30	40.5	46	35	30	25	35
Utilitarian preferred to aesthetic appeals	24.5	22	27	42	43	41	33.5	35	32
Verbal stimuli preferred to non-verbal stimuli	19	21	17	53	67	39	28	12	44
Messages to secure loyalty long-term not short-term	29.9	37	22	38	46	30	32	17	48
Content needs to be politically sensitive	53.5	52	55	22	26	18	24.5	22	27
Effective message based on information not persuasion	53.5	52	55	22	26	18	24.5	22	27
Medium issues									
High use of radio	42	32	52	25.5	27	24	32.5	41	24
High use of television	58	64	52	23	27	19	19	9	29

High use of internet	25.5	25	26	29.5	50	9	45	25	65
High use of newspapers	39.5	43	36	51.5	48	55	9	9	9
High use of magazines	27.5	38	17	53	58	48	19.5	4	35
High use of PR	32	38	26	44.5	54	35	23.5	8	39
High use of promotional offers	60.5	44	77	24	39	9	15.5	17	14
High use of trade shows	22	30	14	44	61	27	34	9	59
High use of direct mail	12.5	12	13	48.5	66	30	39	21	57
High reliance on personal selling (cf. Australia)	40.5	42	39	45	46	44	14.5	12	17
Low degree of government control of media used	36.5	33	40	34	38	30	29.5	29	30

Receiver issues

Equipment affordability a problem	31.5	4	59	13.5	13	14	55	83	27
Reliability of infrastructure a problem	41	25	57	19	21	17	40	54	26
Messages rarely received in group situation	44.5	63	26	34	29	39	21.5	8	35
Familiarity with marketing yields positive reaction	44.5	46	43	39.5	36	43	16	18	14
Response likely to reflect group norms	52	42	62	25	33	17	23	25	21
Response influenced by literacy/education	54	46	63	23	25	21	23	29	17
Emotional not rational messages yield positive response	45	21	69	34	46	22	21	33	9

Feedback issues

Consumers won't provide opinions of advertisements	49.5	44	55	35.5	44	27	15	12	18
Obtaining feedback on market research difficult	38.5	42	35	42.5	42	43	19	16	22

Table 12A.1 Continued

	Positive(%)			Indifferent(%)			Negative(%)		
	Overall	H/Middle	Lower	Overall	H/Middle	Lower	Overall	H/Middle	Lower
Interference issues									
Message reaction depends on group influence	38.5	25	52	47	63	31	14.5	12	17
Message reaction depends on local/regional loyalties	34	25	43	40.5	46	35	28.5	29	22
Government wishes impact on reaction to messages	47	39	55	31	35	27	22	26	18
Competitor activities impact on reaction to messages	55.5	42	69	40	58	22	4.5	0	9
Environmental/other issues									
Flexible attitude to time influences promotional activities	45	42	48	38.5	42	35	16.5	16	17
Gender attitude influences promotion	51.5	48	55	31	35	27	17.5	17	18
Concern for privacy influences promotion	37.5	52	23	37.5	30	45	25	17	32
Customer's wishes more important than in Australia	27.5	33	22	48.5	54	43	24	13	35
Promotion influenced by access to unofficial markets	40	35	45	31	39	23	29	26	32
More necessary to promote in Thailand (cf. Australia)	47	37	57	51	63	39	2	0	4

Index